THE AMERICAN SENATE

Reprints in Government
and
Political Science

General Editor: Richard H. Leach
DUKE UNIVERSITY

THE

AMERICAN SENATE

By

LINDSAY ROGERS

With a New Foreword and Prolusion by
LINDSAY ROGERS

And a Commentary by
CARL MARCY
CHIEF OF STAFF
U. S. SENATE COMMITTEE ON FOREIGN RELATIONS

JOHNSON REPRINT CORPORATION

New York and London

1968

FOREWORD (1968)

Forty years after this book was published, the Senate of the United States is still the world's most powerful second chamber. During an era when in other constitutional systems quite a few second chambers have become secondary, our Senate has remained of primary importance. Some of its roles have on occasion been more stellar; other roles have for periods seemed somewhat minor. But the Senate of the United States still merits Gladstone's famous description of it: "the most remarkable of all the inventions of modern politics."

I have easily resisted the invitation (no temptation) to undertake a complete revision of my book and to deal with the Senate as of the seventh instead of the third decade of the twentieth century. In the third decade, as I frankly admitted, I was writing with "complete partiality and a bad temper." After forty years I might not be able to recapture those qualities for the making of a revised version. But there is another more important reason why I think a revision would be second best and it is pedagogical. Readers will be able to say to themselves: "What he tells us may at the time have seemed quite acute but it now needs qualification," and hence they will be pleased, as one always is when one thinks that one is correcting or improving on what one is reading. And if my middle-aged book is ever discussed in the presence of those who are suffering from lectures, the man on the rostrum can punctuate his eloquence by remarking that such and such a thing that I had said had become hopelessly out of date. I would hope that occasionally from the suffering listeners there would be a cry: "It is not as bad as you have said it is," or—perhaps more frequently—"It is worse than you think it is."

In some introductory remarks (under the caption, "Prolusion,") there are discussions of several matters which loom large in the context of recent developments. I consider the first three matters: a fourth matter is dealt with by a highly competent gentleman who has been closer to recent events than I have been.

(I) The Filibuster. It is more essential than it was forty years ago that a bare numerical majority shall not be able to impose closure—i.e., to bring debate to an end and to proceed to a vote. William Hazlitt said of George Crabbe: "he rivets our intelligence by being tedious." On important occasions a handful of senators, even though they are tedious, attract attention and rivet intelligence.

(II) Congressional Investigations. I still maintain that the Senate should be able to peer into any dark corners which it thinks contain debris or skeletons, but Senate committees have shown that they cannot do this efficiently and that their reports on what they find become matters of party controversy.

Hearings before Congressional committees on pending legislation have always been a distinctive and extremely useful legislative device and they are now much more important than they used to be. This is the case because bureaucracies in the Executive departments have become more influential as the matters with which they deal have become more difficult for the layman to understand. Hence it is more essential than was formerly the case that the staffs of Congressional committees be able to assist the Solons to know the meaning of the laws they are requested to enact and that hearings be held to bring out the pros and cons of the drafts that are presented. In the British Parliament there is no device similar to American Congressional committees, and there has recently been strong advocacy that the House of Commons segment itself to consider at least some government bills before they come before the whole House. It will not be long before Cabinets yield to this very proper pressure. But the British House of Commons has for years refused to use select committees for inquisitorial purposes, and from no responsible quarter is there any proposal that the Commons should change its mind. When definite charges of wrongdoing are made or when rumors of scandals circulate, the British Parliament farms out its inquisitorial powers to "Tribunals of Inquiry." Since I wrote in 1926, a dozen of such Tribunals have completed their labors and no one of them has been found really wanting. Governments and opposition parties have accepted their findings. Some tribunals have been spectacular successes. I suggest that the American Congress plump for an agency similar to the British one.

(III) The Presidential Press Conference. Calvin Coolidge had a "White House Spokesman," but the gentlemen who have subsequently lived in 1600 Pennsylvania Avenue have used the presidential press conference. This is a unique American political invention which can be used as a formidable political weapon. In providing a forum in which debate is free, the Senate can on occasion be the scene of well contrived defense and counteraction.

(IV) The Senate and Foreign Policy. On January 22, 1917, Woodrow Wilson went before the Senate and said:

> I have sought this opportunity to address you because I thought that I owed it to you as a counsel associated with me in the final determination of our international obligations to disclose to you without reserve the thought and purpose that have been taking form in my mind in regard to the duty of our Government in the days to come when it will be necessary to lay afresh and upon a new plan the foundations of peace among the nations.

The years since have seen a vast change. I quote Edgar E. Robinson, the well known historian: "The growth of the powers of the President in foreign relations appears to be the most important phenomenon in modern history, inasmuch as the exercise of those powers by four Presidents in the past twenty years has determined developments throughout the world."

On what I conceive to be the dwindling role of the Senate the Prolusion's comments will come from my friend Carl Marcy, who saw service in the State Department before it moved (appropriately?) to "Foggy Bottom" and who now, as Chief of Staff of the Senate Committee on Foreign Relations occupies as high a post as can be reached in Washington's legislative bureaucracy (I use the word in no pejorative sense). Mr. Marcy has also been free to comment on any matters that I deal with anew and to say anything else which his knowledge and experience lead him to think is pertinent.

Lindsay Rogers

PROLUSION

1. The Filibuster

Forty years ago, the good words I said about the filibuster were the most controversial part of my book. They have been quoted on the floor of the Senate chamber a score of times, and once, by the tolerance of Senator J. William Fulbright, who ignored alphabetical order, I was put in a galaxy of "Professor Rogers, William S. White, Woodrow Wilson and Mr. Walter Lippmann," who had had "a long history of applying their excellent minds to an analysis of Government matters." On occasions when the Senate majority was insufficient to impose closure on debates delaying important legislation I was often asked whether I held my original opinions. My reply was always "yes." I was always certain that if the pending measure was really in the interests of the country, the necessary majority would be secured. And so it was. Delay and the knowledge of the opposition that it faced a two-thirds majority assured the country that no steamroller was working.

On two occasions I restated my views. In the spring of 1949 the civil rights program had been the victim of a great fight in Congress over closure —a fight which ended in March with the adoption of a new rule providing that debate could only be brought to an end by vote of the senators duly chosen and sworn. (I use "closure" rather than "cloture," which is the term of the Senate debaters.)

In *The Survey* (March 1949) I re-argued my case. The Editor, keen on presenting both sides, followed the article with a dissent by George Field, Executive Director of Freedom House, and in the June issue, Henry Steele Commager, then writing from the eminence of Morningside Heights, contributed a further word on the filibuster. Mr. Commager's main point was that only by ignoring the Negro population in the South could "one justify the logic" of what I had said: that the Southern section of our country was bitterly opposed to civil rights legislation. Mr. Commager's point was irrelevant. My argument was that in a federal system there may be matters on which a minority feels so deeply that a majority should pause and say to itself: "It is not proper for us to insist now; there should be a delay until an overwhelming majority is secured." Legislators everywhere, and particularly in a federal system, should remember some lines in Shakespeare's *Measure for Measure:*

> O! it is excellent
> To have a giant's strength, but it is tyrannous
> To use it like a giant.

For the January 8, 1959 issue of *The Reporter* I wrote an article entitled "The Filibuster Debate— Barrier Against Steamrollers" and again the Editor thought the issue so controversial that he simultaneously presented the opposite view. The opposer was Senator Jacob K. Javits.

More recent discussions of closure have centered
not on the question of whether the Senate rules
should permit filibusters, but on the way in which
Rule XXII could be modified. (In 1959 there was a
changeback to two-thirds of those present and voting, and the new proposal was to substitute three-
fifths for two-thirds.) At the opening sessions of
the last few Congresses there have been attempts
to amend Rule XXII in proceedings, when, it was
argued, the rule did not apply so that a majority
could bring debate to an end. Does "the Senate of a
new Congress have power to adopt its rules at the
opening of the new Congress unfettered by the rules
of earlier Congresses" or is the Senate a "continuing
body" whose rules (including XXII) cover all its
business? Consideration of this matter was most extended at the opening of the Ninetieth Congress
and the case of those who held the first view was
stated not only in lengthy debates but in a volumi-
nous brief printed in *The Congressional Record*
(January 18, 1967).

The differing purport of, or the nuances in, the
views expressed by successive Vice Presidents need
not detain us. Vice President Nixon took the position
"that the Senate was a continuing body and that
the rules of the Senate did continue except for any
rule adopted by the Senate which, in the opinion
of the Chair, would inhibit the constitutional right
of a majority of the members of the Senate to change
its rules or adopt any rules at the beginning of a

new session of the Senate." He went on to say that "any provision of the rules previously adopted which would restrict what the Chair considers to be the constitutional right of the majority of the members of the Senate to change the Senate's rules or to adopt new rules would not be applicable." While Nixon was presiding over the Senate, his "advisory opinion" was not implemented. Johnson and Humphrey as Vice Presidents (the former pro- and the latter anti-filibuster) were more restrained than Nixon had been. They ruled that the matter was one for the Senate itself to decide. In January, 1967 anti-filibuster Senators suffered a decisive defeat.

At the opening of the Ninetieth Congress, Senator George McGovern (D., N. Dakota) offered a motion "under Article 1 Section 5 of the Constitution, which provides that a majority of each House shall consti- tute a quorum to do business and each House may determine the rules of its proceedings." He moved "that debate upon the pending motion to proceed to the consideration of S. Res. 6 [changing the two- thirds of Rule XXII to three-fifths] be brought to a close by the Chair immediately putting the motion to the Senate for a 'yea' or 'nay' vote." If the motion was adopted by a majority of those present and vot- ing, there would "be two hours of debate" divided equally between proponents and opponents "and immediately thereafter the Chair shall put to the Senate without further debate the question on the adoption of the pending motion to proceed to the consideration of S. Res. 6."

This motion was confused in its terms and a good many parliamentary inquiries were necessary to secure clarification. But the actions that the Senate took were quite simple.

Senator Everett Dirksen (R., Illinois), the minority leader, at once made the point of order that the motion did not present a constitutional question: "The motion simply is a dressed up 'previous question'. It contains some surplusage and other matters; but when it is resolved into its solid component, it amounts to nothing more than an effort to shut off debate. That can only be done by a two-thirds vote." It could be done by a majority in the House of Representatives which had different rules. "But under every other parliamentary procedure insofar as I am familiar with the authorities on the subject, including Roberts' *Rules of Order,* Section 29, this is a summary motion to chop off debate in this body; and that is tantamount to asking for the previous question. . . . So, no constitutional question being involved, and this being a summary motion, it flies in the face of the present rules of the Senate and of all other parliamentary procedure and is in my judgment clearly subject to a point of order." Senator McGovern's motion to table the Dirksen point of order was rejected by a vote of 37 "yeas" to 61 "nays." The Chair then put to the Senate the question of whether the Dirksen point of order should be sustained, and the vote was 59 "yeas" to 37 "nays."

At later sessions the Senate considered the proposed amendment of Rule XXII but its deliberations were governed by Rule XXII, and there was filibustering. Finally Senator Mansfield, the majority leader (who favored changing to three-fifths but who the week before had thought the Dirksen point of order well made) filed a motion signed by the required number of Senators to invoke closure to bring to a close debate on the motion to approve Res. 6. On January 24 the Senate by a vote of 53 to 46 refused to close debate. The attempt in the First Session of the Ninetieth Congress to amend Rule XXII was a dismal failure.

"We decided by an overwhelming vote," said Senator Mansfield, "that the uniqueness of this body should be maintained; that reflection and deliberation should be assured of all proposals from whatever quarter. The choice last week was in my opinion a wise choice. A majority of the Senate could have decided otherwise. A majority failed to adjudge abuses under the present rules sufficient to justify an extraordinary method to effect a change in the rules." The abuses have not been numerous and their consequences have not been serious.

"Seven times out of 36 endeavors,"—the rhetoric is Senator Dirksen's—"this Senate has voted cloture, going back to 1919. Do not tell me you cannot get it, because I got it, just as others did. You can get

it again when you have a case, but when you have a
bill of goods to sell to the Senate, a bill of goods
that is under suspicion and not in the national interest, it should not be sold. That is the point. If
we are going to protect the Republic against wild
schemes and fantacies [*sic*] and favorite legislative
brain children, the thing to do is to protect our
rules."

Civil rights measures were more than "fantasies"
or "brain children"; federal legislation was highly
desirable and filibusters delayed it sometimes from
Congress to Congress. In one sense that was highly
regrettable. Viewed differently it may not have been
a bad thing. When closure ended the filibusters and
permitted action, the opposing minorities knew that
they were heavily outvoted.

A Civil Rights Bill reached the Senate for consideration on February 26, 1964. Actual debate began March 26 and closure was voted on June 10
("yeas" 71; "nays" 29). "The Senate of the United
States made a three-months' spectacle of itself on
a bill so overwhelmingly passed," said one critic. I
wonder. Closure was also successful on the 1965
Voting Rights Act. Debate was not nearly as prolonged as debate on the 1964 law, and the verdict
(May 25) was 70 to 30. Closure was also ultimately
successful in the 1968 Civil Rights Protection Act.
After three failures the closure motion passed March
4 by a vote of 65 to 32.

Between 1946 and 1968, the Senate refused to pass a number of closure motions which sought to end filibustering. No failure of the Senate to close debate had harmful results. Civil rights legislation was delayed, but when enacted, there were better chances of its being accepted. In Table I, I list the closure motions and record the "yeas" and "nays." The figures show that in no case was there a sizable majority in favor of stopping debate.

In November, 1919 (Treaty of Peace with the Germans); January, 1926 (World Court); February, 1927 (Establishment of National Bank Branches); February, 1927 (Bureau of Prohibition in Treasury Department); August, 1962 (Communications Satellite Act) the Senate agreed to closure. As has been said, three closure motions have been adopted on Civil Rights Acts.

Ours is the only major country with a two-party system where the laws that get on the Federal statute books, or efforts to get them there, usually have bipartisan support and bipartisan opposition. In academic quarters one sometimes hears laments that American political parties are not "disciplined": that their leadership is sometimes shadowy or undiscoverable, and that they do not present to the electorate clashing bodies of doctrine. But in a country as vast as the United States, with different sectional interests, a political providence has been good in seeing to it that legislation does not result

TABLE I
VOTES IN SENATE ON CLOSURE MOTIONS

	Votes for closure	
Bill	Yea	Nay
Fair Employment Practices Commission (February 9, 1946)	48	36
British Loan Bill (May 7, 1946)	41	41
Anti-Strike Bill (May 25, 1946)	3	77
Anti-Poll Tax Bill (July 31, 1946)	39	33
Fair Employment Practices Act (May 19, 1950)	52	32
Fair Employment Practices Act (July 12, 1950)	55	33
Amendment of Atomic Energy Act of 1946 (July 26, 1954)	44	42
Civil Rights Act (March 10, 1960)	42	53
Amendment of Cloture Rule (September 19, 1961)	37	43
Civil Rights (literacy tests) Act (May 9, 1962)	43	53
Civil Rights (literacy tests) (May 14, 1962)	42	52
Amendment of Cloture Rule (February 7, 1963)	54	42
Reapportionment (September 10, 1964)	30	63
Right to Work (October 11, 1965)	45	47
Repeal of 14(b) of National Labor Relations Act (February 8, 1966)	51	48
Same subject (February 10, 1966)	50	49
Civil Rights Act of 1966 (September 14, 1966)	54	42

TABLE I (*Continued*)
Votes in Senate on Closure Motions

| | Votes for closure | |
Bill	Yea	Nay
Same subject (September 19, 1966)	52	41
Higher Education Act Amendments (October 10, 1966)	41	37
To amend Cloture Rule XXII—To provide for closing debate by three-fifths of Senators present and voting in lieu of present two-thirds requirement (January 24, 1967)	53	46
Civil Rights Protection Act (February 20, 1968)	55	37
Same subject (February 26, 1968)	56	36
Same subject (March 1, 1968)*	59	35

* Finally, on March 4, 1968, after private negotiations as to acceptable amendments, a fourth attempt to impose cloture on debate on the Civil Rights Protection Act was agreed to: yeas 65, nays 32.

from a powerful majority lording it over a determined party minority; that on policies our parties prefer concessions to a success which would enable one to say with Pyrrhus: "Yes, but if we have another such victory, we are undone." The filibuster is undemocratic if "democracy" means that anywhere, and particularly in a Federal system, any majority should be able to do what it wishes on any issue at any time. Federalism was the means of forming the nation and it remains the means of preserving it. Congress, as well as the Supreme Court, is the Federal system's manager, and a Senate filibuster is well worth while if, on occasion, it prevents the Congressional manager from being tyrannical. The possibility of a filibuster can make it certain that a party majority cannot prevent a committee from proceeding with an investigation that the party leaders might wish to avoid.

II. Senatorial Investigations

In 1926 I was strongly in favor of Congress' being able to inquire into every dark corner of an administration, and I still am. I was then aware of the fact that Congressional committee investigations were often not as competent as they should be and that they sometimes smeared persons who had previously been immaculate and who deserved to continue to seem so. During the last forty years there have been a plethora of investigations, and which of them deserves a modicum of applause? Frequently Senate committees on investigating rampages have drawn criticism that was not mitigated by approval from any quarter. What House of Representatives committees have done better? What findings by committees of either House have won general acceptance and have silenced party controversy?

I still believe that the Senate should be able to investigate and even on occasion to conduct inquisitions, but I think that, *save when pending legis-*

lation is the subject matter, the duty of inquiring should be handed over to a more efficient piece of governmental machinery. Two such pieces operate in places outside of Washington—one in New York State and the other in Great Britain. In 1926 I should have taken note of the former, but there was an excuse for my failure to mention the latter. It is only in recent years that the British device has demonstrated its real efficiency. Not content with general acceptance and the absence of any serious criticism, the House of Commons recently authorized a Royal Commission to inquire into the inquiring device. The verdict-handed down was generally favorable.

I could fill many pages with details of committees' playing politics and demonstrating incompetence in respect of functions, like those of a grand jury or a court of law, but I shall try to be brief. Martin Dies, John Rankin, J. Parnell Thomas, Joseph R. McCarthy, and many others: what can be said in praise of any of them? The Mother of Parliaments would not tolerate similar performers. Representatives and Senators have misused investigations to wreak personal vengeance and to publicize their unattractive figures in headlines and newsreels, and on the wireless and television. The spectacle of irresponsible Congressional inquisitors riding high, wide, and unhandsomely makes responsible Senators and Representatives uneasy and the outstanding Solons in Washington shun duties as inquisitors. The House of

Representatives indeed lacks a sense of the ridiculous.
Why a House Committee on "Un-American" Activities when the freely elected legislatures of other
states would never dream of having Committees
on "Un-Canadian," "Un-British," or "Un-French"
Activities?

After he retired to Gettysburg, Dwight D.
Eisenhower recalled rather ruefully that when there
were scandals in his administration the Democrats
had controlled both houses of Congress and that the
investigating committees were therefore politically
hostile to him. Republicans now maintain that the
Johnson administration is blessed by having party
majorities in Congress. When, in the Eisenhower
administration, a special House Subcommittee on
Legislative Oversight made its report, three Republican members charged that the subcommittee
had given a "very careful and minute description
of the association" between Sherman Adams and
Bernard Goldfine but had said nothing about a
"similar association disclosed by our hearings on
the part of Mr. Goldfine and prominent public officials in the Democratic party."

On occasion those who worked on Capitol Hill
have seemed to terrorize the hired men who worked
in the vicinity of 1600 Pennsylvania Avenue. Competent reporters have described the atmosphere in
Washington as one of "panic" with officials unable
to give sufficient attention to policy. This is not
impressive because Washington is no place for thin-

skinned men, and confusion in or lack of policy cannot be justified so simply; and Congress will always contain would-be inquisitors who will make their consciences subservient to their cravings for headlines and will not be scrupulous in following the obligations or procedures that may be prescribed by law.

Some years ago Douglas Cater turned up a memorandum outlining how a House investigating committee could seek to get a maximum amount of publicity:

> 1. Decide what you want the newspapers to hit hardest and then shape each hearing so that the main point becomes the vortex of the testimony. Once that vortex is reached, *adjourn*.
>
> . . .
>
> 5. Do not space hearings more than 24 or 48 hours apart when on a controversial subject. This gives the opposition too much opportunity to make all kinds of counter-charges and replies by issuing statements to the newspapers.
> 6. Don't ever be afraid to recess a hearing even for five minutes, so that you keep the proceedings completely in control so far as creating news is concerned.
>
> . . .

It would be interesting to know how many Congressional investigating committees have used this memorandum as a procedural guide. And now a word about incompetence.

In the 1949 investigation of the "Five Percenters" —those whom a Senate subcommittee called "an unsavory fraternity of individuals who reported to businessmen that they could affect government decisions by pressure or influence," the Committee was unable to agree on whether what had been turned up was nefarious or innocuous. When the inquiries into the Billie Sol Estes case came to an end, what the facts were and what they meant were disputed. The same judgment can be made on Robert G. ("Bobby") Baker's emergence into an unpleasant limelight. Both gentlemen were indicted but the courts were called upon to deal only with the fragments of political malfeasance that had been criminal. I could give many other examples of Congressional investigations that were inefficient. As inquisitors Congressmen have been fumbling and the reason is that they have been amateurs attempting jobs that required professionals.

"Cross-examination is beyond doubt the greatest legal engine ever invented for the discovery of truth," wrote John H. Wigmore, the eminent authority on the law of evidence. "The many possible deficiencies, suppressions, sources of error, and untrustworthiness which lie underneath the bare untested assertion of a witness may be brought to light and exposed by cross-examination." How can Senators or Representatives, even if they think they are professionals and not amateurs, be efficient inquisitors when they are able to devote only parts of mornings or afternoons to their job and then must turn to legislative tasks and constituents' entreaties? An effective cross-examiner must take time to master his case; he must devote not only much conscious but some subconscious thinking to how he will demonstrate "suppressions" or "untrustworthiness."

Senators and Representatives, even if they have talents that are adequate, do not have the time that is necessary. Nor is the situation much improved when a Committee has an able counsel. In the Five Percenter Inquiry, for example, the Senate Committee allowed counsel to do most of the questioning of the less prominent witnesses, and so long as Senators did not interrupt, his cross-examination was workmanlike. When Major General Harry H. Vaughan, President Truman's military aide, was a witness, large headlines were naturally in prospect. Counsel was told to rest and six unbriefed Senators questioned General Vaughan repetitiously, and inconclusively. Some committees have two counsel—one listed as being of "the minority."

Members of Congressional committees might do a better job if they agreed to divide their labors: one member might prepare himself to question one witness with his colleagues remaining silent until, the examination over, they thought some points were still obscure. But no! Most committee members wish to question every witness and oft-times do so in order of seniority and sometimes under a five- or ten-minute rule. No matter how crucial the stage that has been reached, cross-examination is frequently suspended when there is a quorum call. Committee members who have been absent because they anticipated the quorum call (or for other reasons) arrive late, express their regrets that they have not heard the previous testimony, and ask to be told if their questions are repetitious. Any reader of testimony as printed in the *Hearings* will be amused; he will also be appalled.

But to repeat, for Congress to preserve its inquisitorial powers in full measure even though it may sometimes prostitute them is more important than the elimination of reprehensible practices. A more vital consideration, however, is that the inquisitorial powers are inefficiently used. Hence they should be farmed out to an agency that can really be efficient and will command public confidence. There are two such agencies that might be imitated.[1]

Section Eight of the New York Executive Law (the Moreland Act) empowers the Governor whenever he so desires to appoint a Commissioner or

[1] Some of this discussion borrows from my articles, "When Congress Fumbles for Facts," *N. Y. Herald Tribune,* March 29, 30, and 31, 1950 (reprinted *Congressional Record,* A2864 (April 11, 1950), A2880 (April 12, 1950); and in Hearings before the Joint Committee on the Organization of the Congress: 89th Congress, First Session, Part 13, pp. 2040–2046). I also contributed an article, "The Problem and Its Solution," to a "Symposium on Congressional Investigations," *University of Chicago Law Review,* Vol. 18, pp. 464–477 (Spring, 1951).

Commissioners "to examine and investigate the management and affairs of any Department or Bureau or Commission of the State."[2] The Commissioner can subpoena persons and records and swear witnesses. He can employ counsel, investigators, detective agencies, and experts. The Legislature assures the Governor a free hand by making continuing appropriations for the payment of the Commissioners' honoraria (fixed by the Governor) and of the expenses of the investigation. Reports go to the Governor for submission to the Legislature.

Since 1907 when the Act was passed there have been more than fifty commissioners who peered into dark corners. Only one Governor has used the Moreland Act improperly. He was William Sulzer, an "over-enthusiastic investigator" who within ten months after his inauguration (January 1913) ordered eight separate investigations. "A former Tammany Congressman, he antagonized his own party, as well as the opposition, by his investigatory zeal," writes Ernest Henry Breuer.[3] "As a result the Legislature found grounds to impeach and remove him from office in October 1913." Rarely if ever has any member of the Legislature (or any critical newspaper) been able to charge that the Governor had selected as Commissioner a partisan or a nonentity;

[2] The statute was originally enacted as N.Y.L. (1907) c. 539 and was amended by N.Y.L. (1928) c. 131.

[3] New York State Librarian, who has published an important monograph, *Moreland Act Investigations in New York: 1907–65 (New York State Library Bibliographic Bulletin* 85, August 1965).

methods of investigation have rarely stirred criticism. The reports of Moreland Commissioners have been convincing to legislatures and to interested publics.

The reason, to repeat, has been that Governors were careful in their choices and that practically all of those commissioned have been men who had reputations that they wished to preserve. They have been judges, like Frederick E. Crane and John B. McEvoy; journalists and educators like John H. Finley, Henry L. Stoddard, and Edward L. Thorndike; lawyers like George W. Alger and George Gordon Battle; and public servants like Robert Moses and John H. Delaney. Such men were careful to provide themselves with efficient counsel and investigators and did not seek headlines. They devoted the major part of their time to their jobs until they were completed and their inquiries have ranged over the whole field of New York State's administration.

Rarely has the New York State Legislature been hostile to investigations ordered by the Governor. Indeed, there have been occasions when legislative committees which had already started to probe matters yielded the field to a Moreland Commissioner. The "absurdities and difficulties which inhere in a race to subpoena witnesses and documents," said the Assembly Speaker on one occasion, "require us to restrict our activity." And a legislative committee already investigating a bureau of the state government ceased to function and left a free hand to the Moreland Commissioner appointed by the Governor to investigate that agency. No one appreciated this forbearance more than myself for I was then (1928) a Moreland Commissioner investigating widely publicized charges of fraud in the Bureau of Workmen's Compensation.[4]

If there were a Federal Moreland Act, Senators and Representatives might be willing to restrict themselves in the same fashion as the New York Legislature has and to wait for a report. My first Moreland Report on fraud said that a tiny fire had caused a great deal of smoke. The Legislative Committee which had hitherto been silent then asked me to appear before it and attempted a little grilling. The chief criticism went to press releases but I had a perfect alibi in that the full report had been

[4] An item or two on the relations between one Governor, the Honorable Alfred E. Smith, and one of his Commissioners whom he had never met before he appointed him. When we did meet (January 1928), the only thing the Governor said was: "Do as good a job as you can and as quickly as you can. If there are any crooks, they should be rooted out without delay. And when you finish with fraud, give me any recommendations that you think are worthwhile for the improvement of the administration of the Bureau as a whole. I helped to create it and I want it to be as good as possible." During the following months I saw the Governor several times. Our conversations dealt with national and international politics, and the Bureau of Workmen's Compensation was never mentioned even though the Democratic National Nominating Convention was approaching, and sensational findings of malfeasance in a New York State Department would have been embarrassing to the occupant of the Executive Mansion in Albany, who was a candidate for the Presidential nomination.

sent to every recipient of a press release. So the Committee and I parted with respect that I think was mutual.

Some members of Congress might express fears that a President would appoint a Commissioner who would seek to protect an occupant of the White House, but if he ever did so, a President would invite political hurt as great as any that might have come, say, from full disclosures in the "Bobby" Baker case. The President would see the danger of appointing someone so unknown that he could not be criticized; if the report lacked luster, the blame would fall on the White House. Unlimited debate in the Senate would make this certain. The President would know that the only course politically wise would be to appoint commissioners who valued their own reputations so highly that they would not care where the political chips fell. Curiously enough, Franklin Roosevelt, who as Governor of New York had used the Moreland Act quite successfully, was unwilling to propose a Federal counterpart. When his Committee on Administrative Management (1937) suggested it to him informally, he would have none of it.

More than half a century ago the British House of Commons, which is just as insistent as is the American Congress that there be inquiries into possible official wrongdoing, decided that investigations by select committees were undignified and inefficient. In 1912, rumors circulated that members of Herbert Asquith's Liberal Government had bought Marconi shares in the hope that they would rise in value when the British Post Office concluded a contract for the transmission of its telegrams by wireless. A Select Committee was set up to investigate. Its Conservative members seemed hostile to witnesses who were Liberals, and the Liberals on the Committee seemed overanxious to protect their party associates. The Select Committee produced majority and minority reports and neither the House of Commons nor the public was satisfied. Since then the House of Commons has refused to use select committees to inquire into the British counterparts of American situations like those I have mentioned.

The British operate under what is called the "Tribunals of Inquiry" (Evidence) Act of 1921. When it appears that there should be an inquiry "into a definite matter" of "urgent public importance," Parliament authorizes the appointment of a Tribunal which has "all such powers, rights and privileges as are vested in the High Court." The Tribunal can enforce the attendance of witnesses, examine them on oath, and compel the production of documents. If witnesses refuse to attend or to produce documents or "answer any question to which the Tribunal may legally require an answer" or do any other thing "which could, if the Tribunal had been a court of law having power to convict for contempt, have been in contempt of that court," contempt proceedings can be instituted in the High Court. The Tribunal meets in public unless it decides that "for reasons connected with the subject matter of the inquiry or the nature of the evidence to be given" it should meet in private. It may authorize representation by counsel of any interested person or it may refuse that representation. The Tribunal's Chairman is usually a high judicial officer. (In Great Britain there is no reluctance to take Judges off the bench temporarily even when they must investigate the possibly improper conduct of highly placed politicians; but great care is taken in choosing the Judges.) The Chairman's two colleagues are ordinarily Queen's Counsel. They devote their entire time to their task for as long as is necessary. No report by a Tribunal has been severely criticized in Parliament or in the press.

When in 1926 I discussed Senatorial investigations, I made no reference to the device of Tribunals of Inquiry. This, if not excusable, was at least understandable because Tribunals had only functioned four times and their terms of reference had been of minor importance: a Royal Commission on Lunacy and Mental Disorder had been given powers under the Act and Tribunals had investigated the destruction of documents by Ministry of Munitions officers and two allegations of misconduct by police. It was not until 1936 that a Tribunal was called upon to deal with a matter that involved the behavior of high government officials, as had the

Marconi inquiry of 1912. This was the unauthorized disclosure of information relating to the budget. As a result of the Tribunal's report, "Jimmie" Thomas, Chancellor of the Exchequer, departed from British politics. In 1948 the Tribunal of Inquiry procedure really proved its competence again and American publicists should have viewed it as a political invention that the Congress of the United States should consider adapting for its own effective use.

The postwar British Labour Government had not been in office very long before rumors began to spread that Ministers had taken bribes. Speaking in the House, the Prime Minister, Clement Attlee, said that the Government's attention had been drawn to four specific matters: a license to import a quantity of amusement machinery; an application for a building license; a request to issue capital for the formation of a public company operating football pools; and the withdrawal of a paper-control order. The Attlee government asked the House to authorize a Tribunal of Inquiry but suggested that the terms of reference be limited to transactions involving Ministers of the Crown or other public servants. Thus private persons, whose names had been bandied about, would not be called as witnesses unless their activities had had some connection with the acts of Ministers and civil servants. Wrongdoing by private persons, apart from contact with officials, was a matter for the police and the criminal courts.

In the House of Commons there was no partisan

debate on Mr. Attlee's resolution. Winston Churchill, the leader of the Conservative opposition, urged that members of the House refrain from "gossip" until after the Tribunal had reported. He did not need to warn them not to make speeches, for under the standing orders of the House of Commons the Speaker would prevent any discussion of the work of the Tribunal until after it had made its report. Members knew that it would be perilous for them to discuss the investigation in speeches outside Parliament; they might be cited for contempt of Parliament in discussing a matter *sub judice;* or the Tribunal might itself do the citing on the ground that it had been "scandalized." The resolution passed without opposition and the Attlee Government appointed the members of the Tribunal—a judge and two barristers. There was no criticism of the choices.

Who should be the Tribunal's counsel? Even though he was a ministerial colleague of some who were to be involved, the Attorney General, Sir Hartley Shawcross, an extremely able cross-examiner, offered the services of himself and of "two learned friends"—barristers who were in private practice. As Attorney General, he had obligations in connection with the administration of the criminal law concerned with the prevention of corruption that he felt he should not abdicate. He told the Tribunal that he would act "with complete independence of the Government, and I must add, with complete indifference as to political and personal results." The Tribunal accepted this offer. (When the hearings were over, no one was able to say that Sir Hartley had been lenient with friends and colleagues.) After its first meeting the Tribunal adjourned for a fortnight so that counsel could prepare their case.

When it reassembled, the Attorney General took a morning and part of the afternoon outlining the evidence that was to be presented, named the half dozen witnesses who would be called first, and proposed that the four persons against whom the allegations were most serious be called last, after they had had an opportunity of listening to possibly incriminating testimony. This procedure was agreed to. The Tribunal thereupon sat morning and afternoon for twenty-one days, recessing only over weekends. Twelve different counsel appeared on behalf of thirteen of the witnesses. After the Attorney General was through they could reexamine their clients and endeavor to make their stories seem less damaging; they could cross-examine witnesses who made accusations against their clients.

Counsel were not limited by any ten-minute rule, but they knew that if they were repetitious the Tribunal would admonish them and they were all successful in avoiding reproofs. Only rarely did one attorney interrupt another attorney's questioning or did the members of the Tribunal intervene. After the testimony was completed, the twelve counsel argued for three days in defense of their clients and the Attorney General addressed the Tribunal for a day and a half. The Report, issued a month later, used three hundred thirty numbered paragraphs for a detailed examination of the evidence and considered the cases of every minister or civil servant whose name had been mentioned. The members of the Tribunal were unanimous in differentiating between conduct that was culpable, innocently indiscreet, and entirely blameless.

The tale that had been told was tawdry. The *eminence grise* had been one Sydney Stanley, né Solomon Kohsyzcky, alias Rechtand, an undischarged bankrupt, who got on intimate terms with certain Labour Ministers, entertained them lavishly, and gave them presents. Wartime controls were still on in Great Britain and licenses were necessary to import certain commodities, to get paper supplies, to repair business properties, and so on. Stanley had boasted of his ability to expedite action and even to persuade a Minister to overrule his civil servants. One business man whom he solicited as a client had gone to the police and their investigations soon resulted in the rumors to which Mr. Attlee had referred.

From Stanley, the Parliamentary Secretary to the Board of Trade had accepted a gold cigarette case, a suit of clothes, and much hospitality, knowing, said the Tribunal, that the benefactions had been made "for the purpose of securing expeditious and favorable consideration by the Board of Trade and other ministries of any application made by any person whom" the donor would introduce. Two persons had given the Parliamentary Secretary gifts without corrupt motive, but a liquor merchant had made presents of wine and spirits "for the purpose of securing favorable and expeditious treatment by the Board of Trade of his applications for licenses to import sherry casks." The Parliamentary Secretary had received these gifts, "knowing the purpose for which they were made, and in return for these gifts intervened to secure the grant of the licenses." Before the Tribunal reported, the Parliamentary Secretary resigned his office and withdrew from the House of Commons.

A prominent trade union official who had been made a director of the Bank of England, had been offered the chairmanship of a proposed new company "as a consideration to induce him to assist in obtaining from the Treasury upon the recommendation of the Capital Issues Committee permission for a public issue" of shares to float a new company. "We are convinced," said the Tribunal, that this was in the hope of "material advantage to himself," although in fact all that he "received, apart from some trivial gifts, was a present of a suit of clothes." All civil servants were cleared and there was no evidence of the gift of large sums as rumor had reported. Parliament and the public accepted the Tribunal's findings without serious question. The inquiry had lasted two months.

The second inquiry was equally expeditious. In

September 1957 there was a sudden, spectacular increase in the bank rate—from five to seven percent. Soon rumors began to circulate that some persons "in the know" had engaged in "inspired selling" of their gilt-edged securities whose prices were bound to fall when the increase was announced. A Tribunal of Inquiry was appointed and the chairman was again a judge of the High Court. It met at once to consider its procedure and recessed for ten days. It wished time to obtain and examine statements by prospective witnesses. Three hundred and sixty-eight persons were questioned but the Tribunal put only one hundred thirty-two of them on the stand. This took eleven days. Eleven witnesses had counsel, nine of whom addressed the Tribunal on behalf of their clients, and the Attorney General summed up. All this advocacy took less than one day. The Tribunal considered the evidence for three weeks and then reported unanimously that there had been no improper conduct.

As this account suggests, Tribunals of Inquiry work quickly and efficiently and their reports carry conviction. But in another important respect the procedure at Westminster is superior to that in Washington. Congressional inquiries have been properly criticized because they "smear" honorable persons. To an extent this cannot be avoided. "Your name seems familiar; haven't you recently been indicted?" said one character to another in a George Kaufmann play. "No," was the reply, "but I had to testify before the Securities and Exchange Commission." A Tribunal of Inquiry can sometimes wipe a smear away. This a Congressional committee cannot do.

During the investigation of the alleged bank rate "leak" (1957) one Governor of the Bank of England (who was also a partner in a banking firm that dealt in securities) was cross-examined for two and one-half hours. In its report the Tribunal said that it had observed him "under searching cross-examination covering every point in his conduct. Having so observed him, we have unhesitatingly reached the conclusion that he was a witness of truth and that he behaved with complete honesty and propriety in the difficult and embarrassing situation." The Tribunal dealt similarly with other witnesses concerning whom there had been imputations of possibly improper conduct. These witnesses emerged from the investigation with their reputations unbesmirched.

From this aspect, the superiority of British methods over American practices has again been demonstrated by the most recent tribunals of inquiry which had to concern themselves with ramifications that were different from, and possible disclosures far more sensational than, the situations confronting the tribunals whose work I have discussed. Lord Acton once said that during the nineteenth century, assassination had altered the course of history twenty-five times. After quoting Acton, G. M. Young in his *Victorian England: Portrait of an Age* (1952), noted that Victorian history had been twice deflected by divorce proceedings. "The fall of Parnell left England with a dead god instead of a leader, and the fall of Dilke left Liberalism without a brain." The two politicians had been named as correspondents in very unsavory divorce cases. Two situations that confronted Harold Macmillan's Government did not involve any divorces, but they made it relevant to recall Parnell and Dilke.

One William John Christopher Vassall, a civil servant under the Admiralty Board, had been convicted of offenses under the Official Secrets Act and was in jail. While he was serving in the British Embassy in Moscow, Soviet agents had detected his homosexuality and had blackmailed him into acting as a spy. After Vassall's trial and conviction there were rumors galore concerning improper relations between a civil Lord of the Admiralty and Vassall and there were allegations that the Admiralty had contained another spy and that this had been known to the First Lord for eighteen months before Vassall's arrest.

The Chairman of the Tribunal to inquire into the Vassall matter was Viscount Radcliffe, a Lord of Appeal in Ordinary, and his colleagues were a Judge of the High Court and a Queen's Counsel. The Tribunal was appointed on November 15, 1962; it held its first hearing on January 15th and its last on February 8th. During the interval the Tribunal sat *in camera* on 16 days and 6 half days and in public on 7 days and 7 half days. The report was dated April 5, 1963 and cleared the two Ministers. There had been no improper relations between the civil lord and Vassall and there were no grounds for any allegations that "Admiralty officers had known since 22nd March 1961 that a spy was at work inside the Admiralty building." The Radcliffe Report drew some criticism because it had not been severe enough in calling attention to lapses and failures in security vetting techniques. More important, however, was the fact that the Report gave to Ministers, whose names had been loosely mentioned, such clean bills of health that no one in the House of Commons dared or even desired to challenge the judgments.

In a second situation there was a larger cast of characters, and rumors were more rife and far ranging. It would have been pertinent to quote a couplet from A. H. Clough's *The Latest Decalogue:*

> Do not adultery commit;
> Advantage rarely comes of it.

The characters who seemed to have stellar roles were Christine Keeler and an osteopath named Stephen Ward, one of whose non-nocturnal diversions was making sketches. Members of the Royal Family had been among his sitters and he had been an intimate of the Cliveden set. Ward was to commit suicide while standing trial for living on the earnings of prostitutes.

One of Ward's protégés was Miss Keeler and

among those with whom she shared her favors was the Soviet Naval Attaché, Captain Eugene Ivanov, who was anxious to learn when the United States was going to let Germany have atom bombs. Another sharer was said to be John Profumo, the Secretary of State for War. Newspapers had stories but hesitated to print them because they feared libel suits. Metropolitan police and the security services were concerned and there was quite widespread uneasiness concerning the effectiveness of the security measures that the Government was taking.

Five colleagues questioned Mr. Profumo about his personal involvement. They knew that he had written a letter to Miss Keeler, that it was in the possession of the *Sunday Pictorial*, and that the letter began "Darling." Mr. Profumo explained this away by saying that such a degree of intimacy was normal in the world in which he moved and the Ministers accepted this explanation without insisting on seeing the letter. A statement was drafted and the War Minister read it in the House of Commons: "Miss Keeler and I were on friendly terms," Profumo told the House, but "there was no impropriety whatsoever in my acquaintanceship with Miss Keeler."

Rumors increased in number and in definiteness. Dr. Ward did not conceal his knowledge that Profumo had lied. By the end of May (1963) the Prime Minister decided that there would have to be an inquiry and he named the Lord Chancellor

to conduct it. When he heard of this action, the
Minister of War, who was vacationing in Italy,
knew that his number was up. He returned to England and told the truth in a letter (June 4) to the
Prime Minister:

> In my statement I said that there had been no
> impropriety in this association [with Miss Keeler].
> To my deep regret, I have to admit that this was
> not true and that I misled you, and my colleagues,
> and the House. . . . I have come to realize that,
> by this deception, I have been guilty of a grave
> misdemeanour, and despite the fact that there is
> no truth whatever in other charges, I cannot remain
> a member of your Administration, nor of the House
> of Commons. . . .

At once, sociological pollsters got to work: "What
was Profumo's sin?" What had been most important, an M. P. having a mistress, security risks, or
lying to the House? Only 8 percent thought that
having a mistress was important. Twelve percent
listed the security risks but nearly 80 percent
thought that Profumo's real offense had been lying
to the House of Commons. As someone put it in
doggerel form:

> Shame on you, Oh Christine,
> For wrecking our Tory machine.
> To lie in the bed in the nude
> Is far from what you call rude.
> But to lie in the House is obscene.

The Prime Minister concluded that a thorough-going inquiry was desirable; otherwise rumors would continue to circulate. On June 21, 1963, there-fore, he asked the Master of the Rolls, Lord Denning, to act as if he were a Tribunal but with-out the powers that a Tribunal had. There was a great danger of smearing people who were perfectly innocent and so the inquiry should be conducted in private. Lord Denning heard 160 witnesses, some of them more than once. They included the Prime Minister, eight Cabinet ministers, four other min-isters, three law officers, five members of the House of Lords, fifteen members of the House of Commons, several civil servants, the Commissioner of the Metropolitan Police and several of his officers, the Director General of the Security Service, twenty-five members of the newspaper profession including proprietors, editors, and reporters, six girls and nine men who knew Stephen Ward well, and several members of the general public who volunteered information.

In his report Lord Denning said that the inquiry with which he had been entrusted had "two great disadvantages. First, being in secret, it has not the appearance of justice; second, in carrying out the inquiry I have had to be detective, inquisitor, ad-vocate and judge and it has been difficult to com-bine them. But I have come to see that it has three considerable advantages. First, inasmuch as it has been held in private and in strict confidence,

the witnesses were, I am sure, much more frank
than they would otherwise have been. Secondly, I
was able to check the evidence of one witness
against that of another more freely. Thirdly, and
most important, aspersions cast by witnesses against
others (who are not able to defend themselves) do
not achieve the publicity which is inevitable in a
Court of Law or Tribunal of Inquiry"—and it may
be added, to an even greater and more harmful
degree when the proceedings are before a Congressional committee.

Perhaps there are other English jurists who could
have handled the job assigned to Lord Denning,
but there was general agreement that the Master of
the Rolls, because of his personality, his ability,
and his judgment, had succeeded admirably. Two
books have been published on the matters that the
Denning inquiry dealt with: Clive Irving, Ron Hall,
and Jeremy Wallington, *Anatomy of a Scandal: A
Study of the Profumo Affair* (New York, 1963); and
Wayland Young, *The Profumo Affair: Aspects of
Conservatism* (London, 1963). But neither is as
interesting (fascinating?) as Lord Denning's Report (Command Paper 2152 "Presented to Parliament by the Prime Minister by Command of Her
Majesty September 1963").

The report revealed a weakness of administration
in respect of security matters, but there had been
no security leaks. The report made no sensational
disclosures. Never before had the British public

formed such queues in front of Her Majesty's Stationery Offices in order to purchase a public document and they were apparently convinced by what they read. As for the reaction in Parliament? Mr. Profumo's political career had ended but there were no other casualties. "Who could have imagined during the summer and autumn of hard scandal," wrote *The Economist,* "that the House of Commons would bundle away the relics of the Profumo affair this week without even voting?" *The Manchester Guardian Weekly* expressed a similar opinion: "The report ought to be a guillotine on gossip." And it was.

But, successful though Lord Denning's inquiry was, it is doubtful whether it will ever be imitated in the future. Even though there had been no serious criticism of the device of Tribunals of Inquiry, a Royal Commission under the chairmanship of Lord Justice Salmon was set up to survey the past and to make recommendations for the future. The Royal Commission did not like the Denning procedure. It spoke no favorable word for using select committees of the House of Commons. It was firmly of the opinion that Tribunals of Inquiry should continue to be used but it recommended some minor changes of procedures. The Attorney General should not be the prosecutor, as he had been in some of the instances I have mentioned; private sessions should be reduced to a minimum, but in some cases they were desirable to prevent innocent individuals from suffering. The Salmon report (Command 3121, November 1966) also recommended that expenses of counsel for persons involved in inquiries should be paid from public funds. If and when, as I hope, the American Congress considers legislation that will provide a counterpart of the British system, the Washington proponents should give careful attention to the Salmon recommendations. Any American legislation should provide that a Tribunal must be set up if called for by a resolution of either branch of the Congress. Objections to the use of judges on such Tribunals do not seem to be persuasive.[5]

III. Press Conferences

In the introduction to the 1915 edition of his *Law of the Constitution,* A. V. Dicey declared that "'political inventiveness' in general falls far short of the originality displayed in other fields than politics by the citizens of progressive and civilized states." He went on to say that representative government was almost "the sole constitutional discovery or invention unknown to the citizens of Athens or of Greece." When it was made, the Dicey generalization probably went too far; but in the second decade of the twentieth century we in the United States witnessed several political inventions and we were late in recognizing the importance of one of them—the presidential press conference.

[5] See Alphaeus Thomas Mason, *Harlan Fiske Stone: Pillar of the Law* (New York, 1956).

Woodrow Wilson was the "inventor," but when
foreign problems became important—Mexico, neutrality, our entry into the War—he was unwilling
to risk the indiscretions that might result from discussions with a large number of journalists. His
Republican successors thought it wiser not to appear in mental *déshabillé*. When I wrote in 1926,
Calvin Coolidge was using what was called the
"White House spokesman" and Congress was frequently annoyed. Herbert Hoover, wisely, was
something of a shrinking violet. Franklin D.
Roosevelt was not. He could have obtained a patent
on the uses to which he put the press conference.
And now there is television!

In no other major representative government does
a press conference held by the Chief Executive have
the importance that it has in the United States. Occasionally the British Prime Minister appears on
television, but his most important pronouncements
are made in the House of Commons where he has
party supporters but where he also must face some
keen men who are his political opponents. They can
interrupt him; they can show by their jeers that
they think he has gone too far; and he must be
present and listen when opposition speakers deal
critically with the points he may have sought to
make.

A Prime Minister would lose ground politically
if he attempted to subordinate the role that he plays
when he appears in the House of Commons. One

of Winston Churchill's great strengths was that, perhaps to a greater extent than any other recent Prime Minister, he recognized the importance that the House of Commons attached to its role as a critic of the Executive. For example, when Churchill returned to England after his historic meeting with Franklin Roosevelt aboard the British battleship *Prince of Wales* where the Atlantic Charter was drafted, he was extremely reticent with the reporters who wanted to know what had happened. The House of Commons was entitled to hear from him first. President Roosevelt paid no attention to Congress, and announced to the press the matters on which he had agreed with the Prime Minister. In the United States, presidential use of the press and of television makes it essential that on Capitol Hill there be some ready method of reply. This means that the Senate should adhere to its practice of not permitting a bare majority to bring debate to an end.

Many academic and journalistic writers have dealt with what I have described as an important political invention. The most recent addition to this literature, James Reston's Elihu Root lectures at the Council on Foreign Relations, *The Artillery of the Press: Its Influence on American Foreign Policy* (New York, 1966), is of great importance and will often be consulted and cited by those interested in the workings of the American Government. Here I do no more than touch on a few high spots of the ways in which press conferences have advantaged or disadvantaged the occupants of the White House.

In 1938 there appeared the first five volumes of *The Public Papers and Addresses of Franklin D. Roosevelt* and they included stenographic transcripts of 48 of the 337 press conferences that had been held during Mr. Roosevelt's first four years in the White House. Even though he was to be a presidential candidate again, there was little editing and expurgation. The transcripts were in sufficient detail to give the flavor of the conferences and to permit generalizations more accurate than had previously been possible on the importance of this new channel of presidential publicity.

At his first Conference, held in the middle of the banking crisis on May 8, 1933 (and fully reported in *The Public Papers*), Mr. Roosevelt discussed the procedure he proposed to follow. He told the correspondents that they could ask him any questions that they wished to, but that he would use his own discretion as to whether he would reply. They might inquire about some matters on which he would be insufficiently informed and he would not say anything. Some statements would be issued in written form, and on them quotation marks could be used. The press conferences had two other purposes: "The first is 'background information,' which means, material that can be used by all of you on your own authority and responsibility. . . ."

"Then the second thing," continued the President,

"is the 'off-the-record' information, which means, of course, confidential information which is given only to those who attend the conference. Now there is one thing I want to say right now, about which I think you will go along with me. I want to ask you not to repeat 'off-the-record' confidential information, either to your own editors or to your associates who are not here; because there is always a danger that, while you people may not violate the rule, somebody may forget to say: 'This is off the record and confidential' and the other party may use it in a story. That is to say, it is not to be used and not to be told to those fellows who happened not to come around to the conference. In other words, it is only for those present."

Under these rules newspaper correspondents could come to know the President's mind far better than Congress was able to know it. Presidential messages to Congress were outlined in press conferences before they went to the Legislature. In the case of the most spectacular proposal during his second term— additional Justices of the Supreme Court of the United States—Mr. Roosevelt was careful to explain it at a press conference as well as to send it to Congress. After the United States Supreme Court declared parts of the National Industrial Recovery Act unconstitutional (the "sick chickens" decision), the President discoursed for an hour and used a figure of speech that came to be much quoted: "We have been relegated to the horse and buggy definition of interstate commerce." Correspondents asked whether they might quote the "horse and buggy" remark directly. The President said, "I think so." And his secretary added: "Just the phrase." There followed one or two other inconsequential questions and the conference was over. The next day, the newspapers reported the President's views at great length, but only this one sentence was directly attributed to the President.

The importance of the political invention of Presidential press conferences is clear and has been multiplied many times by the advent of television. The President can appear in our living rooms whenever he wishes, but for the moment, I continue to discuss the press conference as it was in Roosevelt's day, and the reader will be able to say to himself, "how television has brought about a change." When a Prime Minister appears in the Commons, what he talks about is determined by the legislative timetable and the questions he is asked by his fellow members of the House. What was discussed in the Roosevelt press conference was within the sole discretion of the President. On occasion he could and did refuse to reply. The newspapers could not report what questions were unanswered. What appeared in the press therefore was only what the President was willing to have appear.

Secondly, a Prime Minister is always confronted by an opposition. In the press conference, although they ask questions freely, the correspondents, out of respect for the Presidential office, must refrain from anything that resembles heckling. Mr. Roosevelt, in other words, was able to get his views before the country without immediate challenge and reply. Newspapers reported "background" information, attributing views to the President, and did not interrupt the reports to suggest that views were inconsistent with views previously expressed or that they were based on inadequate factual material. Analysis and criticism had to come later in editorial pronouncements or in speeches in the Senate.

In the third place, before the advent of television, Presidents could and did use press conferences to prevent the discussion of certain matters. News could be kept from "boiling over." The President could discourse to the correspondents "off the record" and outline some complicated policy so that no mention of it would be made in the press. The injunction of secrecy had to be maintained until he gave his consent to its removal. Intelligent and inquisitive correspondents are often able to discover for themselves that certain policies are contemplated; their doing this and then using the information could be barred by Presidential "off-the-record" utterances which in confidence disclosed information which sooner or later would have been turned up by the correspondents. Finally, with the President being the judge of what he wished to be published, he could use conferences to distract attention from proceedings in Congress or from other matters which were in public controversy.

In the Roosevelt era, informality was the dominant note. He once told a correspondent to put on a dunce cap and go stand in the corner. There were jokes about the first Presidential salary check and the excellence of the beer that President Roosevelt had presented to the Press Club. There was also levity in dealing with matters of great moment. Sometimes there seemed to be an attitude of irresponsibility. I give one illustration taken from a discussion of the London Economic Conference (May 10, 1933). The record as it appears in *The Public Papers* reads in part as follows:

"Q. Mr. President, do you or do you not consider the settlement of the war debts vital to the success of the Economic Conference?

The President. "Have I stopped tickling the toes of my mother-in-law? *[Laughter]* Yes or no?

"I don't know, it is too ticklish a question to answer. Are my mother-in-law's feet ticklish? *[Laughter]* In other words, of course, some cleaning up of the debt issue would be a fine thing, but it is not necessarily tied in with the success of the Economic Conference. The two are not necessarily wired together. They may be, what shall I say, 'platonic friends'?"

Whatever one thinks of the humor, one must have a friendly feeling for a President who does not take himself too seriously; who, in editing his *Public Papers*, does not wield a blue pencil on a colloquy like the one which I have quoted.

Television, as I have said, makes it natural that Presidents endeavor to keep their mental undress from giving impressions that are unfavorable. Viewers are unable to know how far a conference has been planned—*i.e.*, whether the questioners whom the President calls on come up with queries that have been planted or whether the President knew that other questions would be asked in the form that they actually took and so could have carefully prepared his replies. Sometimes the correspondents do a little revealing.

In the *New York Herald Tribune*, for example, shortly after President Johnson's nationally televised press conference of August 25, 1965, Roland Evans and Robert Novak said that, instead of being "the spontaneous free for all" that the general public was to suppose it was, "the August 25th session was very nearly as carefully staged as a Broadway play." What used to be "an informal cluster of reporters crowding around the President's desk in search of answers to questions" was no longer a news-gathering device, but rather "a showcase for Presidents." Habitual question-askers were pumped to find out the queries they had in mind. If it was thought that certain questioners (other than those representing the wire services) were likely to prove embarrassing, they might find that they had not been recognized.

President Johnson has used the television and press conferences far more frequently than did Presidents Eisenhower and Kennedy. And I could discourse at length on what, to an outside viewer, has seemed to be the justification for Walter Lippmann's judgment in the spring of 1967: "There has never been a time when the President and the working press distrusted each other so much as they do today." A member of the House of Commons was once called to order because he had charged a speaker with not telling the truth; using language that was more parliamentary, he said that the Right Honorable Gentleman had been guilty of "terminological inexactitude." In Washington, "credibility gap" is the euphemism that is generally used and the situation, as I have said, should on occasion be of considerable interest to the Senate of the United States.

To an extent (I repeat) the Presidential press conference may be viewed as an American counterpart of a British Prime Minister's appearances before the House of Commons to answer questions put to him by its members. But there is one great difference: if the Prime Minister is on shaky ground, questioning by the Opposition can cause real embarrassment. In Washington the correspondents by and large feel a sense of awe, and cross-examination might smack of lese-majesty. Appearances of Cabinet officers before Congressional Committees do, however, provide some of the rough and tumble public policy discussion characteristic of question periods in the House of Commons. Senators are not easily intimidated by Cabinet members. Indeed, the intimidation may operate in reverse—with Cabinet officers being reluctant to expose themselves and their policies to critical public examination. Until March, 1968, for example, Secretary of State Rusk dodged repeated invitations to appear publicly before the Committee on Foreign Relations to discuss Administration policies toward Southeast Asia; but he has shown no similar reluctance to hold press conferences or appear on public platforms where he is able to control any hecklers. While one thinks of the newer instruments of communication as means of promoting the exchange of ideas, it should not be forgotten that controlled communications may be dangerous to our system. I would hope the Senate would not submit meekly to any erosion of its practice of requesting that the heads of government departments appear before Senate Committees under such conditions as the Committees deem desirable.

Lindsay Rogers

IV. The Senate and Foreign Policy (by Carl Marcy)

In the field of foreign policy, "...the cards are stacked against the President. American foreign policy is determined not by him and two-thirds of the Senate, but by one-third of the Senate...." So wrote Lindsay Rogers in 1926. Four decades later,

Senator J. W. Fulbright, Chairman of the Committee on Foreign Relations, took a different view: "The reduced role of the Congress and the enhanced role of the President in the making of foreign policy are not the result merely of President Johnson's ideas of consensus; they are the culmination of a trend in the constitutional relationship between President and Congress that began in 1940, which is to say, at the beginning of this age of crisis."[1]

He included a section in his best seller, *The Arrogance of Power,* entitled "Decline of the Senate." And out of personal experience he illustrated "the extent to which the trend toward Executive predominance has gone and the extraordinary difficulty a Senator has in trying to discharge his responsibility to render useful advice and to grant or withhold his consent with adequate knowledge and sound judgment."

Illustrative of the erosion of Congressional power in the field of foreign policy, a presidential spokesman told the Committee on Foreign Relations in 1967: "... I think the expression of declaring a war is one that has become outmoded in the international arena."[2]

Subsequently President Johnson stated to the press that when the Gulf of Tonkin resolution was used as authority for the depth of American in-

[1] Senator J. William Fulbright: *The Arrogance of Power* (A Vintage Book, 1966), pp. 45 & 47.

[2] Under Secretary of State Katzenbach before the Committee on Foreign Relations, August 17, 1967, *Hearings,* p. 81.

volvement in Asia: "...We stated then, and we repeat now, we did not think the resolution was
necessary to do what we did and what we're doing.
But we thought it was desirable and we thought if
we were going to ask them [Congress] to stay the
whole route and if we expected them to be there
on the landing we ought to ask them to be there
on the takeoff."[3]

Mr. Rogers wrote in 1926 that the control over
foreign policy by one-third of the Senate "...is a
control which... unfortunately, cannot be got rid
of by any of the ordinary devices of popular government." But what of the nonordinary devices, or devices that may not reflect popular government?

The ingenuity of the Executive is well known.
"We have even come close," said Senator Frank
Church of Idaho in 1967 ". . . to reversing the traditional rule that minor or routine arrangements
with foreign countries can be made by executive
agreement while significant ones must be made by
treaty. Some months ago," continued the Senator,
"the Senate was asked to ratify, as a treaty, an
agreement with Thailand concerning taxes. It was
of course entirely proper that the tax agreement be
referred to the Senate, but when the matter was
under consideration by the Foreign Relations Committee, I was struck by the ironic fact that the
United States now has 35,000 troops in Thailand,
some of whom are engaged in military support oper-

[3] *New York Times,* August 19, 1967, p. 10.

ations against the guerrillas in northeast Thailand, and that this far more significant commitment was never referred to the Senate for its advice and consent."[4]

In this "age of crisis," are the foreign policy cards still "stacked against the President," as Mr. Rogers suggested? Has the relationship between the President and the Senate, which was set forth in rather imprecise terms in the Constitution, undergone a fundamental change? Is there an irreversible trend toward concentration of foreign policy in the President, or are we simply witnessing the historic swing of a governmental pendulum which the Founding Fathers (either with prescience or understanding of power) incorporated in the Constitution? If there is an irreversible trend, readers of this study forty years hence (if there are any) may at that time contemplate the Senate as a governmental anachronism much as we today view the House of Lords. On the other hand, there are signs that the "trend" was but the upswing of a pendulum which has now reached the apex on the Presidential side.

Writing personally, I am as willing to go out on a limb in 1968 as Mr. Rogers did in 1926 and predict that while there may be a *trend* toward Executive dominance in foreign policy that trend is subject at least to interruption and possibly to reversal.

[4] Page 3, Speech by Senator Frank Church, entitled "President and Congress in Foreign Policy: The Threat to Constitutional Government," given October 29, 1967, Idaho Club, Boise.

Or, put in a more philosophical context, the Founding Fathers who two hundred years ago had much
more time to think, read, and contemplate human
nature than we do today are at least as likely
(probably more likely) to be proven right in their
understanding of relationships between a people and
its government than today's practitioners aided by
computers, scientific devices, and pollsters who
measure everything but a voter's political blood
pressure as he stands face to face with a voting
machine. Unfortunately, while the understanding
of the Founding Fathers may be proven right, that
does not mean their concepts will prevail.

The reprinting of Mr. Rogers' classic study of the
Senate some forty years after it was first published
illustrates in a forceful way why the American
Constitution has survived so long and served the
nation so well. The *doctrine* of the separation of
powers is self-evident in the instrument itself. But
the degree to which the doctrine works in practice
can be illustrated only by looking at it from some
historic perspective. To read *The American Senate*
today is to dig up a time capsule.

The point that can be missed is that forty years
ago the Senate had acquired a "control" of foreign
policy "not contemplated by the framers (of the
Constitution), and which, unfortunately, cannot be
got rid of by any of the ordinary devices of popular
government." By 1967, however, it was the President
who had control and it is fair to add that this

Presidential control was not contemplated by the framers of the Constitution either. Perhaps this control cannot be got rid of by any of the ordinary devices either!

So it is that the reader of this book should, by putting past realities in juxtaposition with today's realities, be able to begin to comprehend the wisdom of those political pragmatists who provided a legal framework for this society, now one of the oldest, continuous Constitutional democracies on earth. The wisdom of the Founding Fathers was not in the precision with which they spelled out who should do what, but in their understanding of the balance of power as applied to the government of a democratic society.

Specifically, the reader and student of foreign policy might contemplate those conditions in 1968 which suggest that the power pendulum is swinging again toward the Senate and the Congress. Certainly during the Ninetieth Congress (1967–68), the President began to encounter foreign policy criticism that transcended partisan politics. The fact that the Committee on Foreign Relations in 1967 rejected an urgent Presidential request for a Congressional resolution in the nature of a blank check for use at a meeting of American Republic presidents at Punta del Este, and held hearings on resolutions designed to express concern at the growing tendency of the Executive to make national commitments without clear Congressional authority to do so, was significant in this respect. In the words of a report of the Committee on Foreign Relations on its so-called "Commitment Resolution": "Whether one approves or disapproves of the present division of authority, it is difficult to deny that it has come about as the result of erosion, inadvertency, expediency, and—in a few instances—usurpation." Conscious of this erosion, the Committee on Foreign Relations moved in 1967 to redress the balance by approving a resolution which reads as follows:

WHEREAS the Executive and Legislative branches of the United States Government have joint responsibility and authority to formulate the foreign policy of the United States; and

WHEREAS the authority to initiate war is vested in Congress by the Constitution; Now, therefore, be it

RESOLVED, That a commitment for purposes of this resolution means the use of, or promise to a foreign state or people to use, the armed forces of the United States either immediately or upon the happening of certain events, and

That it is the sense of the Senate that, under any circumstances which may arise in the future pertaining to situations in which the United States is not already involved, the commitment of the armed forces of the United States to hostilities on foreign territory for any purpose other than to repel an attack on the United States or to protect United States citizens or property properly will result from a decision made in accordance with constitutional

processes, which, in addition to appropriate executive action, require affirmative action by Congress
specifically intended to give rise to such commitment.

Although this resolution would have no effect in
law, the fact that the Committee on Foreign Relations, after four days of public hearings on the
subject, then spent five lengthy drafting sessions to
hammer out a resolution that was approved by a vote
of 17 to 0, gives the resolution great potential
significance in the field of foreign policy. Its implications are much broader than its words. The resolution marks the end of an era of collective defense
pacts by which the United States bound itself
under a variety of circumstances jointly and severally to come to the assistance of nations subjected
to aggression. It seems likely to mark the end
of an era of Congressional resolutions delegating
powers to the President which have been described
as "open-ended commitments" or predated declarations of war.[5]

It will be a long time before the Senate expands
current defense treaty commitments beyond the
present 42 nations or before it consents to open-
ended resolutions authorizing substantial commitment of American forces abroad. On the other hand,

[5] *Collective Defense Treaties,* April 10, 1967, A Committee
Print prepared by the Committee on Foreign Affairs, House of
Representatives (Washington: U. S. Government Printing
Office, 1967).

the President may seek to do those things himself. The procedures may be in flux, but the power issue is not dead.

Perhaps I have put the cart before the horse by predicting a resurgence of the role of the Senate, before disposing of those factors which have been denigrating the foreign policy role of the Senate since 1926.

It is interesting to speculate on the causes for the decline of the role of the Senate in the formulation of foreign policy since Mr. Rogers wrote in 1926. It was in part the reaction of internationalists, intellectuals, and idealists to the Senate's rejection of the League of Nations, which, over a period of twenty years, created a climate of criticism of the Senate that led to a gradual flow of power from the Senate to the President. There was also involved in this the famous *faux pas* of Senator Borah in the summer of 1939 when, during consideration of the repeal of the Neutrality Act, he told President Roosevelt that he (Borah) had better information from Europe than the President and that there would not be a war.

In deference to the 1926 version of the power of the Senate, postwar planners in the Department of State worked hard during World War II to be sure that the postwar international organization would not suffer the fate of the League. They educated the public and they wooed the Senate where a new generation of Senators, perhaps somewhat contrite at the action of their predecessors, sought by speeches, resolutions, and cooperation with the Executive to save the United Nations from the fate of its predecessor. Bipartisanship, or nonpartisanship, during and after World War II, was the mode and became a habit. The Foreign Relations Committee of the Senate for many postwar years took the lead in stopping politics at the three-mile limit and, in general, accepting in a rather noncritical way the prescriptions of the President for the postwar world. Senators drew the wrong lesson from Versailles. Instead of learning to exercise their prerogatives *responsibly,* they took the view that it was irresponsible to exercise them at all. Finally, it was a hardy Senator of either party who was willing to substitute his judgment for that of the President who commanded American civil servants, foreign service officers, and troops stationed throughout the world.

The habit of postwar cooperation was continued during the period from 1952 to 1960 when one might have expected mounting Senate criticism because of new programs and a more free-wheeling attitude on the part of Senators. The Senate (except for two years) was controlled by the Democrats while the White House was in the hands of the Republicans. According to textbook theory this should have been disastrous because party discipline theoretically makes the American system work better if the same party is in control in both the White House and the Senate. In the field of foreign policy, however, this is questionable.[6]

Senators take seriously their constitutional function of advice and consent. Party discipline does not keep Senators voting with their own party leader in the White House in the field of foreign policy. Indeed, administrators who take for granted that party discipline is more important to a Senator than independence in the exercise of the constitutional function of advice and consent are in for trouble sooner or later. President Eisenhower had his troubles with Republican Senators Taft, Knowland, and McCarthy when the Republicans controlled the Senate, just as President Johnson has his troubles with Democratic Senators Fulbright, Mansfield, and another McCarthy. Senators, like most of us, do not like to be taken for granted and when one-third of them can upset a foreign policy embodied in a treaty, it puts a heavy burden on a President to keep them happy.

Tacit recognition of these factors, an increasing

[6] Those who refer to the years of the Vandenberg chairmanship as an example of good Senate-Executive relationships forget that Vandenberg held the whip-hand over President Truman. Without Vandenberg, President Truman would have been powerless to join NATO or to get the Marshall Plan authorized. As it was, Vandenberg dictated to the Administration, telling it that the Economic Cooperation Administration should be an agency separate from State and that its first Administrator should be Republican Paul Hoffman from Michigan. Executive-Senate relations were good in large part because the Administration had to keep Senator Vandenberg happy.

use of executive agreements, emphasis on the need for executive flexibility to meet crises, "commitment" by Presidential declarations, and confusion between policy statements and commitments—all contributed to the power of the President to make foreign policy. Few Senators had occasion to feel any erosion of power and those who did were out of step with the new world!

When disillusionment set in, when America's monopoly on nuclear weapons was broken, when the United Nations provided only an international cloak for stopping aggression in Korea while the United States carried the main burden, and when Sputnik shook the confidence of the American people and much of the world in the eminence of American science and technological achievement, it was perhaps natural for Americans to turn to their Executive for quick decisions as to how the nation should respond to crisis. There was fear that the American democracy lacked the capacity to respond quickly to the new threats of nuclear attack and push-button warfare.

The Senate reflected this concern and seemed willing to go along with Executive requests for "flexibility" in dealing with foreign policy. It approved large foreign-aid programs on the basis of what were described as "illustrative programs"—meaning that when funds were appropriated under broad headings, the Executive might then spend them along the lines suggested, or it might not.

Collective defense treaties bound the United States formally, and jointly or severally, to respond to threats of aggression to 42 nations spread around the world. The Senate approved these treaties without ever clearly facing, and certainly not resolving, the problem of who does what as between the Congress and the Executive in the event a treaty commitment were to be presented for collection.

Testimony on these treaties revealed some ambivalence on the part of administration witnesses as to the respective roles of the Congress and the Executive in regard to the "constitutional processes" by which the United States might take action under some of these treaties. Secretary of State Acheson, however, had no doubts. The authority of the President over the use of the armed forces, Acheson told the Foreign Relations Committee in 1951, "may not be interfered with by the Congress in the exercise of powers which it has under the Constitution." "We are in a position in the world today," Acheson added, "where the argument as to who has the power to do this, that, or the other thing, is not exactly what is called for from America in this very critical hour."[7]

Probably the Executive apex of this swing of the pendulum was reached when Congress passed the

[7] "Assignment of Ground Forces of the United States to Duty in the European Area," hearing by Committees on Foreign Relations and Armed Services. U.S. Senate, Eighty-second Congress, First Session, on S.Con.Res. 8, Feb. 1–28, 1951 (Washington: U.S. Government Printing Office, 1951), pp. 92–93.

Gulf of Tonkin resolution which, as it turned out, was used by the President as moral (if not legal) authority to commit so many of the armed forces of the United States to Vietnam as to create a situation scarcely distinguishable from war.

These words are written too closely to the beginnings of a shift in power and influence to permit perspective. It seems likely, however, that two factors will prove to have been most important in prompting Senatorial introspection of the Senate's role in the formulation of foreign policy. First is the creeping nature of the involvement of the United States in Vietnam and the frustrations which grew out of that war. Second is the fact that President Johnson was a strong President. A word of explanation on this point:

There is a general assumption that strong Presidents are "good" Presidents in the sense that they acquire power for the Executive branch of the government. But is a "good" President one who strengthens his office at the expense of the other branches of the government, or is a "good" President one who respects federalism and the separation of powers? Fortunately and almost inevitably, our system of government has thus far operated so as to generate countervailing force. Even at a time when six of the last seven Presidents and Vice Presidents came from the Senate (President Truman, Vice-President Nixon, President Kennedy, Vice-President Johnson, President Johnson, Vice-President Humphrey) and might have been expected to revere if not to respect their old establishment ties, power has moved toward the President.

I suggest, however, that this flood tide of power is about to ebb. During the last two years the overuse of the powers of the Presidency by that former leader of the Senate establishment, President Johnson, has set up countervailing forces which presidential successors will need to deal with for a generation—just as the overuse of the powers of the Senate in 1919 and 1920 by Senator Lodge created countervailing forces which weakened the role of the Senate for perhaps a generation.

When Mr. Rogers published *The American Senate* in 1926, the Chairman of the Committee on Foreign Relations was William E. Borah of Idaho—a strong Committee Chairman. On republication of this volume, J. William Fulbright of Arkansas—a strong Committee Chairman—had a younger Idaho Senator on his Committee—Senator Frank Church. Surveying the impact of the Vietnam war and other global involvements of the United States, actual and potential, which have so absorbed American energies, Senator Church commented on the constitutional effects of the new responsibilities of the United States, and said:

> One of the least noticed, but, in the long run, most important of these effects has been the unhinging of constitutional processes in our government, particularly in the making of foreign policy.

As crisis has followed upon crisis in these last twenty-five years, more and more power has accumulated in the hands of the President while the Congress has been reduced to virtual impotence in the making of foreign policy.

The cause of this change has been the long series of crises, each of which necessitated—or seemed to necessitate—decisive and immediate action. As each crisis arose, the President assumed, and the Congress usually agreed, that the executive alone was capable of acting with the requisite speed. No one thought very much about the constitutional consequences of Presidential dominance in foreign policy; we tended to think only of the crisis we were dealing with, of the need for speedy action, and of the importance of national unity in a time of emergency.

Now, however, we have got to think about constitutional problems because nothing less than the survival of constitutional government is at stake. Our democratic processes, our system of separated powers, checked and balanced against each other, are being undermined by the very methods we have chosen to defend these processes against foreign dangers.[8]

Ideally the foreign policy of a democracy is one which combines the maximum amount of expert knowledge with the maximum amount of public support. Under our system of government the way

[8] Speech by Senator Frank Church, entitled "President and Congress in Foreign Policy: The Threat to Constitutional Government," October 29, 1967, Idaho Club, Boise.

we try to get this is through a system of checks and balances. Thus, the foreign policy expert in the field of economic development may know that United States interests in Asia require larger aid programs. But he may not know the impact of what he proposes on many domestic programs. So it is the Congress which provides the check—the broader look. The expert may be too generous, and the Congress too stingy, but that is part of what the struggle between the Executive and the Congress is all about.

The President who tells the American people that if they could just read the cables and if they knew what the State Department knows they would support his foreign policies makes a debater's point which the critic will meet by suggesting that if the secret information is so persuasive, why not tell the people? But that is only half the story. The President must have two ingredients that do not show in the cables—he must have a substantial degree of domestic support and, closely related, he should receive and respect the judgment of representatives who are at least as close to the people as he is.

As pointed out by Professor Ruhl Bartlett in urging that Congress reassert its role in the determination of foreign policy, one must reject this

> . . . idea that foreign relations in their economic, political, and military aspects are so intricate and complex as to be largely beyond the understanding of Congressmen and far beyond the comprehension

of the ordinary citizen [and that] such matters must
be left, therefore, to experts in the Executive branch
of the Government. In addition to being insulting,
this argument is utterly fallacious. Experts are
needed in the mechanics of many things whether
they are called professions or something else, but
there are no experts in wisdom concerning human
affairs or in determining the national interest, and
there is nothing in the realm of foreign policy that
cannot be understood by the average American
citizen.[9]

Or, as another Senator posed the same issue,
"American involvement in Vietnam and what we
do about it has now reached the point where our
American policies must be determined largely by
the exercise of good judgment. Where American
policy goes from here cannot be justified on the
basis of implications that there exists a body of
'facts' to which the Administration is privy...." For
example, "the Joint Chiefs of Staff and the President do not know whether a little more bombing
will bring the other side to negotiations, or whether
the North Vietnamese have the same staying power
as Texans at the Alamo."[10] This is a matter of
judgment.

The expertise which the Executive branch can

[9] Hearings before the Committee on Foreign Relations, U.S.
Commitments to Foreign Powers, S. Res. 151, Ninetieth Congress, First Session, p. 20, August 16, 1967.

[10] Senator Vance Hartke (Ind.), *Congr. Record*, October 24,
1967, p. S15183.

bring to the conduct of foreign policy must be leavened, whether the expert likes it or not, by other judgments and by the yeast of public attitude. As we should perhaps have learned in Korea, and certainly are learning in Vietnam, undeclared wars are hard to explain and hard to wage if dissent is widespread.

Put another way, the President may believe he has the "facts" and he may believe his advisers have the best judgment, but in the final analysis, it may be the legislative branch which has the "votes"— and, human nature being what it is, it is possible, indeed, even likely that the "judgment" of the elected official is, on the average, at least the equal of the expert in the bureaucracy.

It can be argued that the Chief Executive has great advantages in the struggle with the Congress because he has at his command vast resources of information garnered from the ends of the earth by the Foreign Service. On the other hand, Members of the Congress often have a continuity of service at policy levels unmatched by high officials in the Executive branch. A Fulbright or Hickenlooper by 1968 had been active in determining legislative policy toward foreign nations through the terms of five Presidents, seven Secretaries of State, and Heaven knows how many Assistant Secretaries. Senators may be skimpy on detail, but they are long on policy and experienced in judgment. The Chairman of the Preparedness Subcommittee of the Senate has been more accurate in his defense spending estimates in recent years than the Department of Defense. The staff of the Joint Committee on Internal Revenue Taxation has the reputation of developing better budget estimates than the Treasury.

One advantage which will always lie with the Executive in the continuing struggle between the Legislative and Executive branches for power and influence in the field of foreign policy is the monolithic character of the Executive. While there may be internal struggles and debate prior to the adoption of a policy, once the President has decided, it is the duty of his agents to assist in the execution of that policy. Furthermore, the internal debate of the Executive branch remains, for the most part, hidden from public view. The Congress, on the other hand, can—and should—only resolve its policy disputes in the full light of publicity. And once its policy disagreements are resolved by a vote, a narrow margin vote may still keep alive the hope that a change may be brought about.

It is the Congress which for this reason has the duty to hold the Executive with its aristocratic and secret-prone foreign policy instincts to public accountability for foreign policy. It is only by bringing democracy into foreign policy procedures and decisions that a national consensus can hope to be formed. If a national consensus cannot be formed and maintained by public debate in the Congress, the sooner the President knows that, the better—

papered-over dissent is no substitute for democratic support. If Anthony Eden could have foreseen domestic British dissent before he conspired with the French and the Israelis to move into the Middle East, would he have done so? If President Johnson had clearly put the issue of war or peace to the Congress in 1964—or at a subsequent time—might he not have had a foretaste of the domestic dissent of 1967 and would he under those circumstances have escalated in Vietnam in 1965?

Vietnam is teaching Washington a great many things—one of which is the importance of thorough public debate before voting on issues that may involve the nation in war. Handy as it has been for the President to note that the Tonkin Resolution was opposed by only two senators, the paucity of facts, the perfunctory character of public consideration of the issue, and the pressure for precipitate action did not create the consensus or law-abiding support that the President must surely at a later time have wished he had.

I recall some years ago when a Senator was berating the late Senator Taft for his support of an appropriation to pay the United States' share of NATO costs when only the year before Senator Taft had opposed approval of the North Atlantic Treaty. Senator Taft replied that he was a law-abiding citizen and, although he had opposed the North Atlantic Treaty, its approval had made it the law of the land and he felt, therefore, compelled to support the treaty and to support United States' obligations under it. Had Senator Taft been referring to something other than a treaty with a twenty-year life, however, I suspect he would not have been hesitant to re-open the issue. I suspect further that his law-abiding instincts might have been strained by the Tonkin Resolution and its history.

Preoccupation in the previous pages with the swing of power as between the Senate and the Executive should not obscure the fundamental change that has taken place since 1926 in the relationship of the United States to the rest of the world. The Constitution did not survive the Civil War without significant formal amendment. But transition from an isolationist society to a society which is involved in every part of the world has brought no formal changes.

As a former student of Mr. Rogers (although not as far back as 1926), I am confident that a sure path to flunking his course would have been to predict that within forty years the United States, with the approval of the Congress, would have spread foreign economic, military, and technical aid to more than 100 countries (including the Soviet Union) in an amount in excess of $110,000,000,000. Under these circumstances, it is remarkable that the relationship of the Senate and the Executive has not changed more than it has. The pendulum is still there and working.

Since 1926 there has been a complete change in

the composition of the Senate (the senior Senator Hayden came to the Senate in 1927). The east front of the Capitol has been rebuilt; new office buildings have gone up; the old Senate monorail subway has been replaced; Senate staffs have expanded; the Senate Chamber has been rebuilt; flowing senatorial manes have disappeared (but they may come back). But these are superficial changes.

The institution of the Senate changes, and yet it remains the same. It is the institution nearest to the pure democracy that was found in the town meetings of New England. The Senate is on occasion exasperating, petty, or mean but, on other occasions, great. It is indeed the culminating institution in the democratic form of government which Winston Churchill described as "the worst form of Government except all those other forms that have been tried."

Members of the Senate cherish their rights and prerogatives. They feel, as Gibbon wrote in the *History of the Decline and Fall of the Roman Empire,* that the "principles of a free constitution are irrevocably lost when the legislative power is nominated by the executive."[11]

Carl Marcy

[11] Random House, Modern Library Ed., Vol. I, p. 54.

THE AMERICAN SENATE

THE AMERICAN SENATE

by Lindsay Rogers

NEW YORK
ALFRED A. KNOPF
MCMXXVI

"A little group of willful men, representing no opinion but their own, have rendered the great government of the United States helpless and contemptible."

WOODROW WILSON

"That remarkable body, the most remarkable of all the inventions of modern politics, the Senate of the United States."

W. E. GLADSTONE

"Things are seldom what they seem,
  Skim milk masquerades as cream."

W. S. GILBERT

PREFACE

The nature of this brief discourse on the Senate of the United States is indicated by the texts on a preceding page, and the main points of my argument are adumbrated in the following Introduction. Here, therefore, a word will suffice:

The Senate has been much written about, but it now discloses, I venture to believe, certain angles which until recently have not been so obvious, and which have been given little comment. This is to be expected, for the political stock company puts on new dramas; the scenes constantly change, and institutions play different rôles of varying importance. Contrary to the expectations of the Founding Fathers, and to the almost universal experience of constitutional government elsewhere, the upper chamber in the United States is now the more powerful branch of Congress, and, indeed, one of the most powerful legislative assemblies in the world.

Forty years ago, Sir Henry Maine boldly declared that the Senate was "the one thoroughly successful institution which has been established since the tide of modern democracy began to run." The truth is that the Senate is a product of distrust of democracy, and that certain of its executive functions are now so pervasive as to query its success; but, on the other hand—and this is my principal

point—Sir Henry Maine was correct in an undreamed of connection: The Senate is the only
American institution so organized and articulated
as to exert any supervision over the executive, and
this function would be impossible were the rules to
provide for closure.

In arguing this, I have to pay some attention to
recent developments of the House of Representatives and the Presidency, for the American Senate
is a subject which, even narrowly limited, cannot be
considered apart from the congressional system as
a whole. This, of course, is as it should be. The
American Government has been more frequently
and more fully described than any other set of
political institutions that the world has known, yet
there is an amazing dearth of analysis and criticism
of the manner in which our system really functions.
This results partly from the fact that, in Professor
Beard's phrase, American politics has been under
bondage to the lawyers; that constitutionality has
been put above every other earthly consideration.
Partly also the predominance of description (and
the absence of analysis) is due to the practical impossibility of structural change. Why point out
defects or make suggestions if nothing can be done?
But there is, I think, one additional reason: the
American political canvas is so vast that the painter,
if he fills the whole, must himself slur, and can with
difficulty attract the attention of his audience to, detailed relationships. There are, therefore, some
distinct advantages in selecting and concentrating
attention on a single portion of the American po-

litical scene. Its beauty or ugliness will be more apparent, and the way this results from or affects adjacent portions of the picture will be more understandable.

My view then, shortly stated, is this: The undemocratic, usurping Senate is the indispensable check and balance in the American system, and only complete freedom of debate permits it to play this rôle. Its power comes, in large part, from the guillotine to which the House of Representatives submits—a procedure which has attracted scant attention—and is the more indispensable because it is directed against government by favorable publicity through the medium of the White House "Spokesman." Adopt closure in the Senate, and the character of the American Government will be profoundly changed. This is the subject that I discuss in the following essay, and I make no apology if occasionally I may seem to have the qualifications that Byron said Mitford possessed for writing history: "Complete partiality and a bad temper." Considering my purpose and method, this may be an advantage.

                                                    L. R.

Columbia University,
June 1, 1926

CONTENTS

APPENDICES:

THE AMERICAN SENATE

CHAPTER I

INTRODUCTORY

"On all great subjects, much remains to be said."
—JOHN STUART MILL.

"An assembly of old men or elders; hence an assembly or council with the highest deliberative and legislative functions." [1] Thus the lexicographers define a Senate, and the criticism is frequently made that American Senators always try not to belie one of the implications of their name; if senatorial wisdom is sometimes not *sans reproche,* senatorial deliberation is always *sans peur.* Expedition is rare and precipitancy is unknown. The most powerful upper chamber in the world is more execrated for its delay in acting than for the specific decisions which it may reach. Throughout its existence, the

[1] "The place of the heart, on the authority of Plutarch, is filled by the Senate. Now 'senate' according to the opinion of the ancients is the name of an office, and its distinguishing mark is old age; the word senate is itself derived from 'senectus,' which means old age. The Athenians called it Areopagus, as if for the reason that in its members was gathered the strength of the whole people; and although that nation made many notable inventions, they established nothing more wholesome nor more famous than their Senate. For what is more noble than an assembly of elders, who having faithfully completed their terms in the ordinary offices, then pass on to the duty of giving counsel and exercising rulership, and in feeble bodies thus put forth the strength of the mind? They are the better fitted to the business of wisdom in proportion as they

Senate has had more honor abroad than in its own country, and in recent years it has been increasingly under fire for its garrulity and its dominating influence in the governmental system. I say "in recent times," for at first, the House of Representatives was the more influential chamber; the Senate acted principally as a council of revision, and it did not presume to lead the way in legislation, to determine foreign policy, and to attempt supervision of the executive.

The organs of a government always compete for power and authority. Executive and legislature, upper chamber and lower chamber, electorate and representatives, permanent officials and political heads—the struggle never comes to an end. Throughout the world, during the last decade, one unmistakable tendency of this conflict has been the decline of second chambers. The Senates which can triumph in controversies with lower houses are in a decided minority, and occasional victories as in Canada and France only serve to call attention to the customarily subordinate rôle of the upper cham-

are the less able to perform feats of the body. Truly they came into such honor among the Greeks that the leaders of the commonwealth nowhere took any step, and nothing considerable was done, which the appointed elders did not initiate or approve; and what is more, from the foundation of the City [of Rome] their names were inscribed in letters of gold, and they were therefore called by all 'conscript' fathers, as excelling all others in wisdom, age, and fatherly affection. In their hands was the authority of counsel and of carrying out all public undertakings. Moreover, though we have seen that their name was derived from their age, I think that what was meant was not merely age of body but of mind." John Dickinson, *The Statesman's Book of John of Salisbury,* Book V, Chapter 9 (New York, 1926).

ber, and to lead to a demand that it be adhered to; for bicameralism, though it may be advocated in theory, has been greatly attenuated in practice.

The Parliament Act of 1911 was one landmark of this tendency, and practically all of the Constitutions adopted after the Paris Peace Conference put second chambers in a state of nonage similar to that enjoyed by the House of Lords. For the suspensive veto of two years which that body may exercise on legislation, the European systems substitute a suspensive veto that may be quickly overcome by the repassage of the disputed measure by a special majority of the lower house. The Constitutions of Germany, Austria, Czecho-Slovakia and Poland, for example, set up secondary, rather than second chambers, which may only delay temporarily action by the lower houses. There is thus a new measure of truth in the generalization of the late Professor Esmein, that foreign governments had adapted the idea of a second chamber from the idea of the House of Lords. It may be added that the degree of borrowing has been not unrelated to the degree of misunderstanding, but the family of the mother of parliaments continues to grow. The progeny have been different.

The oldest of these descendants is the American Senate—now the most powerful second chamber in the world. This alone makes it deserving of attention; while upper chambers elsewhere wane, the Senate waxes. It is a body whose development has completely falsified the confident anticipations of the framers of the American Constitution: few if any issues have arisen to make the small states require protection against the more populous states, and, instead of being only a check in the congressional system, the Senate is now a senior partner —more influential and venturesome than the House of Representatives.   The Senate is, generally speaking, the principal, if not the only forum of the nation; interests are espoused and aspirations are voiced which have no chance of being presented on the floor of the House of Representatives.   In respect of its executive functions, the Senate is exercising a greater supervision over the President's appointments, and has fought for a control over his removals—a controversy which, after 139 years, pointed to astonishing *lacunae* in the American Constitution.   The trend may be toward "Government of the Senate, by the Senate and for the Senate," a result, which, in the opinion of many, has already been reached in the control of foreign relations: the Senate rather than the Executive determines the treaty engagements of the United States.

This dominance is partly personal, but largely institutional.   When the White House was occupied by Cleveland, Roosevelt and Wilson, it was the presidency that was much discussed, and particularly under Wilson there were many complaints that executive authority was becoming too powerful, and that Congress was being relegated too far to the background.   "The laws", in Burke's classic phrase, "reach but a very little way.   Constitute government how you please, infinitely the greater part of it must depend upon the exercise of powers which are left at large to the prudence and uprightness of ministers of state." Since Mr. Wilson left the White House, presidential prudence has sometimes been synonymous with presidential complaisance in the face of senatorial aggrandizement; but even during the latter part of the Wilson administration, the Senate, at least in the struggle over the Treaty of Versailles, succeeded in being the dominant partner. Since that battle, its authority in foreign affairs has become more and more pervasive. International policy is largely determined in the Capitol instead of the State Department or the White House.

One tremendous advantage that the Senate has in such controversies arises from the fact that it —almost alone among modern legislative assemblies—refuses to permit closure; a minority may obstruct and triumph, and while limitations were put on the League of Nations debate in 1919, and the World Court debate in January, 1926, their price was substantial concessions by the majority. Yet curiously enough, freedom of debate, although sanctioning minority control by avoirdupois rather than by argument, has proved to be a valuable safeguard against executive inefficiency and corruption. Because closure is impossible, Senate minorities are able to force some accountability into the rigid irresponsibility of the American system; if not confronted by the weapon of unrestricted debate, party control, untempered by fear of the electorate, could become a party cloak, effectively concealing what the executive desired to conceal. Whatever may be thought of the rightfulness or wrongfulness of the Senate's power over appointments, treaties, and legislation, there can be no question, I think, of its benefits with regard to checking the executive. Much can be forgiven an aggrandizing body which forces some measure of responsibility into an otherwise irresponsible system, and, as will appear later, this particular senatorial power would be impossible but for unlimited debate.

Thus viewed, the question of closure becomes of crucial importance. Advocates of restrictions on debate rest their case on the clichés of democracy, and transform government by a majority from an imperfect device into an eternal principle. They completely overlook the fact that even if the filibustering minorities kill some meritorious legislation and treaties, the price will be a small one to pay for retaining some measure of legislative control of the executive. Abolish closure and the Senate will gradually sink to the level of the House of Representatives where there is less deliberation and debate than in any other legislative assembly. At present the United States may boast of the most powerful upper chamber and the most ineffective lower chamber in the world. The secret of this transformation is to be found in rules of procedure to which, unfortunately, little or no attention is paid.

To be sure, the standing orders of legislative assemblies are a dull and complex business, yet it is only through understanding exactly how the House of Representatives plays the rôle of a rubber stamp that one may realize the exact nature of the Senate's task; and it is only by keeping in mind the rigid, separated character of the American Government that one may see how indispensable are political debate, investigations by senatorial committees, and attempted scrutiny of executive activities, and how impossible they would be if a majority could act whenever it desired. That a majority of the House of Commons may act whenever it cares to has no bearing on the American problem, for England is governed by a responsible Cabinet, and the United States is not. It is not my purpose here to discuss the merits of the two systems; my only point is that our machinery of government is so different that it requires its own peculiar throttles and safety-valves.[2] In describing these and in discussing the work that they do, my plow (to mix the metaphors) will have to turn up some familiar earth, but the arrangement of the furrows, I venture to believe, will be new, and they will show the Senate in an unfamiliar light.

In short, the United States, which prides itself on adherence to democratic theory, possesses a Senate which is undemocratic in its composition, and which enjoys enormous powers, for the exercise of which it cannot be held accountable; yet at the same time, the Senate is the single American institution that can enforce some measure of responsibility and

[2] There is no bias in my use of metaphors—a danger which has been discussed by Mr. J. A. Hobson. He has suggested that "in modern times, the Constitution is preëminently a piece of machinery, a thing of carefully adjusted parts and balances. Thrust a ramrod into this delicate machinery, you do irreparable mischief. Disturb the nice equipoise of its constituent parts, you bring it to a standstill." Or, regarded as a tree, the Constitution "changes slowly by some internal laws of growth which cannot be safely interfered with by any Parliament or People! Radical reform is thus ruled out by metaphor." *Free Thought in the Social Sciences*, pp. 24–25 (New York, 1926).

mitigate the autocracy and security which may be synonymous with the dogma of the separation of powers. The Senate, originally a compromise, is now a paradox. Once a counterpoise, it is now the grand vizier. These contrarieties I propose to discuss.

CHAPTER II

THE FOUNDING FATHERS AND THE SENATE

"This masterpiece of the constitution makers was in fact a happy accident."

—BRYCE.

The task confronting the framers of the American Constitution was not easy. Government under the Articles of Confederation had been weak and ineffective, and there was general agreement that something had to be done. But what? How reconcile a strong government with colonial particularism and separatism? Yet this was essential, and "the Founding Fathers"—as President Harding called them—could draw on no overwhelming variety of political experiment such as was known to the post-war European constituent assemblies. British and Colonial experience furnished the models which were to suggest adaptations or inventions to the men of the Philadelphia Convention, and one of their most distinctive creations was the American Senate.

Under the Articles of Confederation, the Colonies had equal voices in the Congress; unanimous consent was required for the amendment of the Articles, and the approval of nine (out of thirteen) States in Congress was necessary for all important matters. This was manifestly unsatisfactory, but what change was possible to keep a minority from holding up important decisions and to safeguard the interests of the small as against the larger Colonies? This was the most difficult problem that faced the Convention, and its solution was an important adjustment in an instrument of government which, as finally written, was little more than a bundle of compromises. The Senate, the principal compromise of the Constitution, brought to an end the great controversy over the method of representation—by States or by population.

Before this question was settled, the issues that it raised threatened for a time to break up the Convention. The populous Colonies were, by their size, encouraged to stress the disadvantage of equality of voting, and to argue for representation in proportion to population. The smaller Colonies feared that they would be outvoted and dictated to. The so-called Virginia plan provided for proportionate representation in both houses of a bicameral legislature; the New Jersey plan proposed equal representation in a unicameral body. These were the major drafts that were before the Convention. The first decision was that there should be two chambers. Then, on June 11, 1787, when the Convention had been in session only three weeks, representation in the first chamber according to population was accepted in Committee of the Whole by a vote of seven States to three (the vote of Maryland being divided) and in the second chamber by six to five. On the latter issue at least, the small

States declared that they would not yield, and feeling ran to a high pitch. Much of the discussion turned on the theoretical question of whether separation from Great Britain made the States separate from one another; whether, in other words, they were sovereign and entitled to equal representation. The situation was not relieved by these metaphysical arguments, and it became so threatening that Franklin, whose religious views were hardly orthodox, proposed "imploring the assistance of Heaven" and opening the Convention sessions with prayer. This was objected to by certain of the members, for the reason that it might lead to "disagreeable animadversions" and give the impression that the Convention was hopelessly divided. One story is that Hamilton declared the Convention not to be in need of "foreign aid" but whatever the fact, some comfort or regret may now be found in the creation of the American Senate without the assistance of prayer.

The struggle came to a head on July 2, when the Convention voted on the composition of the second branch of the legislature. The State delegations in attendance were now evenly divided—five to five. The vote of Georgia was split. A Grand Committee, composed of one member from each State was therefore chosen to consider the question. The personnel of this Committee was quite favorable to the small State party,[1] and it was evident that

[1] "One would fain know the political manœuvering that preceded the election of the Committee. The moment that it was chosen, the large-state party was beaten in its effort to have

the proportional principle, as applied to the upper chamber, was doomed. Three days later, the Committee recommended that the lower house should be based on population, and that in the second chamber, each State should have an equal vote. This was carried (on July 16) by a vote of five to four —the small States, of course, voting in the affirmative, with the Massachusetts delegation divided, and that of New York absent. Had the Convention been acting not by representatives of States, but by representatives apportioned according to population, this result would not have been possible. Had the small States been beaten, they would, in all probability, have withdrawn from the Convention. The compromise as proposed was not accepted by the larger States without considerable grumbling, and it failed also to give complete satisfaction to the smaller States, whose representatives had urged at different times that the Senators should be paid by States and should vote by States instead of as individuals.[2] This extreme form of federalism, however, was not accepted. Each State was to have two Senators, elected by its state legislature, for a term of six years, one-third of the terms expiring every two years. The Constitution gave a

proportional representation in both houses; for not one of the really strong men of the nationalists was chosen."—A. C. McLaughlin, *The Confederation and the Constitution,* p. 234 (New York, 1905).

[2] Roger Sherman proposed in the Grand Committee "that each State should have an equal vote in the 2d branch; provided that no decision therein should prevail unless the majority of States concurring should also comprize a majority of the inhabitants of the United States"—Max Farrand, *The Framing of the Constitution of the United States,* p. 98 (New Haven, 1913).

guarantee "that no State without its consent, shall be deprived of its equal suffrage in the Senate" and conferred on the upper chamber certain special functions of an executive and judicial character: confirmation of appointments, ratification of treaties, and the trial of impeachments. In legislative power, the Senate was equal to the House of Representatives, except that bills for raising revenue must originate in the more popular body.

In making these adjustments, the framers were as much concerned by the dangers of democracy as by the necessity of protecting the small States. The Constitution was ingeniously and meticulously contrived to bridle the majority and protect established rights. It created different sources of political power for the several branches of the government, and then, as an extra safeguard, checked and balanced these branches against each other in the exercise of their authority. This hope *The Federalist* frankly expressed:

"If men were angels, no government would be necessary. If angels were to govern men, neither external nor internal controls on government would be necessary. In framing a government which is to be administered by men over men, the great difficulty lies in this: you must first enable the government to control the governed; and in the next place oblige it to control itself. A dependence on the people is no doubt a primary control on the government; but experience has taught mankind the necessity of auxiliary precautions. . . .

"If a majority be united by a common interest, the rights of the minority will be insecure. There are but two methods of providing against this evil: the one by creating a will in the community independent of the majority—that is, of the society itself; the other by comprehending in the society so many separate descriptions of citizens as will render an unjust combination of the majority of the whole very improbable, if not impracticable. The first method prevails in all governments possessing an hereditary or self-appointed authority. . . . the second method will be exemplified in the Federal Republic of the United States. Whilst all authority in it will be derived from and dependent on the society, *the society itself will be broken into so many parts, interests and classes of citizens, that the rights of individuals or of the minority will be in little danger from interested combinations of the majority.*[3]

This breaking up process the Constitution achieved. The leading branches of the American government derive their powers from different sources. The "auxiliary precautions" are well thought out. The House of Representatives is elected by the mass of the people, but the suffrage qualifications are determined by the individual States, subject now to the provisions of the Federal Constitution that negroes and women shall not be denied the right to vote. The Senate was elected by the legislatures of the States, and these, in 1787, were rather generally based on property qualifications. Sometimes this qualification was different for the lower and upper houses of the state legislatures. The President of the United States was to be chosen by an Electoral College, members of which were appointed in such manner as the legislatures of the States determine, and although the Electoral College now is only an automaton, and

[3] *The Federalist,* No. 51.

simply registers the popular vote, it would be possible for any state legislature that so desired to appoint its Presidential Electors itself, or to designate the Governor, or any other agency that it chose to make the selection. Popular participation in the choice of the President rests not upon the Constitution, but upon the consent of the state legislatures. Appointments of judges are made by the President and confirmed by the Senate, but both the appointing and confirming authorities are not subject to direct popular checks and hold office for terms different from the biennial period of the House of Representatives. Indeed, the terms of the major branches of the American government are so arranged as to raise effective shields against gusts of popular passion. Members of the House of Representatives serve for two years, and they do not begin to legislate in a regular congressional session until thirteen months after their election. Senators serve for six years (taking office after the same period) and one-third of the membership is renewed every two years. The President of the United States has a term of four years, and federal judges hold office for life. It is entirely possible, therefore, that a popular demand for particular legislation must continue unabated for six years in order to be effective, and then it may later be made nugatory by judicial review. One could hardly say that the American system makes for undue precipitancy. The "auxiliary precautions" are numerous and effective.[4]

[4] *Cf.* Charles A. Beard, *An Economic Interpretation of the Constitution of the United States,* p. 161 (New York, 1913).

It is worthwhile stressing these intentions of the framers, for one must understand clearly the nature of the system they desired in order to appreciate the present-day importance of the Senate. This importance is quite different from that contemplated by the architects of the Constitution, but it results, nevertheless, from their arrangements to prevent "an unjust combination of the majority." It results, furthermore, from the falsification of two of their major hopes with respect to the Senate. The men in the Philadelphia Convention parcelled out power so that each possessor would be powerless, but the President is now a puissant autocrat unchecked (public opinion apart) save by what scrutiny Congress and its committees may bestow upon him and the departments. The Senate's share in this supervision (much more important than that of the House) was undreamed of by the draughtsmen of the Constitution, and it is so significant because, contrary to expectations, executive separateness may mean bureaucratic security, and nonfeasance or malfeasance. Mitigation of this by the Senate, however, would not be possible if the Philadelphia Convention had realized its hope that the upper chamber would be an aristocratic body. The margin by which this result has not been reached is rather closely proportioned to the Senate's effectiveness in being an actual or latent check on the executive. In this respect the framers were fortunately not fatidical.

Proposals, indeed, were made in the Convention to confine the membership to the propertied classes, and it was suggested that the representation of the different States should vary according to their wealth. Hamilton, as is well known, had a profound admiration for the British Constitution, and he thought the House of Lords "a most noble institution" which formed a "permanent barrier against every pernicious innovation." His idea was that the Senate should be chosen for life by electors who were chosen by the voters, and when the Constitution did not embody his ideas on this point, he had some doubts as to the stability of the system that was set up.[5] Other members of the Convention urged the advisability of a property qualification for membership in the Senate, and it was said that a term of six years and indirect election would be inadequate safeguards "if needy persons" should be selected. It was proposed also that no salary should be paid to Senators, and that since this body "was meant to represent the wealth of the country, it ought to be composed of persons of wealth; and if no allowance was to be made, the wealthy alone would undertake the service." [6]

The Founding Fathers were extremely able men, but they were decidedly not democrats, and this original intention makes recent developments in respect of the Senate more interesting. Even John Dickinson, on whose motion the decision was reached that the Senators should be elected by the state legislatures, "wished the Senate to consist of the most distinguished characters, distinguished for their rank in life and their weight of property,

[5] McLaughlin, *op. cit.*, pp. 218–219.
[6] Farrand, *Records of the Federal Convention,* Vol. I, pp. 426–428 (New Haven, 1911).

and bearing as strong a likeness to the British House of Lords as was possible." Twentieth century Senators will probably agree that Dickinson was prophetic in the case of "distinguished characters" but not prophetic in the likeness to the British House of Lords, certainly in respect of reduction of authority. Madison thought that a "second branch, as a limited number of citizens, respectable for wisdom and virtue, will be watched by and will keep watch over the representatives of the people; it will seasonably interpose between impetuous councils, and will guard the minority who are placed above indigence against the agrarian attempts of the ever increasing class who labor under the hardships of life, and secretly strive for a more equal distribution of its blessings." Gouverneur Morris expressed the hope "that the Senate will show us the might of aristocracy." [7]

Before popular vote was substituted for election by state legislatures, this ideal had on occasion been partly realized. The Senate was called a millionaires' club. Its leadership was strongly conservative, and property was pretty well entrenched. Gouverneur Morris's hope had not been in vain. The fact was, however, that the degree of realization seemed to be increased by the obviousness of the modicum. With a small number of Senators and with unlimited debate, that is to say, one saw the representatives of property and their influence much more clearly than was the case in the House of Representatives where size, ex-

[7] Ford, *The Rise and Growth of American Politics*, p. 53 (New York, 1898).

treme forms of guillotine, and strict party control muddied the currents of the influence of wealth, at the same time that they stifled radical minorities. In the absence of analyses of votes over a long period, generalizations are risky, but it is safe to say, I think, that, by and large, and more especially in recent years, the Senate has been but slightly more "illiberal" than the House of Representatives. On the legislation regulating railroads, on the anti-trust laws, the Senate as a whole was no less willing to act than the House of Representatives. Because of procedural differences, reactionary minorities were more in the open, but the general trends of legislative opinion were not different; and on certain matters, like the Sedition Law of 1918, the Senate has been more solicitous of individual liberty. Party leadership in the House of Representatives was, in 1918, so effective that the measure passed practically unchanged. It was in the Senate that the real protests were made and the bill was amended so that liberty of speech was not completely extinguished—an action which was comparable to that of the House of Lords in the case of the Defense of the Realm Act. Water power,[8] oil lands, and other natural resources have, on the whole, been no more strongly protected by the Senate than by the House. The degree of protection was simply more obvious in the case of the smaller body; its general conservatism and interest in the constitutional question of national power have caused it to delay and move slowly.

[8] See Kerwin, *Federal Water Power Legislation* (Columbia University Studies, 1926).

Over the whole period of its existence, however, the Senate has unquestionably originated more important legislation than has the House of Representatives.

This, indubitably, the framers of the Constitution did not anticipate. Hamilton thought "on the credit of historical examples as from the reason of the thing, that the most *popular* branch of every government partaking of the republican genius, by being generally the favourite of the people, will be as generally a full match, if not an overmatch for every other member of the government." [9] Contrary to this prophecy, the Senate has been a "full match" for every other member of the government, and legislatively it has lorded it over the House of Representatives. The Senate, of course, has an immense advantage in that it is a smaller body. Until recently the turnover among Senators was less than that among Representatives. Members of the upper chamber were elected by their State legislatures for term after term, and acquired expertise which gave them a decided advantage over their inexperienced associates. The Senate has been relied upon to perfect measures as they come from the House of Representatives, and primacy in drafting ability frequently means primacy in determining the policy that measures shall embody. Through its executive functions—appointments and treaties—the Senate gained prestige which helped it legislatively. Its longer term has made for independence, and the power which comes from im-

[9] *The Federalist*, No. 66.

munity from perpetual political preoccupations. A Representative is elected, say, in November, 1924; he begins his work, normally, at the session of December, 1925 (although there may be a special session from March 4 on) and then stands for re-election again in November, 1926.   Much of his time must be taken up with his political fences; he always lives in the shadow of his constituency, and always thinks of the repercussions that his congressional activity may have back home.   Furthermore, since the 6th day of April, 1789, the upper chamber, as Senator Lodge pointed out, "has never been, legally speaking, reorganized.   It has been in continuous, and organized existence for one hundred and thirty-two years, because two-thirds of the Senate being always in office, there never has been such a thing as the Senate requiring reorganization as is the case with each newly elected House. . . . There may be no House of Representatives, but merely an unorganized body of members elect; there may be no President duly installed in office.   But there is always the organized Senate of the United States." [10]   It has had in full measure what Bryce called "collective self-esteem"; it has also shown, he might have added, individual self-esteem.   The consequences are visible in the Senate's insistence on the full enoyment of its executive prerogatives.

[10] Henry Cabot Lodge, *The Senate of the United States and other Essays*, p. 2 (1921).

CHAPTER III

THE SENATE AS AN EXECUTIVE COUNCIL

*"Upon what meat doth this our Cæsar feed,
That he is grown so great?"*

1. *Appointments*

Earlier drafts of the Constitution sought to set up the Senate as a real executive council, and at one time in the deliberations of the Convention, the upper house seemed likely to have more authority than was finally given to it. Judges were to be appointed and ambassadors were to be sent by the Senate, which was "to make treaties of peace and alliance." It was expected that the Senate would sit continuously, and it was urged that salaries be higher than for Representatives, because Senators "would be detained longer from home [and] obliged to remove their families, and in time of war perhaps to sit constantly." [1] The compromise in the matter greatly reduced the Senate's powers, but it is nevertheless incorrect to say with Professor Ford that "in the ordinary procedure of the Senate, all that remains of its privy council functions is the fossil imprint preserved in the phrase that 'the

[1] Farrand, *Records of the Federal Convention,* Vol. II, p. 293.

Senate advises and consents' used in ratifying treaties or confirming appointments." [2]   This was certainly not expected at the time; the clause was objected to because, even as limited, it put dangerous power into the hands of the Senate.   That body, James Wilson declared, would really control the President through the control of appointees.   "According to the plan as it now stands, the President will not be the man of the people, as he ought to be, but the minion of the Senate." [3]   This "fossil imprint" has made some "minions of the Senate" and rarely if ever has the White House been able to rejoice that the privy council functions had become completely moribund.

With respect to appointments it was not anticipated that the influence of the Senate would be great.   As Hamilton wrote:

"There will, of course, be no exertion of *choice* on the part of the Senate.   They may defeat one choice of the Executive, and oblige him to make another; but they cannot themselves *choose*—they can only ratify or reject the choice of the President.   They might even entertain a preference to some other person, at the very moment they were assenting to the one proposed, because there might be no positive ground of opposition to him; and they could not be sure, if they withheld their assent, that the subsequent nomination would fall upon their own favourite, or upon any other person in their estimation more meritorious than the one rejected.   Thus it could hardly happen that the majority of the Senate would feel any other complacency towards the object of an appointment than such as the appearances of

[2] *The Rise and Growth of American Politics,* p. 265.
[3] Farrand, *op. cit.,* Vol. II, p. 522.

merit might inspire, and the proofs of the want of it destroy." [4]

Hamilton was wrong. The Senate was interested in considerations other than "appearances of merit" or "proofs of the want of it," and almost at once it began to interpose vetoes. In Washington's administration the nomination of a naval officer was rejected because he was not approved by the Senators from Georgia. Washington replied with a special message defending his choice, but he had to give way and make a new nomination. Both Adams and Madison consented to interference by the Senate, and the practice of a senatorial veto was thus early established. It is interesting to note, however, that commentators on the Constitution like Kent (1826) and Story (1833) wrote of the Senate as having powers simply of "consent or refusal" and "but a slight participation in the appointments to office." [5]   They did not realize that there was in gestation what we know as senatorial courtesy—one of the most important of the unwritten conventions of the American Constitution.[6]

"Senatorial courtesy" is a kind of liberum veto, and means no more than this: that while the Senate will not suggest particular nominations, it expects

[4] *The Federalist,* No. 66.

[5] Ford, *op. cit.,* p. 260. "The Senate has a controlling voice in the appointment of all important officers, and this right of control cannot be taken from them (*sic*) in the case of even inferior officers, except by their own consent"—*i. e.,* through its consent to a law vesting the appointment elsewhere. H. C. Lodge, *The Senate of the United States and Other Essays,* p. 10.

[6] *Cf.* H. W. Horwill, *The Usages of the American Constitution,* p. 126 ff. (Oxford, 1925).

that the President, in naming certain local office-
holders (*e. g.,* postmasters and collectors of the
customs) will choose persons satisfactory to the
Senator or Senators of the President's political
party from the State in which the offices are located,
or from which the appointees come.   "The strength
of the pack is the wolf, and the strength of the
wolf is the pack"; consequently if Senators are ignored, or if their objections are flouted, the Senate
in most cases will not approve the nominations.   I
say "in most cases" for there have been instances
of presidential victories; but these depend on the
accidents of circumstance: the strength and popularity of the man in the White House, the merit
of the appointee, the standing of the Senators with
their fellows, and the general political situation.
Senatorial courtesy waxes and wanes depending on
the interests of the Senate and the occupant of the
White House.[7]   Presidents have chafed against the
system, but they have usually given way.   Mr.
Roosevelt, with great optimism, announced: "In
the appointments I shall go on exactly as I did while
I was governor of New York.   The Senators and
Congress shall ordinarily name the men, but I shall
name the standard, and the men have got to come
up to it." [8]   But this ideal—like others during Mr.
Roosevelt's administration—had to be compromised
with.

[7] Minor appointees in a Congressional District are named by the
Representative, if he is of the President's party; if he is not, then
the Senators are consulted, and if they are political opponents,
the local organizations are catered to.

[8] J. B. Bishop, *Theodore Roosevelt and His Times,* Vol. I, p.
157; but see pp. 235, 248, 442 and Vol. II, p. 14 (New York, 1920).

The attitude of a President will, of course, be determined in part by what he hopes for from his administration. He can by appointments placate some Representatives and Senators so as to turn them into blind supporters of his legislative projects. If it is a case of having his veto sustained, the weapon is an excellent one for changing votes.[9] As Mr. Wilson said, if the President "rightly interpret the national thought, and boldly insist upon it, he is irresistible"; [10] and an incorrect interpretation can frequently be supported by the appointing authority bestowing *pourboires* on Representatives and Senators. The President nominates 15,000 persons whose annual salaries run into the millions.

Such trafficking, of course, has been bitterly criticized. Proposals have been made to reduce the powers of the Senate and permit the President a free hand,[11] but, as American politics are now

[9] It seemed almost incredible that President Coolidge could not have his bonus bill veto (1924) sustained, but he probably made no great effort, the theory being that his personal record would be kept straight by his disapproval, and that Congress, by overriding the veto, would not put the party in the position of denying the gratuity. Water was thus successfully carried on both shoulders.

[10] *Constitutional Government in the United States,* p. 68 (1903).

[11] The "constitutional position" of the Senate "is not nearly so well intrenched as was that of the British House of Lords, which has been stripped of any control whatever over appropriations or appointments, and is now strictly confined to advisory functions. If the formal language of the Constitution seems to give the Senate discretionary authority over appointments, exactly that was true in actual intention with respect to the discretionary authority of the electoral college; but this has become extinct because the people would not tolerate it. By raising the issue of senatorial usurpation with like vigor, and pressing it with like constancy, as complete a victory may be gained by the people." Henry

carried on, the choice is between evils: party
patronage or personal patronage. Shall the appointments, that is to say, be distributed so as to
strengthen the party organizations throughout the
country, or shall they be used to build up a political
machine for the President himself? It is probably
true that if the Senate did not have the right to
advise and consent, the quality of the appointees
might be improved; [12] but, on the other hand, the
executive's own resources would be too great. It
is of doubtful wisdom to argue that what takes
place now in the South (under Republican administrations) should take place always throughout the
country. Mr. Roosevelt through his southern appointments built up a machine that made Mr. Taft's
nomination in 1908 the more certain; in 1912 with-

Jones Ford, "Usurpation by the Senate," *The New Republic,* January 9, 1915.

[12] "Does the control of the Senate operate to prevent abuses of
patronage by the President? To some extent it does, yet less completely than could be wished. When the majority belongs to the
same party as the President, appointments are usually arranged,
or to use the familiar expression, 'squared' between them, with a
view primarily to party interests. When the majority is opposed
to the President, they are tempted to agree to his worst appointments, because such appointments discredit him and his party with
the country and become a theme of hostile comment in the next
electioneering campaign. As the initiative is his, it may be the
nominating President, and not the confirming Senate, whom public
opinion will condemn. These things being so, it has been doubted
whether this executive function of the Senate is now a valuable
part of the Constitution. It was designed to prevent the President from making himself a tyrant by filling the great offices with
his accomplices or tools. That danger has passed away, if it ever
existed; and Congress has other means of muzzling an ambitious
chief magistrate." Bryce, *The American Commonwealth,* Vol. I,
pp. 110–111.

out his southern delegates (secured through appointments either made or promised) Mr. Taft would have been unable to force his own renomination. President Coolidge selected C. Bascom Slemp as his secretary with an eye on the southern delegates to the 1924 convention, and with results too successful and recent to require comment.

Unfettered presidential discretion would be more plausible if the United States had a real Cabinet —if, in other words, there were some collective responsibility, and if decisions were not taken by an executive unadvised except by politicians, who are outside of the government and whose interventions are not advertised. This is a consideration that should not be lost sight of: executive responsibility for appointments in Great Britain and executive responsibility for appointments in the United States are quite different. The one is collective, the other individual; the one can be enforced, the other cannot. There may be, therefore, grave dangers in a presidential appointing power unchecked by the Senate; certainly the vetoes that the Senate has placed on Mr. Coolidge's nominations have been due to the quality of the appointees rather than any senatorial courtesy, and recent experience fails to suggest that this quality would improve were the President to be able to follow his own sweet will.

On the whole, the Senate has shown restraint in interposing vetoes in the case of major appointments. There is little attempt to control the selection of ambassadors; what investigations of and objections to judicial nominees are made rarely turn on questions of politics, but go to the issue of fitness. Occasionally, in respect of the administrative commissions, objections are made on the ground that certain sections of the country are not represented,[13] but, on the whole, senatorial courtesy is confined to those offices which are more political. Furthermore, the tradition has been pretty well established that the President is entitled to the Cabinet—the heads of departments—he desires, and that the Senate will not interfere even though it may be of the opposite political party.

The shattering of this tradition in March, 1925, was more apparent than real. Not since 1868 had the Senate refused to confirm an appointment to the Cabinet, but it took this action in the case of President Coolidge's choice for Attorney General. Mr. Warren's former close connection with the Sugar Trust (just charged by the Federal Trade Commission with activities in restraint of trade) was the gravamen of the objection; the Senate feared that the trust laws would not be vigorously enforced. This belief was probably intensified by the character of some of Mr. Coolidge's appointments to the Tariff, Federal Trade, and Interstate Commerce Commissions, for these bodies had seemed to be adopting the theory that the prosperity of the country was synonymous with "big

[13] This was the case, for example, with Mr. Coolidge's nominations to the Interstate Commerce Commission in 1925 and 1926.

One of the most extreme instances of senatorial courtesy occurred in 1916 in the case of the appointment of Mr. George Rublee of New Hampshire to the Federal Trade Commission. Mr. Rublee was "personally obnoxious" to Senator Gallinger of New Hampshire.

business" getting and keeping what it wanted. The Senate was influenced also by recollections of its consent to President Harding's appointment of Mr. Daugherty as Attorney General, and its subsequent investigations of his office. The more care, therefore, with the new Attorney General.

Mr. Coolidge for a time proposed to fight.[14] He announced that he would give Mr. Warren a recess appointment, but his resolution weakened when the opposition persisted in face of the threat. He therefore failed to realize his hopes, expressed in a statement to the public, "that the country may have the benefit of his [Mr. Warren's] excellent qualities and the President may be unhampered in choosing his own method of executing the laws." That the President should be unhampered is, generally speaking, sound doctrine; but the Senate has a responsibility, which it cannot avoid. Whether the standard set up in the Warren case was extreme or no is beside the point; if the Senate believes that a nominee is unfit, it should interfere; a reasonable presidential discretion should not be

[14] On March 10, 1925, the Senate refused to confirm the Warren nomination by a vote of 41-39 (*Congressional Record,* 69th Congress, Special Session, p. 107).

On March 12, the nomination was resubmitted. The Judiciary Committee reported that, with the exception of President Tyler, no President had ever ventured to resubmit at the same session a nomination which had been rejected by the Senate. Tyler, on the same day, submitted to the Senate three times the nomination of Caleb Cushing for Secretary of the Treasury (p. 232).

The Judiciary Committee suggested that even if there was no denial of the right of the President to resubmit, the Senate was forbidden by its rules to reconsider (Rule XIII). But the nomination was voted on again (March 16) and rejected 46-39 (p. 280).

presidential license. Similarly—as I will point out
in a moment—the Senate has the right and is even
under a duty to call for the dismissal of "unfit"
members of the Cabinet. This is a familiar oc-
currence in a parliamentary system, and that, as
alleged, frequent senatorial interference might lead
to some responsibility of the Cabinet to Congress
should be a near hope rather than a remote fear.
Were the American Cabinet something more than
an amorphous body of chief clerks there might be
some check on appointments and encouragement of
resignations other than by the President. In Great
Britain, certain of the Cabinet anomalies the United
States has occasionally seen would have been impossible: a Prime Minister would have been unable
to persuade able and eminent persons to enter his
Government if he intended also to include political
pariahs or pilgarlics. The pertinence of this point
will also appear later.

2. *Removals*

Of some actual and possibly of great potential
importance is the Senate's share in removals, and
the controversies over this matter have shown
astonishing ambiguities in our written Constitution.
The question was broached when the First Congress
considered a bill to establish a Department of
Foreign Affairs, which was to be headed by a Secretary "who shall be appointed by the President by
and with the advice and consent of the Senate; and
to be removable by the President." The Constitution had said nothing about removal, and in the

great debate that followed, four different theories were advanced: that the major executive officers held office on good behavior, and could be removed only by impeachment; that the power to remove was incidental to the power to appoint, and was thus vested jointly in the President and Senate; that the power of Congress to create offices was complete and that the power of removal could be vested where Congress chose; and, finally, that the President possessed the sole power by virtue of the Constitution itself. Which of these theories should be accepted was still disputed one hundred and thirty-nine years after the Constitutional Convention.

The debate in the First Congress, and the action taken, was far from conclusive, and has been the subject of varying interpretations, for the legislative opinion was expressed indirectly. An amendment was proposed providing for the care of the records of the Foreign Department, "whenever the said principal officer shall be removed from office by the President of the United States, or in any other case of vacancy." This prevailed in the House by a vote of 30 to 18, and the congressional authorization to remove was thus struck out; that the President possessed the power was taken for granted. The Senate tied when the bill came up, and the deciding vote was cast by Vice-President John Adams, who was not unmindful of the fact that he might become President.[1]   It is interesting to note, how-

[1] In his brief in the *Myers* case (see below) Mr. Beck devotes thirty pages to an analysis of the congressional debate, and argues that Congress recognized that the President's power to make re-

ever, that a majority of former Constitutional Convention members in both the House and the Senate supported the President's prerogative of removal. The House, naturally enough, was unwilling to grant considerable authority to the Senate, and it especially showed reluctance to take any action encouraging ministerial responsibility to the upper chamber, a result which, it was thought, would follow from allowing the Senate to control removals. The significance of the Senate's vote, close though it was, "is the greater when it is remembered that instances where a political body voluntarily deprives itself of power are very few in all the history of government." [2] The deprivation was neither permanent nor complete.

movals arose from the Constitution itself, and not from any federal legislation; that this power was not simply an incident of his power to nominate, but rested also upon the grants to him of executive power and of authority to see that the laws are faithfully executed. Senator Pepper in his brief declares "that no argument in favor of an executive power of removal can be drawn either from the proceedings in the Constitutional Convention, from contemporaneous exposition or from votes and debates in the First Congress." Mr. Justice Peckham in delivering the opinion in *Parsons* v. *United States*, 167 U. S. 324 (1896) gave an elaborate historical review down to the Tenure of Office Act of 1867, and declared that "the continued and uninterrupted practice of the Government from 1789 was thus broken in upon and changed by the passage of this Act, so that, if constitutional, thereafter all executive officers whose appointments had been with the advice and consent of the Senate could not be removed without the concurrence of the Senate in such order or removal."

[2] C. C. Thach, *The Creation of the Presidency, 1777–1789*, p. 150 (Johns Hopkins Studies, 1922). Professor Thach, who has made an exhaustive analysis of the debate, concludes that "the seal of legislative disapproval was set on the concept of a Senate acting as a general council for administrative affairs"; and that

Presidents early began [3] and have continued to exercise a power of removal, but how far this was constitutionally protected remained doubtful. Congressional statutes creating new offices have attempted to prevent their occupants from being completely dependent upon the good will of the executive. Restrictions have also been placed upon the President's power to appoint—his nominees, in some cases, must have certain qualifications or be from both political parties. In respect of removals the attempt has been made to prevent the President from acting except with the consent of the Senate or on the ground that the incumbent is corrupt or incompetent. The number and variety of these restrictions are much greater than is generally realized,[4] and their constitutionality has not been definitely decided. It may be settled when the Supreme Court of the United States decides a case that was brought up in 1924; perhaps only a part of the problem will be dealt with—for when the Supreme Court adds to the Constitution, it prefers to do so by jots and tittles.

The case referred to arose under a congressional

the congressional majority "wished to give an unmistakable quietus to the idea, not unnatural in itself and certainly held by some, that the two clauses allowing senatorial participation in executive matters constituted the Senate a permanent executive council or in fact that it was an executive council at all." (pp. 143, 150.)

[3] Until the end of Johnson's administration the President removed 5614 civil officers. See Carl Russell Fish, "Removal of Officials by the President of the United States," *Annual Report of the American Historical Association for the Year 1899,* Vol. I, p. 67.

[4] A list is given in the Appendix, below, p. 257 ff.

statute of 1876 which provides that "postmasters of the first, second and third classes, shall be appointed and may be removed by the President by and with the advice and consent of the Senate, and shall hold their offices for four years unless sooner removed or suspended according to law." In 1920, without consulting the Senate, President Wilson removed a postmaster, who brought suit for his salary for the remainder of his term. The case came before the Supreme Court of the United States in 1924 [5] and was considered so important that it was assigned for reargument. The Solicitor General, Mr. James M. Beck, was in the peculiar position of urging that the law was invalid. He asserted, indeed, the unconstitutionality of any restriction whatever upon the President's power of removal. The principal counsel on the other side was the Hon. George Wharton Pepper, a Senator from Pennsylvania, who appeared *amicus curiæ* and filed a brief supporting the Senate's rights. His position was that Congress could put on the President any restriction it desired. Between these two extreme views on the constitutional question, there is an ample area in which the Court must chart a course through what at present is a twilight zone. The Court will not have to find out what the law is, because the law does not exist. The Court must determine what the Constitution would have said on such a subject if the Constitution had not been silent, and, as I have suggested, it may keep the Constitution's delayed utterance from being voluble.

[5] *Frank S. Myers* v. *United States,* No. 77, October Term, 1924.

It may even say that the statute quoted in providing that postmasters *"may* be removed by the President by and with the advice and consent of the Senate" is an invitation to rather than a limitation on the President; that it says "may" instead of "may only" or "must" and does not prevent presidential removals without consulting the Senate. This would dodge the main issue, but in doing this the Supreme Court would only be following precedent, for it has refused before to pronounce on the general question.

The removal cases decided by the Supreme Court have been carefully restricted in their application to specific situations; the opinions have been so framed as to avoid passing upon the general question of presidential power or the constitutionality of congressional restrictions on removals. As early as 1839 it was decided that Judges of Districts Courts who had been empowered by Congress to appoint their clerks could also remove them, it being "a sound and necessary rule to consider the power of removal as incident to the power of appointment." [6] In 1897 the Court held that a limitation of the terms of officers appointed by the President by and with the advice and consent of the Senate did not indicate any intention on the part of Congress to forbid the President to remove such officers prior to the expiration of their terms. In this particular case, however, the Senate had confirmed the appointment of a successor before the expiration of the term of the official who had been

[6] Ex parte *Hennen,* 13 Pet. 230.

removed.   Had the case therefore, arisen while the
Tenure of Office Act and the modifying act of
1869 were in force, this action of the Senate would
have deprived the removed official of any rights.
The Supreme Court therefore concluded that the
removed official could not, after the repeal of these
acts, possess rights superior to those which he would
have enjoyed if the acts had remained in force.
This, it is evident, was an ingenious line of argument, but it throws little light upon the general
question of presidential power.   The opinion of the
Court contains a review by Mr. Justice Peckham of
the historical precedents.[7]

Another case which dodged the main issue was
Shurtleff v. *U. S.*[8]   This construed the Customs
Administrative Act of 1890 which provided that
General Appraisers, after appointment by the
President by and with the advice and consent of the
Senate could "be removed from office at any time
by the President for inefficiency, neglect of duty or
malfeasance in office."   An appraiser who was re-
moved by the President on no specification of charges

[7] *Parsons* v. *U. S.,* 167 U. S. 324 (1896).
In 1922 the Supreme Court permitted the President to remove a
Lieutenant Colonel of the Army otherwise than after sentence by
court martial. The officer maintained that since he had been
appointed with the advice and consent of the Senate, he could
not be legally removed except with the consent of the Senate or
in accordance with the Revised Statutes (Section 1230) which
make a dismissal by the President void unless sustained by sentence of a court martial. The Court construed the action of the
President and the Senate in nominating and confirming another
officer to be Lieutenant Colonel as constituting the "consent of the
Senate" as required by the Revised Statutes. *Wallace* v. *U. S.,*
257 U. S. 541 (1922).
[8] 189 U. S. 311 (1903).

maintained that the President had no power to remove him except for the specified causes. "The
right of removal," said the Court, "would exist if
the statute had not contained a word upon the subject. It does not exist by virtue of the grant, but
it inheres in the right to appoint unless limited by
Constitution or statute. It requires plain language to take it away." (p. 316). There was
no "plain language" in the statute, and consequently
the decision did not have to pass upon the constitutionality of congressional prohibitions of removals
except for specified causes "and for no other cause." [9]
Such laws have not yet been before the Court.

It is established, however, that Congress may
prevent removals by a department head. This was
decided in 1886. The case arose under the statute
which provided that no officer in the naval service
in time of peace could be removed except after a
court martial. A naval cadet engineer was dis-
missed by the Secretary of the Navy without a court
martial, and the Supreme Court held that the removal was illegal. Congress had vested the appointment of naval cadet engineers in the heads of
departments, and the Court said, "Congress may
limit and restrict the power of removal as it deems
best for the public interests." This was flatly decided, but the Court also said that "whether or not
Congress can restrict the power of removal incident
to the power of appointment of those officers who
are appointed by the President by and with the advice and consent of the Senate under the authority

[9] See below, p. 265.

of the Constitution (Article II, section 2) does not arise in this case, and need not be considered." [10]

The argument of the Court, in short, was that the constitutional authority in Congress to "vest" the appointment "implies authority to limit, restrict, and regulate the removal." The appointing agent "has no constitutional prerogative of appointment to offices independently of the legislation of Congress; and by such legislation he must be governed." As Professor Powell suggests, the language of the *Perkins* case may be paraphrased, and one may say that the President "has no constitutional prerogative of appointment" to inferior offices "independently of the legislation of Congress." Hence "by such legislation" the President "must be governed not only in making appointments but in all that is incident thereto." From this it follows that:

"the President can at best have a constitutionally protected power to remove only when he has a constitutionally protected power to appoint, unless in some way the power to remove can be implied from other duties of the presidency with which Congress may not interfere.

"The only other presidential duty to which the power to remove can be easily related is the duty to see that the laws are faithfully executed. If the President needs a free hand in making removals in order to ensure the execution of the laws, it might be held that Congress may not restrict him. The Supreme Court has never said that the President gets his power to remove from his duty to see that the laws are faithfully executed. It has said in the *Shurtleff* case that Congress has classed the office of general ap-

[10] *U. S.* v. *Perkins*, 116 U. S. 143 (1886).

praiser 'as appropriately coming under the direct supervision of the President, and to be administered by officers appointed by him (and confirmed by the Senate) with reference to his constitutional responsibility to see that the laws are faithfully executed.' Somewhat naïvely Mr. Justice Peckham adds a little later that 'in making removals from office it must be assumed that the President acts with reference to his constitutional duty to take care that the laws are faithfully executed.' But this refers to that duty, not as the source of the power to remove, but as a guide to its exercise. Mr. Justice Peckham seems to be thinking, not of constitutional law, but of constitutional morality. And *United States* v. *Perkins* makes it clear that the President's duty to see that the laws are faithfully executed does not ensure him a power to dictate the removal of inferior officers. If the head of a department may be denied the power to remove officers appointed by him, Congress may give inferior officers security of tenure. If the President's duty as to the enforcement of the laws does not give him control over inferior officers appointed by the head of a department, it cannot ensure him control over inferior officers whose appointment might have been vested in the head of a department." [11]

This distinction as to inferior officers is, it seems to me, quite important. Neither of the counsel who argued the *Myers* case before the Supreme Court of the United States paid any attention to the fact that the appointing power is granted in two parts: the President shall "nominate and, by and with the advice and consent of the Senate, shall appoint ambassadors, other public ministers and

[11] Thomas Reed Powell; "The President's Veto of the Budget Bill," *National Municipal Review*, Vol. IX, p. 538 (September, 1920).

consuls, judges of the Supreme Court, and all other
officers of the United States, whose appointments
are not herein otherwise provided for, and which
shall be established by law; but the Congress may
by law vest the appointment of such inferior officers
as they think proper, in the President alone, in the
courts of law, or in the heads of departments." [12]
These provisions were interpreted in *United States
v. Germaine*.[13]   Mr. Justice Miller said that the
Supreme Court considered the designation "inferior
officers" as covering all officers inferior to those
specifically mentioned in the Constitution.   If this
distinction is valid, it would mean, in view of the
Perkins case, that for "inferior officers"—that is,
those whose appointment could be vested as Congress saw fit—any legislative restrictions on the
President's power of removal would be constitutional.   As for the non-inferior officers—that is,
those enumerated in the Constitution [14]—the President has a constitutional prerogative to appoint.
The right of appointment presupposes the right of
removal.   But what is the appointing authority?
Is it the President with the consent of the Senate,
or the President alone?   If the former, then Congress may require the consent of the Senate for removals.   If, on the other hand, when the President
nominates, he really appoints (senatorial confirma-

[12] *The Constitution of the United States,* Art. II, Section II.
[13] 99 U. S. 508 (1879).
[14] That "heads of departments" may only be appointed by the
President I take to be implied in the permission given Congress to
vest the appointment of "such inferior officers" in "the heads of
departments."

tion being no part of the appointing authority), then the question is whether his *constitutional* right to appoint includes a *constitutional* right to remove. If it does, then congressional restrictions are invalid. Such a distinction has an important bearing on the Tenure of Office Acts.

These constitute the principal effort of Congress to interfere with removals. The first was passed in 1867 and sought to enable civil officers—the terms used were broad enough to include members of the Cabinet—to continue in office until their successors were appointed by the President by and with the advice and consent of the Senate. The executive power of removal was limited to suspensions for misconduct or crime which had to be reported to the Senate, and if this body failed to approve of the President's action the suspended official returned to his post. Johnson vetoed the Act, but Congress repassed it over his veto. He then attempted to dismiss Mr. Stanton, the Secretary of War, and was impeached by the House of Representatives. The Senate tried the impeachment, and the vote failed to convict.[15] In 1869 Congress amended the Tenure of Office Act by repealing its sections which had related to suspensions. The President might suspend "in his discretion" but was required to nominate persons to fill all vacancies within thirty days after the commencement of each session. This put it in the power of the Senate to obstruct removals by withholding consent to the appointment of a successor if it was not satisfied

[15] D. M. DeWitt, *The Impeachment and Trial of President Johnson* (New York, 1903).

with the reasons for the removal. Grant, Hayes and Garfield all protested against this senatorial power.

The controversy flared up under President Cleveland, who during a congressional recess, removed 643 officers.[16] One of these was a Federal Attorney, and when his successor was nominated the Senate Committee on the Judiciary desired the Attorney General to submit papers concerning not only the qualifications of the nominee but the reasons for the removal of the predecessor. President Cleveland's Attorney General refused to comply, and the Senate, by a vote of 32–25 passed a resolution censuring the law officer and, indirectly, the President. As a result of this controversy, the Tenure of Office Act was repealed on March 3, 1887, and the President has since been free to remove members of his Cabinet, with the exception of the Postmaster General, who is covered by the Act of July 12, 1876.

Enough has been said, I think, to suggest the unconstitutionality of a statutory restriction in respect of the Postmaster General and its constitutionality in respect of postmasters whose appointment could be vested in the head of the department. No such distinction was made when Messrs. Beck and Pepper argued the *Myers* case. The former maintained the unconstitutionality of all restrictions on removal, while the latter took the position that the President had no removal right which Congress could not take away. Whatever the merits

[16] See R. McElroy, *Grover Cleveland*, Vol. I, Chap. VII (New York, 1923).

of the arguments as to what the Supreme Court should make the Constitution say, there are grave political objections to either position.

Hardly anyone would maintain that the Tenure of Office Act was wise legislation. Even Senator Pepper admitted that, on grounds of policy, congressional restrictions were bad. Disunion between executive and legislature should not be encouraged and responsibility for removals should not be divided. To some extent, probably, the House of Representatives could be relied upon not to agree to laws preventing the President from removing the major officials of the Government except with the consent of the Senate, but if the Supreme Court asserts the constitutionality of all legislative restrictions it will extend an invitation to Congress to bind the President. Senatorial courtesy might be extended to removals and the President's responsibility for efficient administration would be confused. Madison wrote in 1834:

"Should the controversy on removals from office end in the establishment of a share in the power, as claimed for the Senate, it would materially vary the relations among the component parts of the Government, and disturb the operation of the checks and balances as now understood to exist. If the right of the Senate be, or be made, a constitutional one, it will enable that branch of the Government to force on the Executive department a continuance in office even of the Cabinet officers, notwithstanding a change from a personal and political harmony with the President to a state of open hostility towards him. If the right of the Senate be made to depend on the Legislature, it would still be *grantable* in that extent; and even with the exception of the heads of departments and a few other officers, the augmentation of the senatorial patronage, and the new relation between the Senate directly and the Legislature indirectly, with the Chief Magistrate, would be felt deeply in the general administration of the Government. The innovation, however modified, would more than double the danger of throwing the Executive machinery out of gear, and thus arresting the march of the Government altogether." [17]

This is not to say, however, that, as the American government is now organized, certain officials should enjoy no safeguards against the President. The members of such administrative bodies as the Federal Reserve Board, the Federal Trade Commission and the Tariff Commission should have, I think, a protected position, and the case for this has been strengthened by certain recent incidents. Mr. Coolidge has endeavoured, it seems clear, to remake these commissions with members of his own

[17] Quoted by Solicitor General James M. Beck in his Substitute Brief for the United States in the case of *Myers* v. *U. S.*

In the debate in the House in the First Congress, Madison had pointed out the objections to senatorial participation in removals:

"Is there no danger that an officer, when he is appointed by the concurrence of the Senate, and has friends in that body, may choose rather to risk his establishment on the favor of that branch, than rest it upon the discharge of his duties to the satisfaction of the executive branch, which is constitutionally authorized to inspect and control his conduct? And if it should happen that the officers connect themselves with the Senate, they may mutually support each other, and for want of efficacy reduce the power of the President to a mere vapor; in which case, his responsibility would be annihilated, and the expectation of it unjust. The high executive officers, joined in cabal with the Senate, would lay the foundation of discord, and end in an assumption of the executive power, only to be removed by a revolution in the Government." *Annals of Congress*, Vol I, p. 480.

way of thinking; his appointees have opposed governmental interference with the business interests; they have taken a highly protective view of the tariff schedules. Now, if a check is desired on such appointments, it may be found in the requirement of senatorial confirmation, but when the President attempts to influence policy or to make removals in order the more completely to remold the commissions, much is to be said against him having a free hand.

Thus on August 27, 1925, President Coolidge telegraphed to Bert E. Haney, Democratic member of the United States Shipping Board: "It having come to my attention that you are proposing to remove Admiral Palmer contrary to the understanding I had with you when I appointed you, your resignation from the United States Shipping Board is hereby requested." In reply Mr. Haney denied that he had made any pre-appointment bargain with the President and refused to resign. He said:

"Obviously, Mr. President, to have given you any such promise as that implied by your telegram would have amounted to a total disregard of my oath of office and my obligation to Congress, whose sole agent I am. Such a promise and disregard of my official oath and the consummation of such an understanding would have obligated me to support the administration of the Merchant Marine Act by the President of the Fleet Corporation, however inefficient, notwithstanding the fact that the law imposed upon me, as a Commissioner of the Shipping Board, the duty to support and maintain an efficient administration.

"The board, when once appointed by the President in conformity with the statute, is an independent agency of the United States Government and is vested by the statute with large and important discretionary powers which the members thereof are compelled to exercise independently of any other governmental agency so long as the law is in force, and, with the exception of the power of removal for causes specified in the act, the members of the board are responsible only to the legislative body."

The congressional intention to have the Shipping Board an independent agency is shown in the requirement that the appointees must represent both political parties. But apart from the impropriety of the President's attempting in such a manner to influence the Board's decisions, there is the question of removal. The law provided that members may be removed for "inefficiency, neglect of duty, or malfeasance in his office." Unless the Supreme Court should decide that the members of the administrative commissions are in a different position from customs appraisers (the language of the statutes is the same) the President could remove for other causes. Mr. Coolidge, however, was not rash enough to venture such an action. There might have been some severe public criticism.

Similarly, the President has sought to influence the Tariff Commission in specific matters and to get rid of certain members not of his way of thinking about protection. The term of David J. Lewis, one of the Democratic members, was about to expire. The President, according to evidence presented to the Senate, asked Mr. Lewis for an undated letter of resignation as the price of sending the reappointment to the Senate. Mr. Lewis refused.   He was given a recess appointment, but his name was not resubmitted when the congressional session began in December.   Similarly the President was not unwilling to get rid of W. S. Culbertson, and he was found an ambassadorial post so that the President could appoint men of his own way of thinking about the indispensability of a high tariff to protect the country's infant industries.   These are really amazing instances [18] of executive interference with commissions that Congress intended should be semi-judicial bodies; if they are repeated, public confidence will be shaken in the non-partisan character of these boards, and they constitute an argument against an unrestricted power of presidential removal.   The proper limitation, however, would not be the joinder of the Senate in removals; it is the statement in the laws of the several grounds for removal and the clear implication that the President would be acting improperly if he removed for other, and perhaps unspecified causes.[19]

[18] An account of them is given in a speech by Senator Norris, *Congressional Record,* January 16, 1926, p. 1819.   On March 11, 1926, the Senate authorized the appointment of a special committee to investigate the Tariff Commission. *Ibid.,* p. 5153.

[19] Two congressional policies have been manifested in the statutes creating the executive departments.   The Secretary of State is required by law to "perform such duties as shall from time to time be enjoined on or entrusted to him by the President" relative to foreign affairs and to "conduct the business of the department in such manner as the President shall direct."   So also the Secretary of War is similarly an agent of the executive and the Attorney General must give his advice and opinion whenever required by the President.   The other Cabinet members, however, have their duties more specifically described by statute and in some cases, as that of the Secretary of the Treasury, subordination to Congress rather than amenability to the Chief Executive

One officer of the government is completely protected against the President, and his status may be
dependent upon the decision of the Supreme Court in
the *Myers* case. The Budget and Accounting Act
of June 10, 1921, created "an establishment of the
Government, to be known as the General Accounting Office, which shall be independent of the executive departments, and under the control and
direction of the Comptroller General of the United
States." The duties of this office, generally speaking, are to see that no expenditures are made except
according to law. Congress, in other words, desires
an audit under the control of the legislature rather
than the executive, which should not be permitted
to make its own interpretation of the legality of its
acts.[20] Thus, the Comptroller General and Assistant Comptroller General are appointed by the
President with senatorial confirmation for a term
of fifteen years, and "may be removed at any time
by joint resolution of Congress after notice and
hearing, when, in the judgment of Congress the
Comptroller General or Assistant Comptroller
General has become permanently incapacitated, or
has been inefficient, or guilty of neglect of duty, or
of malfeasance in office, or of any felony or conduct

is the status sought after. With respect to most of the government departments, therefore, the President's power to have his
administrative policies carried out is dependent upon having
Cabinet members or subordinates who see eye to eye with him;
he is, in other words, Chief of the Executive only through his
power of removing appointees who are recalcitrant and unwilling
to follow his wishes.

[20] The post-war constituent assemblies were solicitous about
this matter. See McBain and Rogers, *The New Constitutions of
Europe*, pp. 193, 229, 285, etc. (New York, 1922).

involving moral turpitude, and for no other cause and in no other manner except by impeachment."

Mr. Wilson vetoed this law, because:

"It has, I think, always been the accepted construction of the Constitution that the power to appoint officers of this kind carries with it as an incident the power to remove.

"I am convinced that the Congress is without constitutional power to limit the appointing power, and its incident power of removal derived from the Constitution."

According to the distinction drawn in the *Germaine* case [21] the Comptroller General is an inferior officer, and had his appointment, say, been placed in the Secretary of the Treasury—as Congress could have vested it—the *Perkins* case [22] is authority for the constitutionality of the restriction on removal. It would seem, therefore, that Mr. Wilson was in error when he thought that this provision was unconstitutional.[23]   Apart from the legal question,

[21] See above, p. 41.

[22] See above, p. 38.

[23] See Powell, *loc. cit.* Mr. Wilson's veto message said that the act "undertakes to empower the Congress by concurrent resolution" (when the Act was repassed in the next Congress "concurrent resolution" was changed to "joint resolution") "to remove an officer appointed by the President with the advice and consent of the Senate.

"I can find in the Constitution no warrant for the exercise of this power by the Congress. There is certainly no express authority conferred, and I am unable to see that authority for the exercise of this power is implied in any expressed grant of power."

As to whether this section of the law is unconstitutional presents a different question. Each House of Congress may appoint and remove its own officers, but there is no constitutional provision for joint officers. The Comptroller General, even though an inferior officer, is an officer of the United States, and according to moreover, it is proper for Congress, charged with responsibility for appropriations, to have an accounting officer independent of, and able to restrain, the executive.

This naturally is an extreme case. The opposite case is that of a Cabinet member. He, it is agreed, should be removable by the President, but I see no objection to resolutions by the House or the Senate calling attention to inefficiency or neglect of duty. A branch of a legislature is entitled to express its opinions;[24] it may pass silly resolutions and rush in where angels fear to tread, and it may pronounce upon subjects not strictly within its constitutional competence.[25] Sufficient checks will be found, I think, in the amusement or disdain that will greet foolish or improper resolutions. Congress is the forum of the nation, and it would be unfortunate if its branches could not voice their opinions.

the Constitution he must be appointed by the President and Senate, or the President alone, or the Courts, or heads of departments. It is doubtful whether he could be appointed by joint or concurrent resolution, and such an absence of power is certainly no warrant for basing upon it the incident power of removal. The Constitution provides the method of impeachment for getting rid of officers of the United States. The opinion may be ventured that Mr. Wilson was right when he found in the Constitution "no warrant for the exercise of this power" of removal "by the Congress." The Comptroller General, therefore, would seem to be entitled to his office until impeached.

[24] This question has been exhaustively discussed by M. de Bornier, "Les résolutions des Chambres," *Revue du droit public,* July-August-September, 1925.

[25] The right of the House of Representatives to adopt a resolution favoring the entrance of the United States into the World Court is upheld in an elaborate and able report prepared by Representative Burton, Sixty-eighth Congress, 2d Session, House Report No. 1569.

These views were not held by certain Senators who objected to the resolution passed on February 11, 1924, declaring it to be "the sense of the United States Senate that the President of the United States immediately request the resignation of Edwin Denby as Secretary of the Navy." Senator Borah thought that the Senate should not interfere. He drew a distinction between resolutions asking the President to call an Arms Conference or such a round robin as thirty-nine Senators drew up warning Mr. Wilson that the Senate would carefully scrutinize any proposed League of Nations.[26] Senator Lodge, who was never hesitant about senatorial aggrandizement in respect of foreign affairs, thought that the resolution would go beyond the generally recognized functions of the Senate:

"I think the undertaking to make or unmake Cabinets by votes of the Senate is wholly beyond the power of the Senate. The power of the Senate is confined, so far as actual power goes, to giving its advice and consent to nominations. There is no one more jealous of the prerogatives of the Senate than am I, but it seems to me that this would be trespassing on the undoubted rights of the executive. . . . It would be an attempt on the part of Congress to assume executive duties, and to a certain extent control of the executive in functions which are purely executive." [27]

These are mere words. The Senate, of course, cannot unmake a Cabinet, but it can express its opinion on the fitness of a Cabinet member, and leave it to public opinion to determine whether to support the

[26] *Congressional Record*, Feb. 8, 1924, p. 2072.
[27] *Congressional Record*, January 31, 1924 (66th Congress, 1st Session), p. 1719.

executive or the body which assumed some responsibility when it confirmed the appointment. I see no objection to such a resolution by the House of Representatives,[28] but surely the Senate, which has put its stamp of approval on the fitness of a Cabinet member can say to the country that it has changed its mind. This is all that happened in the Denby case. After the resolution was passed, Mr. Coolidge issued a statement which said:

"No official recognition can be given to the passage of the Senate resolution relative to their opinion concerning members of the Cabinet or other officers under executive control. . . .

". . . The dismissal of an officer of the government such as is involved in this case other than by impeachment is exclusively an executive function."

This is a correct statement of the law, but on which side the merit lay may be guessed from the fact that the Secretary of the Navy speedily resigned from the Cabinet. Irrespective of the merits of particular cases, however, it is important that Congress should not be barred from expressing opinions on, and attempting to increase, the efficiency of the administration. This, as I shall argue at some length, is an important duty of the legislature. It is, in the United States, the peculiar function of the Senate. This body has its opportunities and responsibilities, not in respect of removals, but in acting as a forum where criticisms of the executive may be freely expressed.

[28] See Hinds, *Precedents of the House of Representatives,* Vol. II, sec. 1581 ff. (Washington, 1907).

3. *Treaties*

Not the least interesting feature of the American Government—in its subsequent development more than in its constitutional statement—was the arrangement for the control of foreign policy. What the dichotomy of the Constitution means has been much discussed since President Wilson and the Senate locked horns over the Treaty of Versailles, and the precedents have been exhaustively dealt with.[1] I do not propose to rehearse this controversy as to the respective powers of the President and the Senate. The policy of the adjustments—the way in which they work—rather than constitutionality is my subject, and it warrants brief consideration, for the Treaty debate by no means marked the apotheosis of senatorial influence. Truer today than they were in 1898, or in 1919, are the words that John Hay used to Henry Adams: "I have told you many times that I did not believe another important treaty would ever pass the Senate," [2] except perhaps after much mutilation. The treaty checks and balances, that is to say, give a minority of the Senate such great power

"that it has been made impossible for America to speak with a bold and united voice. Nearly every important treaty the country has been called upon to make has be-

[1] E. S. Corwin, *The President's Control of Foreign Relations* (Princeton, 1917); Q. Wright, *The Control of American Foreign Relations* (New York, 1922); J. M. Mathews, *The Conduct of American Foreign Relations* (New York, 1922).

[2] Thayer, *Life and Letters of John Hay*, Vol. II, p. 170 (Boston, 1915).

come a bone of contention between the Executive and the Senate. It is certain that in the years to come, if we are to go forward in the new paths and stand for a clear-cut world policy, we must devise some method of speaking to the world promptly, and with an undivided voice. Our present system leads to utter weakness, muddle and delay: it forces both sides to play politics, and instead of meeting the issue squarely, to indulge in a vast controversy over the prerogatives of two coördinate branches of the government. The deadlock between the Executive and the Senate every time we face a really critical foreign problem is intolerable. It not only disgraces us before the nations, but in some future world crisis may ruin us." [3]

Mr. Baker suggests that, in the case of the Treaty of Versailles, Wilson saw this difficulty, and thought that he might circumvent it by keeping public opinion in America alive, and so committed to his principles that it would force unity of action. Mr. Wilson, as the world knows, was unsuccessful; perhaps a greater attention to public opinion and less intransigeance would have made his position stronger, but in any event the cards are stacked against the President. American foreign policy is determined not by him and two-thirds of the Senate, but by one-third of the Senate, which will withhold its consent. That is minority control which "leads to utter weakness, muddle and delay." It is a control which, naturally, was not contemplated by the framers, and which, unfortunately, cannot be got rid of by any of the ordinary devices of popular government. Disagreement between Executive and Senate in the

[3] Baker, *Woodrow Wilson and World Settlement*, Vol. I, p. 316 (New York, 1922).

American system of government, that is to say, cannot be settled by an election. When Senators refuse to consent to a treaty, they are in a much stronger position than was the House of Lords when it refused its assent, say, to the Lloyd George Budget of 1909 or the Parliament Act. They are well nigh invincible for two reasons: (1) the Lords knew from the results of two general elections that if they did not give way public opinion might come to desire the abolition of the British upper chamber, and (2) they could not successfully hold out against such action or against the Parliament Act because of what Bagehot called the "safety-valve" of the British Constitution—that is, the executive's power to create Peers to overcome a majority in the upper chamber. On the other hand, the United States never has a *general* election; Senators are chosen at different times for different periods on different issues. Our republican institutions, furthermore, put one-third of the Senate in an absolutely impregnable position: it can prevent the adoption of a resolution submitting a constitutional amendment to the state legislatures. It is this aspect of the Senate's power over treaties—not the *constitutional* question of what the President may or may not do—that is so important at the present time.

The framers of the Constitution were all nervous of unrestrained authority, whether it was possessed by an executive or a legislature. With the exception of Alexander Hamilton, who was conspicuous in the minority, the men in the Philadelphia Convention desired to get away from a strong government, and by checks and balances to avoid tyranny by any branch of the political establishment, or even by a majority of the people acting through their elected representatives. This system of checks, as I have said, pervades the whole Constitution, and is carried so far that practically but one power is conferred without a corresponding restraint on its exercise—the power of executive clemency, and even in this case the President would be accountable directly to the Senate in an impeachment proceedings for its corrupt exercise, and indirectly in case of a reëlection, for its indiscriminate use.[4] Hence it is natural to find the treaty powers checked against each other, and the control over foreign relations none too explicitly stated.

One of the early drafts of the Constitution provided that "The Senate of the United States shall have the power to make treaties, and to appoint ambassadors and judges of the Supreme Court." This was objected to by Madison on the ground "that the Senate represented the States alone, and that for this, as well as other obvious reasons, it was proper that the President should be an agent in treaties."[5] There were, however, certain general causes which operated to incline the Convention to favor collegial control of foreign relations. Hamilton apart, the framers desired to get away from

---

[4] John W. Davis, *The Treaty-making Power in the United States*, p. 6 (Oxford, 1920).
[5] Farrand, *Records of the Federal Convention,* Vol. II, p. 183.

the English precedent of treaty negotiation and ratification by the Crown;[6] they feared possible autocracy in case the function was given to one man. There was the theory that, since other clauses in the Constitution prohibited the States from making individual treaties, they should be compensated for this loss through the power being enjoyed by their representatives in the upper house; they would thus be safeguarded against injury by federal treaty action. Finally, under the Articles of Confederation the exclusive power of entering into treaties and alliances had been vested in "the United States in Congress assembled," and nine—that is two-thirds —of the thirteen States voting as units in Congress had to assent to engagements. Congress had been so determined to keep foreign matters in its own hands, that when a Foreign Secretary was appointed in 1782, he was instructed by resolution to submit to Congress for its inspection and approbation all letters to ministers of foreign powers relating to treaties, and the plans of treaties themselves. That this was clumsy machinery could not be denied, but clumsiness in machinery, the workings of which are known, sometimes seems more to be desired than

[6] "On the face of the Constitution of the United States, the resemblance of the President of the United States to the European king, and especially to the King of Great Britain, is too obvious for mistake . . . the mental operation through which the framers of the American Constitution passed was this: they took the King of Great Britain, went through his powers, and restrained them whenever they appeared to be excessive and unsuited to the circumstances of the United States. It is remarkable that the figure they had before them was not a generalized English King nor an abstract constitutional monarch; it was no anticipation of

a nice balance of machinery that may run too rapidly. Late in the Convention, only a fortnight before adjournment, the treaty-making clause was changed to join the President with the Senate. It was proposed that ratification by the House of Representatives should be necessary also, but the desire for secrecy seemed inconsistent with general legislative sanction and so, when the Committee on Style reported, three days before the adjournment of the Convention, the present language appeared for the first time.[7] The clause, as we have it, was the result of a compromise. Had the Convention lasted longer, there might well have been a change. But the more prolonged the session, the more the opportunity for criticism in the country, and it was not without importance that the weather was warm in Philadelphia. The delegates were exhausted. They desired to conclude their labors. Not independent of accidental causes, therefore, was the emergence of the provision that "He [the President] shall have power, by and with the advice and consent of the Senate, to make treaties, provided two-thirds of the Senators present concur." These tergiversations in the Convention, however, should serve to remind us that there is nothing particularly sacred about this clause of the Constitution; the arrangement pro-

Queen Victoria, but George III himself whom they took for their model . . . now the original of the President of the United States is manifestly a treaty-making King, and a King actively influencing the executive government."—Sir Henry Maine, *Popular Government,* pp. 211–213 (London, 1909).

[7] C. C. Tansil, "The Treaty-making Powers of the Senate," *American Journal of International Law,* July, 1924.

posed is the child of chance rather than logic or experience.

The difficulty now is that the advice and consent and concurrence of the Senate are interpreted not as authorizing affirmatives or negatives, but as inviting the substitution of senatorial judgment for executive judgment. The Senate, in other words, may dictate to the President. "One more than one-third of our number," the ultimatum reads, "will defeat the treaty in its present form, but we will be willing to agree if changes are made in certain particulars which we specify. Our judgment is better than yours; public opinion cannot touch us until it has forgotten or is distracted by other issues; we care nothing about delays or embarrassment *vis-à-vis* other nations, so you had better agree to accept the only conditions on which our minority will not exercise its constitutional veto." Such an ultimatum may of course be presented on proposed legislation, but it is proper that statutes should emerge from a conflict of different views, and even that minorities should receive some concessions. Mutilation of a bill is rarely so important or so final as mutilation of a treaty and there is no foreign contracting party to consider. Furthermore, a minority has no constitutionally protected veto on legislation. It may not be true, as John Hay maintained, that "there will always be 34 per cent of the Senate on the blackguard side of every question that comes before them," [8] but there will always be percentages representing individual prejudices and sectional or racial

8 Thayer, *op. cit.,* Vol. II, p. 254.

interests.   Not a few Senators also are profoundly
convinced that their wisdom is greater than that of
the executive, and with the back-scratching and
capricious accommodation which exist in every assembly not subject to responsible leadership, it is
easy to create a minority larger than 34 per cent to
substitute its programme for that submitted by the
executive.

This, indubitably, the framers did not contemplate, even though there may be some dispute as
to their exact intentions in respect of the Senate's
rôle as a privy council for foreign affairs.   That
they thought of the Senate—then quite a small body
—as consulting with the President seems clear.
Such collaboration, indeed, may be justified by the
language of the Constitution.   Thus Senator Lodge
pointed out:

"that the carefully phrased section gives the President
absolute and unrestricted right to nominate, and the Senate
can only advise and consent to the appointment of, a given
person.   All right to interfere in the remotest degree with
the power of nomination and the consequent power of selection is wholly taken from the Senate.   Very different is
the wording of the treaty clause.   There the words 'by
and with the advice and consent of' come in after the words
'shall have power' and before the power referred to is de-
fined.   The 'advice and consent of the Senate' are therefore coextensive with the 'power' conferred on the President, which is 'to make treaties,' and apply to the entire
process of treaty-making." [9]

[9] "The Treaty-Making Powers of the Senate," in *A Fighting
Frigate and Other Essays and Addresses*, pp. 231–232.

To be sure, the Senate can not initiate a negotiation, since it has no authority to send or receive
ambassadors, but this apart, it stands on an equality
with the President. When it refuses to confirm
John Doe, it does not do so with the proviso that
the office is to be conferred on Richard Roe.   More
extensive, however, is the authority in respect of
foreign affairs.   Pierce Butler thought that treaties
would "be gone over, clause by clause, by the President and Senate together and modelled"; [10] but, on
the other hand, some held that the two agencies
could give only simple affirmatives or negatives.[11]
But whatever the intention, Washington's experience
with the Senate discouraged the idea of collaboration. Here again the accident of early incidents
determined the development of a constitutional
practice which is even more important than the constitutional language.

In his memoirs John Quincy Adams gives a much
quoted account of President Washington's having
gone to the Senate with a project of a treaty, and
of having been present while the Senators de-
liberated upon it.   "They debated it," wrote Adams,
"and proposed alterations, so that when Washington
left the Senate chamber he said he would be damned
if he ever went there again, and ever since that time
treaties have been negotiated by the executive without submitting them to the consideration of the
Senate." [12]   This states the result rather extremely,
but it is true that Presidents have not consulted

---

[10] Quoted by Tansil, *loc. cit.,* p. 462.

[11] Thach, *The Creation of the Presidency,* p. 163.

[12] *Memoirs,* Vol. VI, p. 427. A detailed account of the incident

formally with the Senate.[13] Washington occasionally sought the Senate's advice, and succeeding Presidents have paid attention to the probable attitude that the Senate would take if the executive proposed a certain policy. This has been done through consultation with senatorial leaders and not in executive session.[14] If the President is wise, as Lord Bryce remarked, "he feels the pulse of the Senate, which like other assemblies, has a collective self-esteem, leading it to strive for all the information and power it can secure, and, while keeping it in good humor, can foresee what kind of arrangement it can be induced to sanction." [15] But the growing size of the Senate made it increasingly improbable that Washington's experience would be repeated. The rules of the Senate still provide for executive sessions with the President,[16] although, as

is given in Senator Maclay's *Journal* (pp. 128–132) and is quoted by Tansil, *loc. cit.*, p. 464.

[13] Jackson, on May 6, 1830, asked the Senate for its advice on a proposed Indian treaty "fully aware that in thus resorting to the early practice of this government by asking the previous advice of the Senate in the discharge of this portion of my duties I am departing from a long and for many years unbroken usage in similar cases." In his message on the Oregon Boundary Settlement in 1846, President Polk remarked that "this practice, though rarely resorted to in later times, was in my judgment eminently wise, and may on occasions of great importance be properly revived."—Davis, *op. cit.*, pp. 10, 11.

[14] On the suggested consultation of the Senate as to the attitude it would take toward the Covenant, see Lodge, *The Senate and the League of Nations,* p. 123 ff. (New York, 1925) but this account should be corrected by reference to Mr. Henry White's statement in the Associated Press Reports of November 9, 1925.

[15] *The American Commonwealth,* Vol. I, p. 107 (New York, 1911).

[16] Rule **XXXVI**.

Senator Lodge remarked (January 24, 1906), "I think we should be disposed to resent it if a request of that sort was to be made to us by the President." [17]

This formal separation of President and Senate had an influence on our constitutional development apart from the control of foreign relations. It helped, curiously enough, in the institution of an executive Cabinet and in creating a legend that this body had some importance in the scheme of government.[18] Whatever anticipation there had been that the President and Senate acting together would carry on administration was squelched. In the South Carolina convention to ratify the Constitution, James Lincoln had said: "Pray, who are the United States? The President and four or five Senators." But when Washington found the Senate an extremely uncongenial adviser, he put a stop to a tendency that might have drawn in administrative matters other than treaties and appointments; and subsequent Presidents turned more and more to the heads of the executive departments—the executive's personal appointees. They are his subordinates and have no collective responsibility, but they have

[17] *Congressional Record,* 59th Congress, 1st Session, p. 1470. On August 19, 1919, President Wilson met the Senate Committee on Foreign Relations at the White House and for more than three hours answered questions concerning the League of Nations Covenant and the Treaty of Versailles. See *Hearings before the Committee on Foreign Relations United States Senate, 66th Congress, 1st Session, on the Treaty of Peace with Germany,* Senate Document No. 106, p. 499 ff., reprinted in Lodge, *op. cit.,* pp. 297-397.

[18] See below, p. 207 ff.

at least helped to keep the Senate from becoming a privy council.

The necessity of placating the Senate has led some Presidents to consider the appointment of Senators as negotiators of treaties. Thus President Madison selected for the conference at Ghent which closed the War of 1812, Senator James A. Bayard of Delaware, and Henry Clay, who was then Speaker of the House. They were of the opinion, however, that such diplomatic service would give them a double rôle; that they might have to decide between their duty to their associates in Congress to disclose matters within their knowledge, and the duty of secrecy to their colleagues in the peace conference. Accordingly, both resigned from Congress.[19] President McKinley sent to the Paris Conference concluding the Spanish-American War a peace commission of five, of whom three were members of the Senate. This time the anomaly of the appointment was objected to, and the Senate Com-

[19] "No Senator or Representative shall, during the time for which he was elected, be appointed to any civil office under the authority of the United States, which shall have been created, or the emoluments whereof shall have been increased during such time; and no person holding any office under the United States shall be a member of either house during his continuance in office."—*The Constitution*, Article I, Section VI, Clause 2. This inhibition (part of which was introduced in the British Constitution in the reign of Queene Anne but never became effective) was in question when President Harding appointed a Senator and a Representative as members of the World War Foreign Debt Commission. A sub-Committee of the Senate Judiciary Committee was divided on the question whether the appointments were in technical violation of the Constitution. See *Congressional Record*, February 22, 23, and 24, 1922, and Senate Document No. 115, 67th Congress, Second session.

mittee on the Judiciary considered a resolution disapproving the practice. The resolution was not reported to the Senate, because the Committee was reluctant to take any action which might be considered a reflection upon the Senators chosen, but President McKinley told Senator Hoar that he was aware of the objections that had been made, and that such appointments would not take place again.[20]

President Harding, however, returned to the practice at the time of the Washington Conference on Reduction of Armaments. Of five Commissioners, Senator Lodge, Chairman of the Foreign Relations Committee, and Senator Underwood, leader of the minority party, were chosen from the Senate. Largely because of Mr. Harding's membership in the Senate before his nomination and his friendship with Senators, this action was not severely criticized. But from the standpoint of the Senate there are certain obvious objections. The President does seek for special influence—particularly if he placates the minority—and only by logomachy can it be said that there has been no violation of the clause of the Constitution forbidding Senators and Representatives from holding offices under the United States. The unwisdom of this clause in many cases may be admitted, but, at least technically, it is violated by the appointment of senatorial envoys and plenipotentiaries.

To the objection that such a manœuvre may disturb the balance between Senate and President, I attach little importance, since, as I have said, the

Senate now enjoys overweening advantages. Nor
does such a sop to the Senate make a treaty any
less "like a bull going into the arena." It is still
true, as Hay sadly remarked, that "no one can say
just how or when the blow will fall—but one thing
is certain—it will never leave the arena alive." [21]
Thus McKinley's attempted placation of the Senate
did not avoid an acrimonious debate which, for a
time, threatened the ratification of the peace treaty.
Nor was senatorial objection shut off in the case of
the treaties drawn up by the Washington Conference; the price of the ratification of these—in spite
of the advocacy of Senators Lodge and Underwood
—was a series of reservations. Mr. Harding, a
senatorial reservationist in 1919, was forced to be a
President accepting reservations in 1922. This
situation was not without its ironical features, and
President Harding's opinions underwent some
change. It makes a difference whose ox is being
gored.

Such insistence on substituting senatorial judgments for the judgment of the executive is by no
means new. It was begun early, for it was the
only method by which the Senate, denied consultation with the President before and during the negotiations, could make use of its great powers of
advice and consent and concurrence. These are *ex-
post facto* but for this reason more important and,
in some cases, harmful. The Senate first showed
its strength on the Jay Treaty with Great Britain,
which was submitted to the Senate in June, 1795.

[21] Thayer, *op. cit.,* Vol. II, p. 394.

The proposal first was that the Treaty be ratified on condition that the twelfth article (relating to the West Indian trade) be suspended. While this was pending, Burr presented a motion postponing further consideration of the Treaty "and that it be recommended to the President of the United States to proceed without delay to further friendly negotiations with His Britannic Majesty in order to effect alterations in the said treaty" in seven particulars which the resolution proceeded to specify. If adopted, this would have been a fairly extreme assertion of senatorial participation in negotiation, but the resolution was defeated,[22] and the single reservation prevailed. A somewhat similar resolution had been passed in 1793 with reference to an Indian treaty. "It is probable," remarks Mr. Hayden,

"that the passage of this resolution would have modified the subsequent development and exercise of the treaty-making powers of the Senate. Washington might well have considered such an act as notice that, in the future, the Senate would expect to participate in the determination of the conditions under which a proposed treaty would be signed; at the very least it would have suggested forcibly the expediency of always consulting them before opening negotiations. It might also have led the Senate to expect such consultation and thus have made it easier for Senators or groups of Senators to demand it. A legislative body eagerly creates and tenaciously clings to precedents which increase its power and enhance its dignity and importance. At the time Jay's nomination was before them, however,

[22] J. R. Hayden, *The Senate and Treaties, 1789–1817*, p. 79 (New York, 1920).

the necessities of the situation and the political influence of the Federalist leaders were powerful enough to keep the Senate from demanding the instructions which were to be issued to him. The same forces were now sufficient to lead the Senate to waive for the good of the nation and of the Federalist party what it might well have regarded as its established prerogatives. Thus the precedent which was established weakened rather than strengthened its position in treaty-making. The first great treaty under the Constitution had been negotiated by the executive alone." [23]

But if the Senate was weakened in respect of negotiations [24]—a result which the increasing size of the Senate would have inevitably accomplished whatever the early precedents—this was counterbalanced by the great source of strength which was discovered in the device of ratifying on conditions, which would have to be accepted by foreign governments. From 1795 to 1901 there were fifty-seven treaties amended by the Senate, and afterwards ratified by the President; twenty-four treaties were so amended that they were either not satisfactory to the other signatory powers, or were not proceeded

[23] *Ibid.*, pp. 79–80.
[24] Mr. Tansil suggests that "If during the course of the negotiation of treaties the President had continued to ask the advice of the Senate, then the right of the United States to amend or alter conventions tnat had been drafted in conformity with definite instructions would have been certainly questionable. The power of the Senate to amend at will would probably not have reached its present development. But when active coöperation with the Senate during the actual process of treaty-making ceased to be resorted to by Presidents, and when their sanction was sought only after the treaty had been negotiated, then the Senate's right of amendment or rejection became of increasing importance."— *loc. cit.*, pp. 462–463.

with by the President.[25]   The important thing,
however, is not the total number but the subjects
with which the treaties deal. When one recalls
the experiences of Roosevelt and Taft with the
Senate on arbitration treaties, and the struggles over
the Treaty of Versailles and the World Court Protocol, it is not the frequency, but the character of
senatorial dominance that matters. Ample incidents can be cited to show the Senate's power and
to suggest the truth of Hay's belief that no important treaty can pass the Senate without being
changed.

Hay, perhaps, is a prejudiced witness, for no
less than seventeen of his treaties were mutilated by
the Senate, and his complaints were frequent and
bitter. "The fact that a treaty gives to this country a great, lasting advantage seems to weigh nothing whatever in the minds of about half the Senators.
Personal interests, personal spites, and the contin-
gent chance of petty political advantage are the
only methods that cut any ice at present." [26]   This
is certainly true in some cases, but there are also
certain more general considerations. Our constitutional arrangements, as I have remarked, are a
direct incitement to dissension between executive and
Senate, and the President must ingratiate himself,

[25] These figures differ slightly from those given in Senator
Lodge's essay (Scribner's Magazine, January, 1902, reprinted in
A Fighting Frigate and Other Essays and Addresses) and by other
writers on the subject. The corrected lists are to be found in
Tansil, *loc. cit.,* p. 477.

[26] Thayer, *op. cit.,* Vol. II, p. 274.

or risk antagonism.[27] Senatorial enmity is lessened in appointments through the practice of senatorial courtesy; but even the operation of the courtesy system permits occasions when there is temporary warfare. No such placation is possible in respect of foreign affairs. If the Senate is of the President's own political party he will have difficulties because in all probability he will not have a two-thirds majority composed of his own party associates; even if he did have such a party following, certain elements of it would wish to show their power. If a majority of the Senate happens to be of the opposing political party, discrediting the executive is a normal method of party warfare.

Another important factor is that American legislators are elected almost exclusively by the districts in which they live, and they have to think largely in terms of locality. The constitutional requirement is that Senators must be connected by residence with their states; the constitutional provision for Representatives is the same, but in actual practice, practically all Congressmen are elected by their residential districts within their states. This makes localism the universal rule, and nowadays most treaties stir up local currents of opinion. Even Senator Lodge, "scholar in politics" that he was, and advocate of having party lines end at the water's edge, spent much of his time running around Wash-

[27] In his celebrated letter to the London *Times* for January 31, 1920, Viscount Grey said that the American Constitution "not only makes possible but, under certain conditions, renders inevitable conflict between the executive and legislature."

ington getting jobs for his constituents, and was always willing to introduce resolutions pleasing to the Greek or Irish voters of the State of Massachusetts. His attitude toward the Treaty of Versailles was not unconnected with the nature of the electorate that he represented.   Such parochialism in the case of international questions is the more important in the Senate because of the veto power given a minority of 34 per cent.

There is, furthermore, a peculiar senatorial habit of mind which can be better described than explained. John Hay—to continue the anthology of his opinions of Senators—wrote that he had "never struck a subject so full of psychological interest as the official mind of a Senator." [28]   Election to the Senate seems to result in the person chosen becoming more opinionated and more timorous.[29]   Take, for example, the League of Nations debate of 1919–1920. It was literally true that the strength of convictions and the length of speeches were directly proportioned to the ignorance and tyrociny of Senators in

[28] Thayer, *op. cit.*, Vol. II, p. 226.   Henry Adams said that he had only two criticisms of Henry Cabot Lodge: that he was a Senator, and that he was a Senator from Massachusetts (*The Education of Henry Adams*, p. 354).   Roosevelt once remarked that the more he saw of the Kaiser and the Tsar, the more respect he had for American Senators, to which Hay replied that he himself was unable to make such fine distinctions.—Tyler Dennett, *Roosevelt and the Russo-Japanese War*, p. 39 (New York, 1925).

[29] Senator John Sharp Williams on July 15, 1919, read to the Senate an amusing parody of the fears which would be expressed if that body were to begin to debate and make reservations to "Now I lay me down to sleep."   See *Congressional Record*, Vol. 58, p. 2615.

foreign politics. Too many Senators made addresses based on the knowledge of a mediocre college undergraduate, increased by resort to a couple of war books and the *Encyclopædia Britannica,* and presented with the argumentative skill of the average lawyer. This will be evident to anyone with sufficient leisure to read the speeches in the Senate debate. Secretary Lansing apparently recognized this, for he anticipated that only Senators Knox and Lodge would really understand the treaty, and "that Mr. Lodge's position would become purely political, and therefore ineffective." [30] Many Senators, however, had in full measure the qualification which the young journalist applying to Lord Morley for a position as leader writer described as "a great gift for general vituperation." [31] Senatorial imaginations were uncurbed; terrible threats to American institutions were discovered—threats, it may be added, which were not peculiar in their application to the United States, and which, strange to relate, were not discovered in foreign parliaments. The art of imagining dire possibilities if American isola-

[30] *Hearings Before the Committee on Foreign Relations, United States Senate, 66th Congress, 1st Session,* p. *1277.*

[31] The speeches on the World Court, with a few exceptions, were much abler, as a reader courageous enough to make the comparison will discover. Ths may be accounted for in part by the fact that Senators had received their preliminary education in international questions at the time of the League debate, but probably of more importance was the assistance given both protagonists and opponents by expert collaborators who advised on strategy and furnished ammunition. These academic gentlemen who assisted the leaders on both sides have been unhonored and unsung, but were much quoted without quotation marks, and they contributed heavily to raising the debate to a higher level.

tions is abandoned was so successfully nurtured in the League debates in 1919 that more horrendous international goblins were seen in the World Court proposal. These fears did not come from transitory senatorial nightmares; the phobia was much more serious. It results in part from ignorance of foreign politics and international relations, and from inexpertise in discussing them.

It is due also, I venture to suggest, to the fact that American politics is always in the penumbra of possible unconstitutionality. The rules of the governmental game are written out minutely. No trust is placed in the sportsmanship or good sense of the players; reliance is on the rule and in case of dispute as to its meaning, on interpretation by an umpire—the Judiciary. American Senators, therefore, habituated to legalistic manœuvres, want nothing left to the good sense of a World Court, a League Council or anyone else, even the President. The provisions governing advisory opinions must be written in treaties; illegality, rather than impropriety, being relied upon to prevent the Court from usurping authority and extending its jurisdiction. That a body like the World Court, with its future utility dependent on its own wisdom and discretion, would be restrained by a fear of acting improperly or unwisely is a consideration in which Senators can find scant comfort. This is a recent illustration of a general habit of mind. It raises large questions which are not germane here: whether a government runs better by convention and good sense or by a meticulous contract. The senatorial view is that liberties may suffer if good sense is relied upon and that they are unaffected by wars over words.

This habit of mind, incidentally, is much more characteristic of the Senate than of the House of Representatives, even though the latter body is also dominated by lawyers. The future historian pondering the Senate's continued reluctance to enter the World Court is going to be greatly puzzled by the fact that the House of Representatives voted in March, 1925, by 302–28, its earnest desire that the United States adhere to the Court Protocol, and this in spite of doubts expressed in the debate that the House of Representatives had a constitutional right thus to assert its opinion on foreign relations, which are more particularly the prerogative of the executive and the Senate. This constitutional dubiety, I think, neutralized the fact that the House had no responsibility and kept its vote from being a gesture. On the contrary, this action indicated that either the House and the President (for they agreed) or the Senate tremendously misrepresented American public opinion.

My own view is that the House vote—302–28 —pretty accurately reflected the sentiment of the country on the World Court proposal, but my guess cannot be proved right or wrong, and herein is the real difficulty—the chief defect of the American Constitution. The supremacy of public opinion is the prize fallacy of our governmental system unless this concept is so qualified as to time and effect as to be meaningless. How can public opinion—assuming that there is such a thing—be discovered? If, for example, in the case of the World Court, the Senate had thrown the proposal out, what could have been done about it? How could it be accurately ascertained whether the House or the Senate had followed the country's wishes? How, indeed, can it be discovered whether the President and two-thirds of the Senate have the country with them? It is this omission of the American Constitution that is responsible for the daring *amour propre* of Senate minorities. It is the fact that one-third may veto and go unscathed—unless perchance the issue should be a stupendous one—that directly invites the Senate to substitute its anfractuosities for the executive's desires.[32] The Constitution encourages rather than checks senatorial caprice.

Thus, when President Wilson thought that the people of the United States were in favor of the League of Nations, he desired "a great and solemn referendum" for the expression of this popular will. Such a referendum, however, was well nigh impos-

[32] In controversies between the Senate and the President history has not always shown that the Senate was on the right side. Thus in 1844 the Senate defeated a treaty for the annexation of Texas, but in two years Texas had become a State of the Union by joint resolution of Congress. The annexation of Hawaii was rejected in 1854, but forty-four years later was permitted. In 1864 the Senate refused to permit the purchase of the Virgin Islands from Denmark for $7,500,000. The Islands became American territory half a century later at treble the price. In 1888 the Senate refused to settle the old dispute with Canada concerning the Atlantic fisheries but twenty years later this controversy came to an end.

sible,[83] and even if it could have been held, its moral influence would have been negligible. The President is elected every four years, and the House every two years, but only one-third of the Senate goes to the people at a biennial election. Consequently to change the balance of parties in the Senate, two elections are frequently necessary,[34] and even though there should be an unmistakable popular mandate shown in the vote for President or members of the House of Representatives (a rather doubtful result in view of the sectional nature of American politics), the American Senate would not bow in the way that the House of Lords, for example, did with the Parliament Act of 1911. Ex-President Taft was one of the few politicians whose views on the great struggle over the Treaty of Versailles were not twisted by party rancor. In 1920 he appealed for the election of Mr. Harding, the Republican candidate, and his argument was in-

[83] As Bagehot once wrote: "The American Government calls itself a government of the supreme people; but at a quick crisis, the time when a sovereign power is most needed, you cannot *find* the supreme people. You have got a Congress elected for one fixed period, going out perhaps by fixed installments, which cannot be accelerated or retarded; you have a President chosen for a fixed period, and immovable during that period: all the arrangements are for *stated* times. There is no *elastic* element; everything is rigid, specified, dated. Come what may, you can quicken nothing and can retard nothing. You have bespoken your government in advance, and whether it suits you or not, by law you must keep it."—*The English Constitution*, p. 98.

[34] The way in which changes in the political composition of the Senate have lagged behind changes in the country is shown by C. H. Woody, "Is the Senate Unrepresentative?" *Political Science Quarterly*, June, 1926.

teresting. It was that among the two-thirds of
the Senate not up for reëlection were "the Republican Senators who will have the power, and
will reject Article X and defeat the treaty." Hence
he urged the country to vote for a Republican candidate who would compromise with his own party associates and not for a Democratic candidate who,
*even though the country had pronounced unmistak-
ably in his favor, would be met by senatorial recal-
citrance.*

Such a situation, I suggest, is almost unique in
governments that are professedly popular; [35] it
could assuredly not be found in any parliamentary
system, and this is an aspect of the matter that
foreign critics overlook. It is not *ratification* that
causes the difficulty; neither is it *senatorial* ratification, nor the *two-thirds* majority considered by itself. Despite these difficult conditions, consultation
of the Senate would be tolerable and procurable
were there any possibility of holding a "solemn
referendum" on the issue in dispute. As it is, many
consider that the Constitution—to quote Hay for
the last time—makes "an irreparable mistake" in
putting "it into the power of one-third plus one of
the Senate to meet with a categorical veto any treaty
negotiated by the President, even though it might
have the approval of nine-tenths of the people of
the nation." [36]

Similar, although lesser, difficulties appear in

[35] President Harding in a Lincoln day address called "ours, the
only popular government that I know of in the world."

[36] Thayer, *op. cit.*, Vol. II, p. 219.

battles over legislation. Senatorial minorities occasionally procure amendments and sometimes obstruct and veto, but these situations avoid being scandalous for the reasons that time is rarely of the essence of the matter; a simple majority suffices, and foreign nations are not concerned. Logically, I think, there are great advantages in, and no objections to, having treaties ratified like ordinary laws—by simple majorities of both houses.[37] There would still be the serious danger that a President of the opposite political party would have his international programme sabotaged by party rancour and that deadlocks could not be resolved by an appeal to the people; but at least these difficulties —inevitable so long as our form of government is not radically changed—would not be intensified by the requirement of *two-thirds of the Senate*. As it is, only geography saves the United States from serious consequences: the "irreparable mistake" can

[37] See Q. Wright, "The Control of Foreign Relations," *American Political Science Review,* February, 1921.

"The treaty-making machinery of the United States has become so complicated as to be almost unworkable. Only by the exercise of great powers of conciliation or of domination by the President, or by awakening and directing upon the Senate a vigorous public opinion, can any progress be made in international relations. A body of ninety-six men of such diverse characteristics and opinions as the members of the Senate is almost hopeless as an executive force. But it is ideal for purposes of obstruction. If the United States is to move forward in helpful coöperation with the other nations of the world towards the attainment of international peace, it will only be through the expression of a widespread and strongly expressed public opinion, which the Senate may apprehend is to be translated into votes."—G. W. Wickersham, "The Senate and Our Foreign Relations," *Foreign Affairs,* December, 1923.

be endured for the reason that it is American; were any European government to copy it disaster would immediately follow.

As it is, also, the phrenetic Senate, relying on the letter of the Constitution, invites unconstitutionality. Its impregnable position and its sense of power lead to assertions of authority that are unwise politically and improper constitutionally. Thus the provision inserted in the post-war treaties, "that the United States shall not be represented or participate in any body, agency or commission, nor shall any person represent the United States as a member of any body, agency or commission in which the United States is authorized to participate by this treaty unless and until an Act of Congress of the United States shall provide for such representation or participation," is a serious interference with the President's duty of seeing that the laws are faithfully executed and with his constitutional prerogative in foreign affairs. It means, in practice, the consent of the Senate rather than the consent of Congress, for the House of Representatives will not refuse to act in any case where its approval is requested. This "unconstitutional invasion of the executive power by the Senate" was, as Mr. Wickersham has said, "one of the significant steps recently taken by the Senate in assuming an extra-constitutional control of our international relations." More than this, such a senatorial attitude terrorizes the executive. To be sure, it may be argued that Presidents and Secretaries of State should not fear criticism by a minority of the Senate; that they should not be content with the rôles of domestic relations attorneys endeavoring to keep the members of their party household from quarreling, and that party harmony—secured by shelving all disturbing questions—should not be the principal and sole good. This is probably asking too much, and it is therefore true, as Mr. Wickersham has said, that "the whole policy of the Department of State since March, 1921, has been dominated by the general desire not only to avoid criticism on the part of the Senate, but studiously to avoid any act or expression which might indicate either sympathy or coöperation with that great international organization for the preservation of world peace, the League of Nations, which is anathema to certain senatorial minds. This undoubtedly was a counsel of prudence. But it inevitably led to the abandonment of the highest avowed ideals with which the administration assumed control of the government."

One result of the Senate's certainty to delay and proneness to reserve has been greater executive secrecy, and a more frequent reliance on private understandings not contemplated by the Constitution. Executive agreements have, of course, related to many matters not of the kind that should be submitted to the Senate for formal action.[38] In other cases, however, the executive has chosen courses where there was complete freedom from senatorial scrutiny; declarations are made of the *policy* of the American Government. Our constitutional ar-

[38] John Bassett Moore, "Treaties and Executive Agreements," *Political Science Quarterly*, September, 1905.

rangements, however, are so well known abroad that
there has been little secret diplomacy.   Mr. Roosevelt entered into a secret understanding [39] with Japan promising her a free hand in Korea and Man-
churia as a sort of *quid pro quo* for a recognition of
American rights in the Philippines, but instances of
this sort are few in number.   The fact should not
be lost sight of, however, that the American Constitution permits the State Department to pursue a
more autocratic course than would be possible in a
parliamentary government, where there is at least
a slight measure of Cabinet responsibility.   Senatorial ratification of treaties, the power of Congress
to declare war and to join in treaties requiring appropriations or legislation are but the formal trap-
pings that help to distract attention from the fact
that the American democracy has little control of
its day by day diplomacy.   With reference to such
matters as the recognition of new governments, the
disposal of the armed forces of the United States,
protests against restrictions on American property

[39] The memorandum embodying this understanding is published
in Dennett, *Roosevelt and the Russo-Japanese War,* pp. 112–114.
  Roosevelt was anxious to broaden the Anglo-Japanese Alliance
by the inclusion of the United States, but he knew that this could
never be gotten through the Senate. He told George Kennan,
who urged such action, that he was talking "academically." "Have
you followed some of my experiences in endeavoring to get treaties
through the Senate? I might just as well strive for the moon as
for such a policy as you indicate. Mind you, I personally entirely agree with you, but if you have followed the difficulty I
have had even in getting such obvious things done as those connected with Panama and Santo Domingo, you would get some
faint idea of the absolute impossibility of carrying out any such
policy as you indicate in your letter." (pp. 115, 116.)

or citizens in foreign countries—matters which are frequently far more important than those covered by treaties—the President and Secretary of State have complete immunity until their terms expire no matter how much *Demos* desires a different policy. The attitude of the United States toward Russia, to be more specific, is determined by the President and his Secretary of State, who can do pretty much as they please; no congressional committee has any influence, and they can keep public opinion reasonably quiet by giving the newspapers selected "facts." The Senate's share in foreign policy is therefore severely limited to treaties, and from the standpoint of controlling the executive, this is a great defect. A change, however, may be in slow process of being effected.

Both of the recent Chairmen of the Senate Committee on Foreign Relations, as Mr. Walter Lippmann points out, have been particularly sensitive on the prerogatives of the Senate. Senator Lodge was chiefly concerned in maintaining the rights of the Senate as against the executive; [40] and previous Chairmen have relied upon the vague language of the Constitution to maintain the position that it is the right of the Senate to be consulted during negotiations, to make alternative proposals to foreign nations and, indeed, to *share* with the President the treaty-making authority. Senator Borah, on the other hand, seems to look upon the Senate as a body which may secure some measure of open

[40] But see above, p. 52, for a case in which he did not wish the Senate to interfere.

diplomacy. He desires the Senate to be powerful and even to mould the President to its way of thinking, but in this view he is supported by his faith in the people and in the representation which they should have in the branch of the legislature charged with authority over treaties. Senator Lodge simply demanded that the President consult certain Senators, and bow to their individual views; Senator Borah believes that the Senate should in every doubtful case force the President to make disclosures and to wait for an informal assessment of public opinion.[41]

The Constitution, as I have said, is vague on just what the Senate may do. What does "advice and consent" really mean? The framers of the Constitution assuredly did not anticipate that by this language they were opening up treaty negotiations to public scrutiny; they did not contemplate such tactics as those of Senator Borah. The authors of *The Federalist* were no advocates of open diplomacy. They thought that foreign relations should be pretty well removed from popular control. Since the President was to be "chosen by select bodies of electors" there would be no danger that "the activity of party zeal, taking advantage of the supineness, the ignorance and the hopes and fears of the unwary and interested" would place "men in office by the votes of a small proportion of the electors," and since the indirect method would be used as well for Senators—since they would be

---

[41] Walter Lippmann, "Concerning Senator Borah," *Foreign Affairs,* January, 1926.

chosen by state legislatures which would "in general be composed of the most enlightened and respectable citizens"—it was reasonable to suppose that the upper chamber would be made up of men "who have become the most distinguished by their abilities and virtue, and in whom the people perceive a just ground for confidence." Collaboration of the President and the Senate on treaties would insure "every advantage which can be derived from talents, information, integrity, and deliberate investigations on the one hand, and from secrecy and despatch on the other." [42]

This ideal has not been realized. Even if the House of Representatives were admitted to a share in the treaty-making authority, there could hardly be less information, deliberate investigation, secrecy,

[42] *The Federalist,* No. 64.

In a later number of *The Federalist,* Hamilton returned to the same subject, and argued specially against the admission of the House of Representatives to a share in the formation of treaties. In this connection he said:

"The fluctuating and, taking its future increase into the account, the multitudinous composition of that body, forbid us to expect in it those qualities which are essential to the proper execution of such a trust. Accurate and comprehensive knowledge of foreign politics; a steady and systematic adherence to the same views; a nice and uniform sensibility to national character; decision, secrecy, and despatch, are incompatible with the genius of a body so variable and so numerous. The very complication of the business, by introducing a necessity of the concurrence of so many different bodies, would of itself afford a solid objection. The greater frequency of the calls upon the House of Representatives, and the greater length of time which it would often be necessary to keep them together when convened, to obtain their sanction in the progressive stages of a treaty, would be a source of so great inconvenience and expense as alone ought to condemn the project." —*The Federalist,* No. 75.

and despatch than on occasion are shown by the Senate. The fact that this body is not immediately amenable to popular control makes it act in an irresponsible manner. What this means in respect of the substitution of the judgment of Senate minorities for the judgment of the executive has already been discussed. It means also that Senators will make speeches dealing with vague rumors, and, with inadequate information, express definite opinions on international questions.

An excellent illustration of this was in March, 1926, when Mr. Houghton, American Ambassador to Great Britain, while on a visit to Washington let it be known that he took a gloomy view of the European situation, which was reverting to the pre-war basis of national hatreds. Mr. Houghton, following the practice of his superiors (a practice which is discussed in some detail later), did not himself stand sponsor for his opinions. These were, it was explained, "communicated to official sources to filter through to sources of public information." The results were resentment in Europe, vagueness as to the attitude of the administration, great exaggeration of Mr. Houghton's alleged views (for these were stated much more extremely by correspondents than he would have been willing to state them over his own signature), and a stormy Senate debate which was based on the anonymous ambassadorial utterances.[43] Senators discussed the intrigues and plots and machinations of European states. Such talk could do no good, and might have

[43] Cf. *Congressional Record*, March 22, 1926, p. 5775.

done a great deal of harm.[44]   It results from the
fact that, powerful in respect of treaties, the Senate
desires to make a pretense of being powerful in
respect of American foreign policy in general.   It
is possible because germaneness is not insisted upon
and a Senator may discuss almost any subject at
almost any time.   From this angle, unrestricted
debate is an evil, but it is an evil that has its com-
pensating advantages.

[44] Executive sessions are discussed by Senator Norris, "Secrecy
in the Senate," *The Nation,* May 5, 1926.

CHAPTER IV

THE SENATE AS A LEGISLATIVE
CHAMBER

"If a second chamber dissents from the first, it is mischevious; if it agrees wtih it, it is superfluous"
—ABBÉ DE SIÉYÈS

The Senate's success with its executive powers has, of course, contributed largely to increasing its influence as a legislative chamber—as a check on the House of Representatives. "There used to be a singular idea that two chambers—a revising chamber and a suggesting chamber—were essential to a free government," wrote Walter Bagehot. "With a perfect Lower House, it is certain that an Upper House would be scarcely of any value. If we had an ideal House of Commons, perfectly representing the nation, always moderate, never passionate, abounding in men of leisure, never omitting the slow and steady forms necessary for good consideration, it is certain that we should not need a higher chamber. The work would be done so well that we should not want anyone to look over or revise it, and whatever is unnecessary in government is pernicious. . . . But though beside an ideal House of Commons the Lords would be unnecessary, and therefore pernicious, beside the actual House a

revising and leisured legislature is extremely useful, if not quite necessary." [1]

The House of Representatives is not an ideal
chamber. It meets hardly one of Bagehot's conditions, which are essential to the validity of the
Abbé de Siéyès' oft-quoted dilemma. This must be
qualified also, by reason of the fact that, in the
United States, there is no prior veto on legislation
by a Cabinet which possesses complete initiative of
bills and control of the time of the chambers.
When members of a lower house have a free and
equal right to propose legislation; when there is no
executive control, and, indeed, no control whatever
except that of the committee chairmen who become
such through longevity rather than ability and
have no collective programme or responsibility;
when legislation is drafted by Representatives whose
competence [2] comes as the gentle dew *vocis populi*
—then there must be a second, revising chamber,
and it must have real authority. This is not to
deny that, were Congress a unicameral legislature,

---

[1] *The English Constitution*, pp. 174–175.

[2] "I am unwilling to make the admission that if I have a piece
of legislation that I think ought to become the law that I am incapacitated, that people who are elected in other districts are incapacitated to do their own thinking and prepare their own bills.
. . . I am unwilling to make the admission that the House of Representatives must have an expert legislative bill-drafter to whom
to go to draft bills. . . . I realize we are getting away from representative government. The old monarchical idea of having
men to do this work is growing rapidly. I have not an idea of that
kind. I still believe people are capable of electing Members of
Congress who can do their own work. I know that the representatives of the People do good work."—Mr. Sisson in the House of
Representatives, January 20, 1923, *Congressional Record*, p. 2154.

the House of Representatives would feel a greater sense of responsibility and would refrain from passing, as it now does, incomplete, ambiguous and poorly drafted measures, confident either that the Senate will not consider them at all, or, if it does, that it will correct their defects. If the Senate were abolished, the legislative grist of the House of Representatives would be of a much higher grade, but in the absence of responsible leadership, a homogeneous programme, and the requirement of trained draughtsmanship, a revisory chamber is necessary. This function the Senate is well adapted to perform.

Two chambers of equal powers permit, and even invite deadlocks. This is the price (believers in throttling down the governmental machine will consider it a small price) that the congressional system pays for an upper chamber that represents the states *qua* states—that rests on the federal principle.[3]   Yet what a federal principle: the *equality* of

[3] "It is said that there must be in a Federal Government some institution, some authority, some body possessing a veto in which the separate States composing the Confederation are all equal. I confess this doctrine has to me no self-evidence, and it is assumed, but not proved. The State of Delaware is *not* equal in power or influence to the State of New York, and you cannot make it so by giving it an equal veto in an Upper Chamber. The history of such an institution is indeed most natural. A little State will like, and must like, to see some token, some memorial mark of its old independence preserved in the Constitution by which that independence is extinguished. But it is one thing for an institution to be natural, and another for it to be expedient. If indeed it be that a Federal Government compels the erection of an Upper Chamber of conclusive and coördinate authority, it is one more in addition to the many other inherent defects of that kind of government. It may be necessary to have the blemish, but it is a blemish just as much."—Bagehot, *op. cit.,* p. 166.

the commonwealths of the United States is the purest sort of legal fiction! Other federal systems have carefully eschewed basing their federal assembly on such a fable, which history and tradition have made palatable but not justifiable. This equality of representation, however, has not made it impossible for—perhaps it has even invited—the Senate to shelter spokesmen for minorities that otherwise would have been without congressional advocates. It is, moreover, not the least interesting aspect of the American Senate that, set up as the "great compromise" of the Constitution to protect the small states against the large states it could have been impotent throughout the whole of its history and the statute book (from this standpoint) would have substantially the same contents. The federal currents of legislation, in other words, have neither been kept from nor led into different courses by the Senate. Lecky declared that this "illustrious body" had "excited the envy and admiration of many European statesmen and writers on politics," because it had played "so important a part in American history." [4] This "part," however, must be understood as "important" in spite of the theory of representation and contrary to the idea of the Senate as a federal body.

The Senate of the United States is probably the worst rotten borough institution in the world.[5] Squaring senatorial representation with any known

[4] *Democracy and Liberty,* Vol. I, p. 445 (New York, 1913).
[5] *Cf.* Burgess, "The Election of United States Senators by Popular Vote," *Political Science Quarterly,* Vol. XVII, p. 650 (1902).

principle is a sciamachy. New York with ten million people has two Senators, as has Nevada with
less than eighty thousand. If the Senate were
based on the proportional principle, New York
would have 270 Senators. The eighteen smallest
states just about equal New York in population;
they have forty-five Representatives to New York's
forty-three. The population of Pennsylvania is
larger than that of all New England, but Pennsylvania has two Senators, while New England has
twelve. States containing less than one-fifth of the
population of the country return a majority of the
Senate. Anomalies could be multiplied. In other
federal systems the contrasts are by no means so
striking. Under the Constitution of the German
Empire, the smallest state was only represented
forty or fifty times more heavily than Prussia. In
Switzerland, Uri, the smallest canton, is represented
about thirty times more strongly than Bern, the
largest canton.

These disproportions have frequently been
pointed out, but for a number of reasons—not the
least important being the fact that the Senate has
engaged in few great controversies with the House
of Representatives—there has been little agitation
for change. Now, however, the vagaries of representation are coupled with the political opinions of
Senators from the small states and the combination
is said to be particularly dangerous. This reverses
one of the most emphatic of the arguments against
the abolition of the "rotten boroughs" in England.
When the Reform Bill of 1832 was being debated

it was urged that Old Sarum and Gatton served as "nurseries for statesmen." Great parliamentary figures—the Elder Pitt, Fox, Burke, Sheridan— were cited as having been nominated for the House of Commons; and when Macaulay became eloquent on the astonishment of a stranger visiting England and finding that the green mound called Gatton had two members and Manchester none, it was pointed out that Macaulay himself sat for the rotten borough of Calne. The same stranger might be as much puzzled by Nevada and New York each having two Senators; the contrast is greater than that between a deserted village and Liverpool which were equally represented in the Commons. It is doubtful whether the Senators from the "rotten boroughs" have raised or lowered the general average of ability, but certain it is that the occasional third-party representatives have come from the less populous states of the West and that equality of representation has given greater prominence to Senators who are spokesmen for the farmers.

This farm influence in the upper house of Congress may, I suggest, be considered as a bulwark of conservatism. It is modelled in part on a great precedent. The House of Lords was long defended because it represented the landed interest.[6] Similarly it may be argued that the agricultural bloc Senators represent the "landed interest" of the United States. To be sure, the House of Lords

[6] Even now 242 peers represent landowning interests and 227 of them own 7,362,009 acres of land. See *Labour and Capital in Parliament,* p. 10 (Labour Research Department, 1923).

was concerned with protecting great landowners against having their estates taxed or broken up, whereas the agricultural bloc desires protection of small landowners in securing a livelihood.[7]   Is this difference really material?   The theories are not dissimilar, but curiously enough, the basis of representation in the Senate is criticized because, although it affords some protection to the "landed interest," it encourages radicalism.   Thus it has been argued boldly that:

"The system of representation encourages the formation of agricultural and other 'blocs' which negative majority rule and foster class legislation wholly inconsistent with the spirit of democracy.

". . . The Senators from the six states in the Northwest who have been most conspicuous in the 'agricultural bloc' represent only ten millions of people, while the Senators from the six New England states from whom the ascendancy in Congress has been wrested have only about seven million constituents.

"The states which are overrepresented in the Senate offer easy opportunities for the radical and the demagogue to intermeddle with the enactment of legislation." [8]

Now, voting by majorities is a device, not an eternal principle, and it needs some definition (and justification) before it is linked with "the spirit of democracy" as an absolute norm for a representative system.[9]   If it were accepted—even in its most ob-

---

[7] Arthur Capper, *The Agricultural Bloc* (New York, 1922).

[8] W. S. Carpenter, *Democracy and Representation,* pp. 60–61 (Princeton, 1925).

[9] This is not the place to discuss the question of majorities.   The subject, which has received scant attention from the historians, is

vious form—it would mean a rewriting of the Constitution: a changed method of amendment; new systems of popular election; a different treaty-ratifying authority, and no presidential or judicial vetoes. The United States, orally, sings a pæan to the theory of majorities; institutionally, it sings a palinode. A more important consideration, however, is that the agricultural "bloc" Senators may not represent the ten millions of people in six states; they may only represent bare majorities of them, but there are also minorities in other states which perhaps feel that they get more adequate representation from the "bloc" Senators than they do from their own straight party Democrats and Republicans. Consequently the agricultural "bloc" should not be spoken of as supported by one small area. Our "landed interest" is more extensive.

To say, furthermore, that "the states which are overrepresented in the Senate offer easy opportunities for the radical and the demagogue to intermeddle with the enactment of legislation" is not arguing but calling names. The opportunities for intermeddling come rather from long service in the Senate than from equality of representation. Thus Senator Aldrich, of Rhode Island, was for some years a most powerful leader in the Senate; his "intermeddling" was far more pervasive than was warranted by the size of his constituency. In the Sixty-eighth Congress, Senators Smoot and Warren,

dealt with by Th. Baty, "The History of Majority Rule," *Quarterly Review,* January, 1912, and J. G. Heinberg, "History of the Majority Principle," *American Political Science Review,* February, 1926.

representing the small states of Utah and Wyoming, controlled revenue and appropriations.[10] Eighteen states with only slightly more inhabitants than Pennsylvania elect thirty-six Senators, whose "intermeddling" with legislation is perhaps no more influential or pernicious than the "intermeddling" of Matthew Stanley Quay. Considering the personnel of the Senate in the last quarter of a century —reactionaries and radicals—it cannot, I think, be said that the latter have done the country any more harm than the former; nor do I assert that the latter have done more good than the former. There should be room in a legislative assembly for both. The names of Quay, Aldrich and Platt were anathema in the West; certain radical Senators have been despised in the East. But it is hardly convincing to argue against the present senatorial representation on the ground that the small states send radical Senators to Washington. There are radical minorities in Pennsylvania, and in New York, that were more nearly alike in political views with La Follette or Magnus Johnson than they were with Quay or Platt. It may seem on occasion that the Senate is "the cockle of rebellion, insolence, sedition," [11] but it is nevertheless the more representative branch of Congress, the only forum of the nation.

Furthermore, inveighing against "blocs" which negative majority rule is tilting at windmills. There have always been "blocs" in American politics, and the principal difference between them

[10] See below, p. 109.
[11] *Coriolanus,* Act III, Scene 1.

and the agricultural "bloc" is that the latter group is described by a French word. In tactics there has perhaps been the difference of frankness, but for those who desire to protect not the landed interest but the tariff beneficiaries and business interests to inveigh against the agricultural "bloc" is a case of the pot calling the kettle black, with the exception, as I say, that the pot is camouflaged, while the kettle asseverates its inky expansiveness. For the fact is that American parties have always acted through sectional and class compromises. Sometimes, as in the Democratic Party, the compromise is between the conservative South and the Progressive West; in the Republican Party it is between the progressive West and the extremely conservative East. Except for the Wilson administrations, congressional control of both parties has been pretty clearly in conservative leaders. The Middle West chafed for years under the dominance of New England in Congress, and its controlling interest in the Republican Party.[12] When the balance of power shifts to the West, New England objects, but the chief difference, as I have said, is that the agricultural "bloc" works in the open; it is supported by minorities in Pennsylvania, Massachusetts, and Alabama as well as by western farmers, and, incidentally, it has been present in the House of Representatives, where its influence was less public due to numbers and closure, and less strong, due to the strict control of the House by its leaders.

[12] For a discussion of this influence, see Frederick Jackson Turner, "Sections and Nation," *The Yale Review*, Oct., 1922.

This hospitality of the Senate to representatives of minorities has been a much more interesting result of the bicameral scheme than any special protection by the Senate to the small states. The great disproportions now are in respect of wealth and taxes. It was argued originally that equal representation was necessary to protect the small states. These, however, have now become so numerous that if the *protecting* theory were once valid it might be expected that this would now be supplanted by a *grasping* theory; that a combination of small states might be formed against New York, Pennsylvania, Illinois and Michigan which contribute more than half the annual contents of the National Treasury. Nor would these states have any effective strength in the lower house, since their representation there is but 119 out of 435. From this standpoint unrestricted debate in the Senate is a safeguard which these wealthy states should not lightly give up; but the whole question is speculative, for such divisions do not occur. In the votes on the "grants-in-aid"—federal funds to be expended by the states on roads, agriculture, etc.—there have been no lines drawn between small states and large ones; no raids by the poor on the wealthy.

Such an antagonism, indeed, has not developed on any legislative issue.[18] An examination of the

[18] "There has never, in point of fact, been any division of interests or consequent contests between the great States and the small ones, but the provision for equal representation of all States had the important result of making the slave-holding party during the thirty years which preceded the Civil War eager to extend the area of slavery in order that, by creating new slave States, they

Senate votes on the major battles in Congress—such issues as the Alien and Sedition laws, the declaration of war against England in 1812, the incorporation of the Bank of the United States, the Missouri Compromise on slavery in 1820, the annexation of Texas, and free silver—discloses that the average population of states opposed has not differed greatly from the average population of states in favor. There are no traces of a combination of small states.[14] It may, of course, be shown that Senate majorities represent population minorities,[15] but it would be strange indeed if this were not the case,

might maintain at least an equality in the Senate and thereby prevent any legislation hostile to slavery." Bryce, *The American Commonwealth*, Vol. I, p. 99.

Hamilton did not anticipate that there would be any conflicts:

"Gentlemen indulge too many unreasonable apprehensions of danger to the State Governments; they seem to suppose that the moment you put men into a national council they become corrupt and tyrannical, and lose all affection for their fellow citizens. . . . The State Governments are essentially necessary to the form and spirit of the general system. As long, therefore, as Congress have a full conviction of this necessity, they must, even upon principles purely national, have as firm an attachment to the one as to the other. This conviction can never leave them unless they become madmen." *Elliott's Debates on the Federal Constitution*, Vol. II, pp. 303–304 (Washington, 1836).

[14] Moffett, "Is the Senate Unfairly Constituted?" *Political Science Quarterly*, Vol. X, p. 248 (1895).

[15] The Missouri Compromise of 1820; the renewal of the Bank charter, 1832; the adoption of the Bank charter renewal over Tyler's veto, and the Tariff of 1842 were approved in the Senate by votes which represented a smaller population than the votes in opposition. When, on February 1, 1896, the Senate substituted a free-silver bill for the Treasury Relief bond bill passed by the House, the minority of 35 (against 42) represented a popular majority of 8,000,000. *Cf.* Ford, *The Rise and Growth of American Politics*, p. 273.

particularly when the Senate is controlled by Democrats who are elected by the smaller states. Even in the House, based though it is on population, the single member constituency results occasionally in a minority of voters having a majority of Representatives, and an examination of rollcalls would disclose the fact that majorities of members not infrequently have behind them minorities of the population.[16]

Such vagaries are inevitable, but it is a curious fact that, in a country as vast as the United States, representation by area has played such an inconsiderable rôle in elections and congressional decisions. If, for example, from the first administration under the Constitution each state had been allowed only one vote, and that vote had been cast in accordance with the majority of the popular vote in the state, the Presidents, with two exceptions, would have been the same as those actually chosen by the Electoral College. In 1848 and 1880 there would have been ties.

This is not so remarkable, for the truth of the matter is that nowadays most interests run across class lines: agriculture concerns the farmers of New England as much as the farmers of the Middle West; the tariff is important to southern manufacturers as well as to those of New England. These interests prevail irrespective of the size of the state. It is plausible to argue that in the Senate New

[16] Woody, "Is the Senate Unrepresentative?" *Political Science Quarterly,* June, 1926.

York's ten million population should have a greater weight than the smaller population of Delaware, but New York's population is hardly ever a unit on a particular issue. It is the size of a political majority in a state that matters. In 1884, for example, New York cast more than a million votes for the presidential candidates, while Nevada cast only 12,000, but in New York, the votes of half a million Democrats were cancelled by those of half a million Republicans, and the 36 electoral votes of the state were given to Cleveland by 1,047 persons who furnished the Democratic plurality. In Nevada there was a net Republican majority of 1,615, which cancelled the Democratic plurality in New York with 568 votes to spare.[17] In short, when one begins to argue on the basis of electoral statistics, he can get macaronic results and can support amphigoric theories.

Of sectionalism, naturally, the Senate has shown many traces,[18] but then American politics are in-

[17] Moffett, *loc. cit.*

[18] It is interesting to recall that Gouverneur Morris anticipated sectional divisions, and was rather suspicious of representation that would proportionately reduce the weight of the East in the councils of the nation. "He looked forward to that range of new States which would soon be formed in the West. He thought the rule of representation ought to be so fixed as to secure to the Atlantic States a prevalence in the national councils. 'The new States will know less of the public interest than these; will have an interest in many respects different; in particular will be less scrupulous of involving the community in wars, the burdens and operations of which would fall chiefly on the maritime States. Provision ought therefore to be made to prevent the maritime States from being hereafter outvoted by them.' He thought this might

curably parochial.   The House, in Burke's phrase, is "a confused and scuffling bustle of local agency." A Representative, almost invariably connected with his district by residence, thinks and acts so as to placate his constituents and secure reëlection.   He is interested primarily in getting things for his district and the House proceedings in the *Congressional Record* are a compendium of provincial demands and interests.   The Senate—and this is a tremendous factor in the greater power of the upper house —by reason of its broader basis of representation can take a broader view.   This is at times venal and parochial in respect of appointments; it is frequently capricious and not national in respect of treaties, but it at least relates to a wider area than a congressional district; although, strange to say, on foreign questions, the World Court for example, the House is much less particularistic than the Senate.[19]   Combinations of Senators from the great geographical divisions of the country sometimes appear, and in such cases the Senate may fulfil its original purpose, although in a much modified form.

easily be done by irrevocably fixing the number of Representatives which the Atlantic States should respectively have, and the number which each new State will have."   Farrand, *Records of the Federal Convention,* Vol. I, p. 553.

Morris thought that "the busy haunts of men, not the remote wilderness was the proper school of political talents. If the western people get the power in their hands they will ruin the Atlantic interests. The back members are almost always averse to the best measures." *Ibid.,* p. 583.

[19] *Cf.* the action of the House in favoring American entrance into the World Court by a vote of 302 to 28.

I refer, for example, to the "protection" of the South against the Force Bill of 1890; to a similar protection in 1922 against the Dyer Anti-Lynching Bill, and to a hitherto effective veto on legislation reducing the representation of the South in the House under the Fourteenth Amendment.[20] To be sure, the South has not a sufficient number of Senators to make an effective resistance on a rollcall; it must act by parliamentary obstruction [21] rather than by argument, but in these battles the Senators seem definitely to represent *areas* rather than *States*. Occasionally also a vote on some economic issue shows a cleavage along sectional lines. Thus the Senate in February, 1926, defeated Senator Norris' amendment providing publicity for income tax returns. The vote was 49 to 32, and of the majority Senators all but four came from East of the Mississippi River and North of the Mason and Dixon's Line. In other words, practically the entire

[20] "Representatives shall be apportioned among the several States according to their respective numbers, counting the whole number of persons in each State, excluding Indians not taxed. But when the right to vote at any election for the choice of electors for President and Vice-President of the United States, Representatives in Congress, the executive and judicial officers of a State, or the members of the legislature thereof, is denied to any of the male inhabitants of such State being twenty-one years of age, and citizens of the United States, or in any way abridged, except for participation in rebellion, or other crime, the basis of representation therein shall be reduced in the proportion which the number of such male citizens shall bear to the whole number of male citizens twenty-one years of age in such State." *The Constitution,* Amendments, Article XIV, Section 3.

[21] See below, pp. 169, 181, note.

support of the publicity proposal came from the West and the South. It is rare that the Senate divides so sectionally.

Groupings by areas appear also in the committee assignments, and as parties change, the seniority rule makes different sections seem to have control of legislation. When the Democrats have a majority of the Senate, most of the important committees are headed by Senators from the southern states; the South is always said to be in the saddle, but this is to be expected, considering the geographical distribution of party control. Similarly when the first session of the Sixty-seventh Congress was organized, choice minority committee assignments in the House went to southern Representatives; the Republican landslide in 1920 had been so complete that only 20 of the 131 Democratic Representatives came from sections other than the Solid South.[22] If the Democrats ever control the House, the operation of the seniority rule will deprive the West and the North of the control of committees. Dominance by the Republicans varies from section to section; at one time New England, and at another time the West seems to have control. Thus in the Sixty-seventh Congress, 37 Republican Senators and 172 Republican Representatives came from the West; twelve of the nineteen major House committees and a majority of the Senate committees were headed by Westerners, but the primacy of a section is by no means so complete as in a Democratic Congress.

[22] See the remarks of Representative Pou, *Congressional Record*, April 22, 1921, p. 531.

These sectional influences rarely determine the course of legislation to any important degree. They are not so abnormal as to hurt the Senate's authority. A principal factor in preserving this is the absence of any great battles with the House of Representatives when the House has been on the popular side. In England opposition to the programme of Mr. Asquith's Liberal Government, culminating in the rejection of the Lloyd George Budget of 1909, made it necessary for the Liberals to assault the citadel of the Lords and to reduce them, legislatively, to a stage of nonage. There has been no similar struggle in the United States; the Senate has not fought against the lower chamber on questions which stirred up popular feeling. Indeed most of the differences of opinion with the House of Representatives have been on questions of detail and degree rather than of principle.

If there are no factors that have reduced the influence of the Senate (there might have been had the method of election not been changed) [23] there

[23] In 1896 a majority of the Committee on Privileges and Elections reported in favor of an amendment for popular election of United States Senators. The report said:

"It is a fact that must be apparent to all that during recent years an impression, deep-seated and threatening, whether well founded or otherwise, has obtained in the American mind and among the masses of the American people to the effect that the Senate of the United States has become a sort of aristocratic body—too far removed from the people, beyond their reach, and with no especial interest in their welfare. The Senate has, in the past few years, been assailed, as we believe causelessly, from time to time by many of the leading and most influential journals of the country of both political parties.

"The tendency of public opinion is to disparage the Senate and are several reasons contributing to the Senate's primacy in the congressional system. Some of these I have already mentioned: [24] the Senate is in continuous existence; the longer term makes for greater independence and willingness to submit to leadership; membership is more attractive than in the House of Representatives—those chosen to the latter body strive for promotion to the Senate. Frequently, moreover, Senators control, or at least are in close relations with, their state political machines, and with American parties organized entirely outside the government this is no unimportant matter. The members of the upper chamber are powerful in nominating conventions that select presidential candidates. Thus in 1920, President Harding was designated as the Republican party's standard-bearer by a group of Senators who could dictate the

depreciate its dignity, its usefulness, its integrity, its power. If there is any cause for this tendency in the public mind, it should be removed without delay. Although the Senate of the United States should be and, in fact, is the most dignified, as well as the most important legislative body in the world, the tendency in public journalism and in the popular mind is in a large degree to detract from its importance, minimize its dignity and power, and cast the spirit of obloquy over and around it and its members. While your Committee are of the opinion that the impression which leads to all this is, to a very great extent at least, not well founded, yet it is a fact that cannot be ignored that it exists." 54th Congress, 1st Session, Senate Report No. 530.

[24] De Tocqueville thought that the striking inferiority of the House to the Senate was due to the fact that the latter was a product of double election, and he anticipated that democracies must resort to double election in order to avoid the evils inseparable from placing political functions in the hands of every class of the people. Bryce, *Studies in History and Jurisprudence*, p. 336. (New York, 1901).

votes of the delegates of their states at the nominating convention. They did this not by reason of their offices, but because of their importance in the state party organizations; and if this oligarchy was less influential after than before the election, the reason was no self-denying ordinance or dwindling strength of the oligarchy, but an unexpected, even though spasmodic and not always effective presidential independence. On some matters the Senate clearly won. It was notorious that on foreign policy the executive dared no combat with the Senate. Among other defeats a bill giving free tolls to American coastwise vessels using the Panama Canal was passed against the President's wishes.[25]

The upper chamber, of course, has an immense advantage over the House of Representatives in that it is a smaller body. For the last five years the House has struggled to fix the number of its members on the basis of the 1920 census, a new apportionment bring required by the Constitution. On January 19, 1921, the House passed a bill keeping its membership at 435 as at present. This meant a reduction in the representation of eleven

[25] President Harding, however, tried to play the House against the Senate. Thus he had the House hold up the Emergency Peace Resolution; he desired the House not to concur in the Borah amendment to the Naval Appropriation Bill of 1921 requesting the President to invite Great Britain and Japan to a naval conference (sentiment in favor of this was so strong that Mr. Harding decided he had better yield) and he had the Panama Canal Tolls Bill pigeon-holed in the House after it had passed the Senate. The opposite manœuvre was attempted by M. Briand in February, 1926. He used the French Senate to insert in his budget items that had been rejected by the Chamber of Deputies.

states.[26]   The bill was not considered in the Senate, and the matter went over to the Sixty-seventh Congress. At the first (special) session, a bill increasing the number of members to 460 was sent back to the Committee on the Census. In the debate it was said that if the measure were passed the Senate would act favorably. The upper chamber, it was stated, believed that its strength would be increased by a more numerous House of Representatives, for the larger the House the more willing its leaders would be to resort to an extreme form of guillotine and force formal votes of approval for their proposals. The House would continue to be vociferous, but weak, for the Senate could deal more effectively with the masters of a shackled chamber than with the agents of a deliberative assembly. This interpretation of the Senate's attitude on reapportionment may not have been authoritative, but it at least had the earmarks of reasonableness. Considered in connection with the present dominant position of the Senate, it sheds some light on the operation of the bicameral theory in the congressional system.

Another factor in the Senate's authority is the greater age and experience of members. In the last Congress, out of ten Chairmen of the most important Senate Committees only one was under sixty-five, and eight were over seventy years of age. Venerableness does not necessarily mean ability, but

[26] As the bill was reported to the House it would have increased the number of Representatives to 483, the number necessary if no state is to have its representation reduced.

it is usually synonymous with the desire not to concede, and in the Conference Committees the representatives of the Senate are more powerful than the managers from the House. This machinery which is necessary to reconcile the disagreeing votes of the two houses, the Senate uses to its great advantage.

Appointments to legislative committees rarely depart from the rule of seniority, and the result is —particularly in the relatively small Senate—a disproportionate number of choice committee assignments for members with long congressional service. This means that important legislation is framed by a small number of Senators, and when it goes to conference, these senior committeemen have great authority. The situation is much more extreme in the Senate than in the House, and the figures for the Sixty-fifth Congress are striking. One hundred and five Conference Committees were appointed, but five Senators served on eighty-two of them: Smoot 33; Warren 23; Nelson 11; Lodge 9 and Penrose 6. To prevent this concentration of power in the Senate, appointments are now better allocated, and a Senator may not be Chairman of more than one of the ten most important Committees of the Senate; he may not be a member of more than two. This avoids to some extent the extreme oligarchic control of legislation in conference which was possible before the new arrangement was agreed to, but the concentration of power is still such that the managers for the Senate have a great advantage over those who come from the

House of Representatives. The House, indeed, has complained bitterly of the fact that almost without exception the conferences are held in the room of the Senate Committee having jurisdiction of the bill. "Why should we go over there to listen to their reasons for amending our bill," asked Samuel J. Randall, "when the House asks the Conference and holds possession of the papers?" But it is a fact that the reasons seem more cogent when they are voiced in the Senate wing of the Capitol, and this incident contributes to senatorial aggrandizement.

To be sure, the Constitution seeks to give the House special authority in respect of finance, but the provision that bills for raising revenue must originate in the lower branch is only an empty fiction. It means no more than that the House of Representatives has the right to originate the enacting clause. In 1883, for example, the Senate struck out all after the enacting clause in the Tariff Bill of that year and wrote its own measure, which the House was forced to accept. To the Payne-Aldrich Tariff Bill of 1909 the Senate added 847 amendments. To the War Revenue Bill of 1918 the Senate added 320 amendments and receded on 55. When the Tax Laws were revised in 1921 the Senate wrote a new measure in the form of 833 amendments. The House had its way in only seven cases. Seven hundred and sixty Senate amendments were accepted, and on the other points in dispute there was a compromise. The bill was debated in the House for four days and in the Senate for six weeks. The schedules of the Emergency Tariff Act of 1921 were dictated by the Senate. Representative Fordney, Chairman of the House Committee on Ways and Means, told the House that "if we send the bill back just as it was vetoed by President Wilson they will pass it, but we must make no change in it. If we add anything or take anything out they will not give it consideration." [27] The permanent tariff law of 1922 was reported to the Senate with 2428 amendments, and in the final compromise the House yielded thirty times to the Senate's once. The Senate has been notorious also as more spendthrift than the House of Representatives. It has always added millions to the appropriation bills, although it should be said in partial justification of this action, that certain items have been inserted which were out of order under the general rules of the House. In the Sixty-eighth Congress, however, the Senate only added a net of $4,029,458, the smallest in forty years, and this was a matter for self-congratulation by the House of Representatives.

Senatorial prestige, as I have said, was in a fair way to being lessened by the evils that had developed in the elections by state legislatures. The bribery, other forms of corruption, legislative deadlocks, dominance of state politics by the issue of who was to be Senator—these have been frequently pointed out,[28] and into the arguments *pro* and *con* it is not necessary here to enter. The Senate did give the

[27] See *American Political Science Review*, February, 1922, p. 50.
[28] The whole controversy is admirably reviewed by George H. Haynes, *The Election of Senators* (New York, 1912).

impression of a millionaires' club; [29] Senators were occasionally out on bail [30] and in at least one executive session when the roll was being called a Senator absent-mindedly answered "not guilty."

As early as 1826 a constitutional amendment was proposed in the House of Representatives to have Senators elected by popular vote. Up until that time the political prestige of the Senate was not superior to that of the House; the share of the upper chamber in legislation was revisory rather than initiatory. The congressional caucus selected the presidential candidates,[31] and the Senators were outnumbered. In legislation the House did not distrust, but rather relied upon the Senate. These two bodies did not represent different elements in the country; they were sent to Washington by different gradations in the local classes of politicians. Election of the Senate was by party, and the local organization of party included in its fold Representatives and Senators from the locality. These bonds were powerful. They had to be heeded, or a retirement to private life might be the result. They were therefore unbroken by any jealousies

[29] The House of Commons was at one time dubbed "the best club in Europe" but the accuracy of the definition lessened when the Irish question became the hardy perennial if not the poison ivy of British politics.

[30] This was Vice-President Marshall's *mot* with respect to the Republican majority in 1919 when the Senate was organized by the Republicans and the Committee on Foreign Relations was "packed" against the League of Nations. The Newberry case was then pending.

[31] By 1840 Nominating Conventions had become the usual means of selecting presidential candidates.

which might arise out of the parliamentary situation, and the prominence of one House. Members of state delegations met together to plan concerted action and the result was that the Senate and House fished in the same political pool. Senator Maclay noted in his diary when the First Congress had been in session only one month: "the moment a party finds a measure lost or likely to be lost, all engines are set to work in the upper house." [32]   If Representatives, in other words, were unsuccessful in their body, they sought to win a victory through their local colleagues in the Senate, and there thus resulted not a reluctance, but a desire to give the Senate a free hand.

But after the golden age of the Senate when it contained Webster, Clay and Calhoun, or more accurately perhaps, after the Civil War, the great drive began on the method of election. President Johnson in 1868 made the proposal the subject of a special message to Congress, and in 1893 the lower House passed the proposed amendment. The Senate refused to act, and in 1894, 1898, 1900 and 1902 (the latter vote being practically unanimous) the House went on record in favor of the change. In February, 1911, the Senate voted for the amendment, 54–33, four less than the required two-thirds, but in the next Congress, which met April 4 in special session, ten Senators who had opposed the amendment had retired, and it was forced through the upper house in June by a majority of five more than two-thirds. It received the necessary ratifica-

[32] Ford, *op. cit.,* p. 259.

tion by three-fourths of the state legislatures in May, 1913.

During this long period of agitation, however, the states had set out to accomplish the purpose of the amendment indirectly, and another clause of the written Constitution was being changed by custom. As early as 1875 Nebraska provided for a popular preferential vote on candidates for the Senate. For a time, but little interest was taken in this expedient, but in 1899 Nevada enacted a primary law, and the movement gained rapid headway. Formal election, of course, had to made by the legislature, but the legislature was pledged to ratify the popular choice. By 1912 there were twenty-nine states which had senatorial primaries, and in selecting Senators the legislatures were pretty much in the same position as the Electoral College. In 1908 Oregon had a Republican legislature which elected a Democratic Senator who had been successful in the primaries. Incidentally, this amendment changing the method of election was a rather remarkable one in that two of the three organs concerned in its passage were parties in interest. If the Senators voted to submit the amendment to the states, they would affect their chances of reëlection, and the state legislatures which ratified it voted to give up one of their time-honored privileges which made membership in the legislature of national importance.

It is too early to attempt an estimate of the changes in the Senate's personnel that have resulted

from popular election.[33]   Corporate influences have
certainly decreased; men have been chosen who
would have had little chance of election by state legislatures, and conversely, some persons have doubtless
been passed over by popular selection who would
have been sent to Washington had the Seventeenth
Amendment not been adopted.   The occupational
basis of the Senate has always been rather narrow
and it has been frequently pointed out that lawyers
are overrepresented in both branches of Congress.
Nearly sixty Senators belong to that profession
which, as Burke said, quickens and invigorates the
understanding, but which "is not apt, except in persons very happily born, to open and liberalize the
mind in the same proportion."   De Tocqueville
thought that our lawyers were "the most powerful
existing security against the excesses of democracy."
The question may be raised as to whether they are
not a security against the progress of democracy.
The principal problems of government are now economic, and any special competence that lawyers have
may be purchased in the form of legislative drafting assistance.   Apart from this, the preponderance
in Congress is important, because it gives it a narrow occupational basis at the same time that it
avoids any sharp division of classes.   As might be
expected from our unreal party groupings, it is the
middle class, the bourgeoisie rather than the aris-

[33] But see George H. Haynes, "The Changing Senate," *North
American Review,* August, 1914, and "The Senate: New Style," *Atlantic Monthly,* August, 1924.

tocracy, the plutocracy, or the proletariat, which is represented in the American legislature.[84]

One concomitant, if not a result of popular election, has been a greater turnover of Senators. In 1905 only thirteen members of the upper chamber were without previous experience. In 1914 practically one-half the Senate was in its first term. Indeed, one constant tendency of recent years has been for members of the House of Representatives to have longer terms while Senators had shorter terms.[85] The causes of this are somewhat obscure, but the fact is undeniable. Approximately two-thirds of the Senators have had legislative experience, and one-third have served in the House. To an extent, therefore, the upper chamber drains the lower of its best men. The uncertainty of election is sufficiently great, and connection of Congressmen by residence with the districts that they represent is so general, that the greater lure of the upper body is not the evil that it is in France, where nearly 45 per cent of the Senate has had service in the Chamber. The more rapid turnover in the American Senate, however, has not affected its influence. This, indeed, apart from the causes I have discussed, would remain constant and even increase because of closure in the first house and the absence of closure in the second house. In this difference is to be found a fundamental reason for the strength of the Senate.

[84] See my article, "Where Statesmen Come From," *New Republic*, July 30, 1924.

[85] In the Sixty-ninth Congress 24 Senators had served 10 or more years; 20 Representatives had served for 20 years and 110 had served for 10. Sixteen state delegations in the House were unchanged by the 1924 election.

CHAPTER V

CLOSURE

*"The decline in consequence of this body has been so rapid
of late that we are now reduced to about the same level as
the Electoral College."*—W. BOURKE COCKRAN in the
House of Representatives, August 18, 1921.

*"The Senate of the United States is the only legislative
body in the world which cannot act when its majority is
ready for action."*—WOODROW WILSON.

1. *The House of Representatives*

"In all legislative assemblies the greater the number composing them may be, the fewer will be the
men who will in fact direct their proceedings." [1]
This dictum cannot be challenged, yet much depends
on the manner in which the direction is given and
the methods by which it is made effective. As
modern parliaments go, the House of Representatives is not a huge body; its 435 members compare
not unfavorably in number with the 615 of the House
of Commons and the 600-odd of the Chamber of
Deputies. Yet it can hardly be denied, I think,
that in the House of Representatives there is less
deliberation and debate than in any other comparable legislative assembly in the world. Of talk

[1] *The Federalist,* No. 58.

there is much; the *Congressional Record* is more
plethoric than *Hansard* or the *Journal Officiel,* and
if Representatives are not recognized to speak they
can usually publish their views under "leave to print."
What the House suffers from is not restriction of
garrulity, but extinction of deliberation, for the
more numerous branch of the American Congress
endures subjection to an irresponsible dictation far
more severe than any responsible executive has ever
attempted to impose on its legislature.   This vol-
untary submission by the House to the rôle of a
rubber stamp has become more extreme since 1911
when the Speaker was dethroned; it is increasing
rather than diminishing; it profoundly affects the
character of the American Government, and, as I
propose to show, adds greatly to the influence of the
Senate.

Lord Balfour once said that English politics were
organized so that there could be a continuous
quarrel.[2]   Quarreling is the rule in all American

[2] "It is well to remember that, though the House of Commons is
a council met to deliberate, the deliberation is for the most part
by way of contention and conflict.   This may or may not be the
best way of getting the national business done, and of course it
is accompanied all day long by a vast abundance of underlying
coöperation.   But contention is what engages most interest, kindles
most energy, brings into play most force, is the centre of most effort.   It may not be the most beautiful spectacle in the world—
ceaseless contention never can be; it is not always favourable to the
Christian graces; there is more serenity in a library, though for
that matter books and bookmen have been ablaze with furious contention before now; there is more stillness in a cloister, though all
is not sanctity, all is not exemption from strife and rivalry, even in
a cloister.   In the arena where material interests are touched,
where deep political passions are stirred, where coveted prizes are

legislative bodies as well, although it is perhaps more of a sham than in a system with Cabinet responsibility and a continuous possibility of turning out the Government. Sometimes emotions run high, and Marquis of Queensberry rules would not be inappropriate; but for the most part the fight is carried on irenically. The antagonists hit each other over the head with verbal bladders; there is a maximum of noise and a minimum of damage. For this (now almost continuous) performance, rules are necessary, and the procedural regulations of legislative bodies form a technical maze which can be threaded only after much study and with the aid of shadowy precedents. The layman rarely attempts to pry into this maze, and even the legislator frequently loses himself in its mysteries. Any issue of the *Congressional Record* will show the tyrociny of members and the indecision of presiding officers as to the proper procedure to be followed. Yet the importance of the rules can hardly be overestimated. Once a matter of convenience, and designed to secure order in an assembly where contradictory aspirations struggle with each other,

lost and won, where power and the fleeting breath of a day's fame are at stake, where under the rules and semblance of a tournament men are fighting what is in truth a keen and not an ignoble battle, it is childish to apply the tests of scholastic fastidiousness. We have to take the process as it is, and I very confidently submit that it is now conducted, not with less right feeling, considerateness, elevation, talent, knowledge, and respect for talent and knowledge, than was the case in the memory of living men, as Mr. Lecky says, but with very much more of all these things." Morley, "Lecky on Democracy," *Miscellanies,* Fourth Series, p. 195 (New York, 1908).

they are now too frequently weapons of personal and party warfare. They may have as much influence as the Constitution itself on the conduct of public business; chambers do them equal reverence, and are extremely reluctant to venture changes.

The major problem of parliamentary procedure has been the reconciliation of two irreconcilable principles: certainty of business and liberty of discussion.[3] The leaders of a legislative body must be able to have their programme acted upon, but to accomplish this there must be frequent curtailment of debate. Taciturnity is rarely a characteristic of a person chosen to represent constituents, and there is thus a fairly constant tendency for those who control the procedure of a legislative assembly to sacrifice discussion to their timetable and to deal more and more ruthlessly with the rights of their own followers and of opposing minorities. Changes of rules have had two principal objectives. They have been designed, in the first place, to make it certain that the majority steam-roller would proceed and not be stopped by the minority; and, secondly, to prevent the course of the steam-roller from being diverted through members of the majority venturing to repudiate the leaders and their programme. These two objectives are distinct. Rules of procedure which simply provide for expeditious and businesslike attention to bills may be justified to the extent that they accomplish this purpose, while they become objectionable if, in

[3] Lees-Smith, "The Timetable of the House of Commons," *Economica*, June, 1924.

limiting debate, they stifle deliberation and reduce the assembly to a position where it must act as a rubber stamp. The principal defect of procedure in the House of Representatives at the present time is that rules which were originally adopted for the first purpose have been transformed for the second purpose. The closure on discussion is moderate, but the closure on decisions is unconscionable.

In Anglo-Saxon legislative bodies, closure and guillotine are comparatively recent. It is true that as early as 1604 "to prevent the idle expense of time," the House of Commons resolved that "if any man speak impertinently, or beside the question in hand, it standeth with the order of the House for Mr. Speaker to interrupt him and to know the pleasure of the House, whether they will further hear him." [4] But it was not until 1881 that serious restrictions on debate were imposed in the House of Commons:

"During the eighteenth and the first half of the nineteenth century, the House of Commons was governed by custom and precedent, the *'lex et consuetudo Parliamenti,'* which were left to the Speaker and the clerks at the table to enounce. Speaker Onslow would tell Sir Robert Walpole or Mr. Pitt that the rule was so-and-so, and if the Chair was doubtful or disbelieved, an order would be made to search the Rolls of Parliament, or the Journals of the House to find a precedent. All this answered admirably so long as the House of Commons was what Professor Redlich calls 'socially honogeneous,' *i.e.,* composed of

[4] Quoted by Michael Macdonagh, *The Speaker of the House,* p. 200 (London, 1914).

English gentlemen of similar habits and education, not too much in earnest, who recognized the Standing Orders as the rules according to which a pleasant and exciting game was to be played. The first transference of power from the upper to the middle class took place in 1832, and almost immediately a change was felt. 'Before St. Stephen's Chapel was gutted by the fire of 1834 its occupants became aware of a difference in its atmosphere,' writes Sir Courtenay Ilbert. 'The keen wind of democracy had begun to whistle through the venerable and old-fashioned edifice.' But the spirit of Eton and Oxford survived the first Reform Act for a considerable time, and it was not until forty-seven years later that 'the observance of understandings,' on which every constitutional government depends, was rudely abandoned by the Irish Nationalists.

"Parliamentary obstruction, like most other great inventions, was discovered by a man quite unknown to fame, one Ronayne, an Irish Nationalist member, who communicated his idea to its first and most celebrated practitioner, Joseph Biggar, an elderly provision merchant of dwarfed and deformed figure, representing the County of Cavan. The story goes that Disraeli, coming in one day towards the third hour of one of Biggar's orations, fixedly regarded the apparition through his eye glass. 'George,' he said at last to some one near him, 'what is that thing?' 'Oh, that's Biggar, the new member from Cavan.' 'Ah!' said Dizzy, in his deepest and most reflective tones, 'I thought it had been a gnome sprung from the caverns of the earth.' And Disraeli meant what he said, for he felt that he was confronted by a new and terrible power, and he almost immediately retired to the House of Lords. Parnell, who was elected in 1875, saw at a glance the genius of Ronayne's and Biggar's idea. Once recognize that all parliamentary rules and conventions are, as Biggar said, 'nonsense' and the opportunities of warfare are infinite.

"But it was not until the next Parliament, elected in 1880

with a Liberal majority, that both parties saw the necessity of making essential changes in the rules of business. Parnell and his style of fighting were at first regarded as a phenomenon that would pass as other Irish leaders and their methods had passed. But at length his energy and seriousness 'shook the parties and their leaders out of their sleep. Their eyes were opened, and they saw obstruction in its true character as parliamentary anarchy, a revolutionary struggle, with barricades of speech on every highway and byway to the parliamentary market, hindering the free traffic which is indispensable for the conduct of business.' As Mr. Timothy Healy said one night, 'It is no longer a question of argument, but of avoirdupois.'

"Matters were brought to a head by Speaker Brand's *coup d'état* on January 31, 1881, when after a sitting of forty-one hours, from 4 P. M. on Monday to 9 A. M. on Wednesday, he made a short and dignified speech to the House and simply put the question. From that hour, it was recognized that the rules of procedure, once a method of convenience, were become a weapon of warfare. From that day to this, successive Governments have done nothing but tamper with the rules of procedure, modifying or abolishing old rules, and passing new ones, until the Standing Orders of the House of Commons make quite a complicated chapter of technical knowledge." [5]

[5] Baumann, *Persons and Politics of the Transition,* pp. 27–29 (London, 1916).

In 1881 the House of Commons sat for 154 days and 1400 hours, 240 of which were after midnight. On the Coercion Bill, the House sat continuously once for 22 hours, and once for 41 hours. Debates on the Land Bill took up 58 sittings, and on the Coercion Bill 22 sittings. 14,836 speeches were delivered, 6,315 by Irish members. The Speaker and Chairmen of Committees interposed on points of order nearly 2000 times during the session. "Mr. Parnell, the Speaker notes, 'with his minority of 24, dominates the House. When will the House take courage and reform its procedure?'" But, as Lord Morley adds, "After all, the suspension

Closure of debate in the House of Representatives is also fairly recent. "In the earlier Congresses," wrote Speaker Reed, "members acted with the utmost deference to the wishes of the House. They refrained from making speeches, and withdrew motions if the sense of the House seemed manifestly against them. With such deference on the part of each member to the wishes of all, the House was slow to abridge the right of debate." [6] The previous question was not used until the Eleventh Congress, and from 1811 to 1828, according to Calhoun, was called for only four times. [7] But thereafter it came into more frequent use and went through various permutations as to whether it closes debate on all authorized motions or amendments and includes the bill to its final passage. [8] There is the problem also as to whether forty minutes' debate is to be allowed on the immediate question if no debate has occurred. [9]   This proviso is sometimes interpreted rather strictly. When the House Joint Resolution authorizing the Spanish American War came back to the House in April, 1898 with a Senate amendment in the nature of a

of *habeas corpus* is a thing that men may well think it worthwhile to fight about and a revolution in a country's land system might be expected to take up a good deal of time." Morley, *Life of Gladstone,* Vol. III, pp. 56–57.

[6] Quoted by Alexander, *History and Procedure of the House of Representatives* p. 183 (Boston, 1916).

[7] Benton, *Thirty Years' View*, Vol. II, p. 357 (New York, 1866).

[8] Alexander, *op. cit.,* p. 277.

[9] *House Manual and Digest,* Rule XVII, sec. 1; Hinds' *Precedents,* Vol. V, secs. 5443 ff.

substitute, Speaker Reed ruled [10] that after the previous question had been ordered, there could be no forty-minute debate since the original proposition had had such consideration as the House cared to give it before sending the resolution to the Senate. This tightening of the previous question, plus the rule adopted in 1841 that no Representative could speak for more than one hour except by unanimous consent, was sufficient in one respect to introduce the necessary degree of closure in the House.[11]

But opportunities for obstruction were ample, and remained so until the nineties. In Congress "filibustering" was the term usually used, while in Australia it was called "stonewalling" and in Germany "Dauerreden." [12] Minorities in the House of Representatives, if they could not defeat, could at least delay. The beginning of the end of such tactics came when Reed was Speaker, and he was responsible for the most spectacular change in the rules of the House of Representatives—a change which was comparable to Mr. Speaker Brand's *coup*. A contested election case was pending, and

[10] *Congressional Record,* 55th Congress, 2d Session, p. 4062. Six members of the House opposed the resolution, but none was allowed to state his views. In the Senate, on the other hand, there was complete freedom of debate, and every Senator was allowed to explain his vote to his constituents and the country. When the resolution first passed the House, the previous question was ordered, and there were only forty minutes of debate. *Ibid.,* April 13, p. 3813 ff.

[11] See Benton, *op. cit.,* Vol. II, p. 247, and Luce, *Legislative Procedure,* p. 263 (Boston, 1922).

[12] Bryce, *Modern Democracies,* Vol. II, p. 345 (New York, 1921).

the rollcall showed 162 voting, three less than a quorum. Up until this time, when parties were evenly divided, members of the minority party had been effectively obstructing proceedings by the simple expedient of refusing to answer to their names when the roll was called, and absences of majority members resulted in there being no quorum unless the minority consented. Reed directed that the clerk read the names of forty-one members whom he saw to be present but who refused to vote, and declared that a quorum was present, and that the election case should be considered. The ruling was, of course, bitterly objected to; pandemonium reigned in the House for several hours, and Reed was denounced as tyrant and Tsar. "I deny your right, Mr. Speaker, to count me as present, and I desire to read from the parliamentary law on that subject," shouted a member. But Reed replied: "The Chair is making a statement of fact, that the gentleman from Kentucky is here. Does he deny it?" [13] When the Democrats came into power, they tried to go back to the theory of an oral rather than a corporeal quorum, but they were soon forced to readopt Reed's ruling. This spiked the most effective gun in the obstructionist arsenal. Thereafter, a minority could not delay proceedings simply by attending and refusing to answer to the roll. Reed's *coup*, however, did nothing in respect of obstruction which utilized debate, dilatory motions, and rollcalls.

[13] The details of the parliamentary battle may be read in McCall's *Life of Reed* (Boston, 1914), and in Alexander, *op. cit.*

These were dealt with primarily through the development of the Committee on Rules. That committee, in the early days of the House of Representatives, had had few parliamentary burdens. It was a select committee of three or five members, and its jurisdiction was confined to revising a code that had already been adopted. In 1841, however, the House authorized it to report "at all times" and a month later, when the minority by obstructionist tactics had kept an important measure in the Committee of the Whole, the Rules Committee made a report which permitted a majority of the House to suspend the rules and discharge the Committee of the Whole. Suspension of the rules required a two-thirds vote, which the Whigs did not have; but the report of the Rules Committee could be adopted by a majority. The decision in this case, as Mr. Alexander says, was "cataclysmal. It not only gave a majority power to control debate in Committee of the Whole, but made it master of the House. The bewildering excitement which followed opened the way for the adoption of the still more important resolution of limiting speeches to one hour." [14]

The power of the Rules Committee was curbed, or at least not increased, in subsequent Congresses, but in 1859 the Speaker was made *ex officio* Chairman of the Committee, and in 1880 the revision of the rules made the Committee a standing one. Speaker Randall held that it might report at any time on matters relating to the rules, but the real possibilities of the Committee as a dictator of the

[14] Alexander, *op. cit.*, pp. 191–192.

House were not disclosed until 1882 when Thomas B. Reed was the *deus ex machina*.   An election case was again the bone of contention, and to expedite its consideration Reed presented a report from the Committee on Rules allowing the Speaker to entertain only one motion to adjourn or to take a recess pending "the consideration of any question which may arise on a case involving the constitutional right to a seat."   This report was adopted. It was an enormous victory, since it prevented filibustering in respect of contested election cases and suggested a method by which on other matters the Rules Committee could dictate to the House.   As Mr. Alexander says, "Like Pandora's box, it seemed to conceal surprising possibilities." [15]   In the next session, Reed presented a report from the Committee on Rules making it in order at any time during the remainder of the session to suspend the rules by a majority vote in order to reach an agreement on sending a revenue bill to conference. "Under Speaker Carlisle (1883–89) the new method of guiding business won a fixed position in the House.   In the 50th Congress Carlisle, and in the 51st Congress, Reed, appointed the Chairman of the Committee on Ways and Means and the Chairman of Appropriations with the Speaker as the majority of the Committee on Rules.   The three men, occupying the most powerful places in the House, were thus associated and formed a masterful steering committee." [16]   This trium-

---

[15] *Ibid.,* p. 204.
[16] Luce, *op. cit.,* pp. 479–80.

virate was responsible for the rise of the special order—the device which imposes on the House of Representatives a more stringent closure than is to be found in any other legislative assembly. It is a device which is used not only to prohibit obstructionist tactics, but to prevent any *contretemps*—to make it certain that the programme of the leaders will be accepted *verbatim et literatim* by the rank and file of their party. The Rules Committee, indeed, is the American counterpart of a Cabinet controlling the time and dictating the decisions of a House of Commons, but with two important differences: the Rules Committee is not a responsible leader, securing its way through a threat of resignation in case of repudiation of its proposals. The Rules Committee frequently works by securing in advance an ordinance denying its followers the right of a decision on anything except the enactment of a measure in the form proposed. The House of Commons, on the other hand, is theoretically free at every stage of business.

The gradual rise and more frequent use of the special order need not detain us.[17] Nor is it pertinent here to describe in detail how the Committee on Rules became so dominated by the Speaker of the House of Representatives, and his powers in respect of recognition of members, committee assignments, and rewards and penalties grew by such leaps and bounds that the House revolted and the

[17] See C. R. Atkinson, *The Committee on Rules and the Overthrow of Speaker Cannon* (New York, 1911); H. B. Fuller, *The Speaker of the House* (Boston, 1909).

Speaker was dethroned. The change was considerable in more ways than one, but it may be doubted whether a House thus "unshackled" has increased its prestige. Chiefly is there doubt now as to the location of the leadership, which seems to be shared by the Speaker, the majority leader, the Rules Committee, the Steering Committee, the Committee on Committees, and the chairmen of the more important legislative committees.[18]   When Mr. Wilson was at the zenith of his power and driving the Tariff, Federal Reserve and Trust Acts on to the statute book, there was little doubt as to where leadership was located. That, however, was a situation created by a President who openly assumed the rôle of responsible party leader. There was little doubt either before 1910 when the decisions of the Republican Speaker were canonical —when, that is to say, Mr. Cannon could guarantee to the President what the House could be kept from doing or what it would be forced to do. Things now are different. The leadership of the House is like the grasshopper—it makes sudden jumps—but three things are at least clear: the shackling of the House appears in its discharge or rather non-discharge rule; the use of special orders is not diminishing; and recent and repeated abdications on important measures of all deliberative functions show plainly why the House has suffered in comparison with the Senate.

[18] Atkinson and Beard, "The Syndication of the Speakership," *Political Science Quarterly,* September, 1911, and G. R. Brown, *The Leadership of Congress,* p. 172 ff. (Indianapolis, 1922).

Congressional government is committee government. "We are ruled," wrote Mr. Wilson, "by a score and a half of 'little legislatures.' Our legislation is conglomerate, not homogeneous. The doings of one and the same Congress are foolish in pieces and wise in spots. They can never, except by accident, have any common features." [19] In other words, "The measures born in Congress have no common lineage. They have not even a traceable kinship. They are fathered by a score or two of unrelated standing committees: and Congress stands Godfather to them all without discrimination." [20]

Under these circumstances, the degree of control that each committee may have over the business of the House becomes of great importance, for the House, as a whole, may be completely bound by the accident of the personnel of a committee. This, to an extent, is inevitable; the House is influenced by the text of a measure as reported by a committee, and by committee leadership while the bill is being considered. It is a different matter, however, for the accident of committee personnel to make it difficult for the House to act at all, and this is the present situation. The present rules of the House of Representatives deny the truth of Bagehot's dictum that a legislative assembly is wiser than any of its members; the House is kept from making a

<hr/>

[19] *Congressional Government*, p. 113 (Boston, 1913).
[20] "Responsible Government Under the Constitution," *Atlantic Monthly*, April, 1886, reprinted in *An Old Master and Other Political Essays* (New York, 1893).

"wrong" decision by being kept from making any decision except the one which the leaders desire it to make. A legislative chamber that consents to being reduced to such a state of nonage fails in its duties as a representative assembly or as one branch in a bicameral system. No committee of the legislature like the British Cabinet can exercise such a dictatorship. The Cabinet, indeed, may refuse to let the House of Commons consider a particular matter; but the House may always, by majority action, reverse the Cabinet's decision. What happens, of course, in actual practice is that the whips gauge the feeling of the House and that if members in sufficient number really desire to consider a particular measure, the Government provides facilities. In the House of Representatives, even though a majority would wish, say, to change a tariff schedule, it could not do so without the consent of a majority of the Ways and Means Committee. That body has absolute control. There have been, to be sure, rules for the "discharge of committees" but it would have been more accurate to title them for the "non-discharge of committees," and the anachronism has now been recognized by dropping "discharge" and substituting "instruct."

Before January, 1924, there was a rule which in practice was unworkable.[21] Into its mechanics I need not enter, for the importance of the present situation dates from the revision of the standing orders in the Sixty-eighth Congress. When this

[21] Luce, *op. cit.*, p. 458, and *House Manual and Digest*, sec. 399.

began (December, 1923) objections were made to readopting the old rules of the House of Representatives. Insurgent members joined with the Democrats, and threatened to delay the reëlection of Mr. Gillett as Speaker. The movement in a sense resembled, although it was less violent than, the agitation which resulted in the overthrow of Speaker Cannon and the revision of the rules in 1910, and it was agreed finally that, if the Insurgents gave way and permitted the organization of the House, the rules of the Sixty-seventh Congress would be adopted for thirty legislative days only, and that on January 14, 1924, the House would be given an opportunity to consider the revision of its rules, to offer amendments, and to have record votes.

There were three main grounds of objection to the old rules. It was desired, first, to enlarge the Rules Committee, and to give representation to the Insurgents, so that the control of the House would not be so concentrated in the hands of a few party leaders. The second objection was that under the rules of the House, even when the Rules Committee decided upon a report, the Chairman could hold it up and defer its presentation so long as he saw fit. In the third place, it was urged that the House was entitled to get control over its own business if it desired; that if a majority of the House wished to consider certain legislation, it should be permitted to do so, even though the Committee having the legislation in charge was unwilling to report it. These objections were given specific point by the fact that at the last session of the previous Congress, the leadership of Mr. Mondell, the Floor Leader, and of Mr. Campbell, Chairman of the Committee on Rules, had been considered as dictatorial. The situation was not helped by the fact that both Mr. Mondell [22] and Mr. Campbell had failed of reëlection to the new Congress, and so told the House what it might do and what it might not do for four months after they had been repudiated at the polls. There were specific grievances also on account of Mr. Campbell's activity, or rather inactivity, as Chairman of the Committee on Rules. The Woodruff-Johnson Resolution ordering an investigation of the Department of Justice was introduced in the House on April 11, 1922, and was ordered reported by the Committee on Rules on May 3. Mr. Campbell refused, however, to present it. He carried it around in his pocket until there was another meeting of the Committee at which its favorable action was rescinded. Meanwhile, on May 26, the House decided that Representative Johnson could not, under the rules, get the matter away from the Rules Committee.[23] Similarly at this fourth session of the

[22] Mr. Mondell had run for the Senate and had been defeated.
[23] *Congressional Record,* p. 7741.
In February, 1921, according to Representative Byrns, the Chairman of the House Committee on Appropriations "deliberately and arbitrarily withheld the conference report for days from the House, confessedly because he feared that a majority of the House would override him and make the appropriation" of $10,000,000 for work on the Muscle Shoals dam. "It was not until he was certain that there were sufficient votes to defeat it that he made the report." The House also was denied the privilege of voting on

Sixty-seventh Congress, a number of resolutions ordering investigations were permitted to slumber in the Rules Committee. No less than thirty-three investigations were asked for. Most of them were unimportant, but in two cases it is probable that a majority of the House did desire action: the removal of employees in the Bureau of Printing and Engraving, and the investigation of the War Veterans Bureau (later undertaken by the Senate). Under the rules of the House there was no practicable way of discharging the Rules Committee from the consideration of these resolutions; indeed there was no way of forcing the Chairman to report when the Committee had acted. Thus it was quite easy for an Administration, acting through a half dozen representatives, to choke off embarrassing investigations even when these were desired by a majority of the membership of the House.

Twenty-two proposed changes in the rules were presented to the House on January 14.[24] Most of these related to formal matters—changes in the

the Ford offer to lease Muscle Shoals. "In the strangle hold of the majority leader of the House and the chairman of the Rules Committee to choke off a vote on the Ford offer, the chairman of the Rules Committee has told the House that he represented and spoke for the 'responsible majority of the Republican side of the House.' I deny it . . . if the chairman of the Rules Committee had been willing to be fair and let the Members of the House vote, the Ford offer would have been accepted by a majority of two to one, and maybe more than that." *Congressional Record,* 67th Congress, 4th Session, p. 4522.

[24] *Congressional Record,* 68th Congress, 1st Session, p. 943. There were full opportunities for debate, which ran over several days, and the House was permitted free votes—that is, on amendments to the proposals. With hardly an exception, the debate was

number of members of committees and the creation of new committees. Possibilities of high-handed action by the Chairman of the Rules Committee were covered by a modification of Clause 56 of Rule XI which was made to read: "The Committee on Rules shall present to the House, reports concerning rules, joint rules and order of business within three legislative days of the time when ordered reported by the Committee. If such rule or order is not considered immediately, it shall be referred to the Calendar, and if not called up by the member making the report within nine days thereafter, any member designated by the Committee may call it up for consideration." This change, it was thought, would prevent pocket vetoes like those of the preceding session.

The most vigorously fought change was in respect of the discharge of committees. It was agreed, after four days of debate, to adopt a rule which would work as follows: When a committee had had a bill or resolution for thirty days without reporting, a member might present to the Clerk a motion in writing for the committee's discharge. This motion would require 150 signatures and would be printed on the "Calendar of Motions to Discharge Committees." After such a motion had been on the Calendar for seven days, it could be called up by the member on the first and third Mon-

germane to the rules—a rare event in the House. Indeed, it is not too much to say that in debating the changes in the rules, the House was more of a deliberative body than on any other occasion in the last ten years.

days of the month, "and the House shall proceed to its consideration in the manner herein provided without intervening motion, except one motion to adjourn." Twenty minutes of debate were allowed, one-half in favor and one-half in opposition. If the motion to discharge prevailed, "it shall then be in order for any member who signed the motion to move that the House proceed to the immediate consideration of such bill or resolution (such motion not being debatable) and such motion is hereby made of high privilege; and if it shall be decided in the affirmative, the bill shall be immediately considered under the General Rules of the House. Should the House by vote decide against the immediate consideration of such bill or resolution, it shall be referred to its proper Calendar and be entitled to the same rights and privileges that it would have had had the Committee to whom it was referred duly reported the same to the House for its consideration." (Rule XXVII, Clause 4.) [25]

[25] The other changes in the rules are discussed in the "Record of Political Events," *Political Science Quarterly,* Supplement, March, 1925.

One change of some importance struck out Clause 3 of Rule XXI, which read as follows: "No amendment shall be in order to any bill affecting revenue which is not germane to the subject matter in the bill; nor shall any amendment to any item of such a bill be in order which does not directly relate to the item to which the amendment is proposed." This rule had been in force since 1911. It was adopted then by a Democratic Congress at the instance of Mr. Underwood in order to prevent amendments to the Tariff Bill. The significance of the elimination was that it was in order to offer the Excess Profits Tax as an amendment to the Mellon Tax Bill. Had the Underwood Rule remained unchanged, this amendment would not have been in order.

On its face this rule certainly does not seem too liberal. Considering that committees are recruited by accident and longevity, it is not unreasonable that 150 members of the House, supported by a majority vote, may bring a matter out of a committee for consideration; and the requirement for signatures and delay seemed likely to check any frivolous and frequent use of the motion to discharge. These expectations were realized in the Sixty-eighth Congress which, it should be remarked, by reason of the number of "Progressive Republicans" was somewhat more likely than other Congresses to act counter to the wishes of the regular Republican leaders. The discharge rule was invoked in but a single case: On April 5, 1924, a petition signed by a sufficient number of members was presented in support of a motion to discharge the Committee on Interstate and Foreign Commerce from the consideration of H. R. 7358, "A bill to provide for the expeditious and prompt settlement, mediation, solution and arbitration of disputes between carriers and their employees or subordinate officials, and for other purposes," which had been referred to the Committee on February 28, 1924. The motion to discharge came before the House on May 5, 1924, and was agreed to by a vote of 194 to 181, but on May 19 the Committee of the Whole in effect killed the bill by striking out the enacting clause.[26] The action in discharging the Committee was a non-party one, and the opponents of the measure (who came from both par-

[26] *Congressional Record*, 68th Congress, 1st Session, p. 8939.

ties) helped to kill it by dilatory tactics and motions.

This experience, as I say, did not suggest any serious challenge to the leadership of the House through capricious discharges of committees. When the Sixty-ninth Congress was organized, however, this discharge rule was abolished, and in its place was enacted a rule so stringent that it will be absolutely unworkable. The more honest procedure would have been to have no rule at all, and the camouflage of the following provisions is so obvious that it will not mislead:

"5. Clause 4, Rule XIII: Strike out the word 'Discharge' and insert the word 'Instruct' so that as amended the clause shall read: 'There shall also be a Calendar of Motions to Instruct Committees as provided in Clause 4 of Rule XXVII.'

"6. Clause 4, Rule XXVII: Strike out clause 4 and insert in lieu thereof the following:

" '4. A member may present to the Clerk a motion in writing to instruct a committee to report within 15 days a public bill or resolution which has been referred to it 30 days prior thereto (but only one motion may be presented for each bill or resolution). The motion shall be placed in the custody of the Clerk who shall arrange some convenient place for the signature of Members. A signature may be withdrawn by a Member in writing at any time before the motion is entered on the Journal. When a majority of the membership of the House shall have signed the motion it shall be entered on the Journal, printed with the signatures thereto in the *Congressional Record,* and referred to the Calendar of Motions to Instruct Committees.

"On the 3d Monday of each month, immediately after the

approval of the Journal, any Member who has signed a motion to instruct which has been on the Calendar at least seven days prior thereto, and seeks recognition, shall be recognized for the purpose of calling up the motion, and the House shall proceed to its consideration in the manner herein provided without intervening motion except one motion to adjourn. Recognition for the motions shall be in the order in which they have been entered.

" 'When the motion shall be called up, the bill or resolution shall be read by title only prior to a second being ordered by tellers. After the reading of the bill by title the motion shall not be submitted to the House unless seconded by a majority of the membership of the House to be determined by tellers, and Clause 4 of Rule XV shall not apply to such second; if such motion fails of a second, it shall immediately be stricken from the Calendar and shall not be thereafter placed thereon.

" 'If a second be ordered, debate on such motion shall be limited to 40 minutes, one-half thereof in favor of the proposition, and one-half in opposition thereto. Such motions shall require for their adoption an affirmative vote of a majority of the membership of the House. Whenever such motion shall prevail, the committee shall report said bill or resolution to the House within 15 days thereafter, and said bill or resolution shall be referred to its appropriate Calendar.' " [27]

This was adopted with little discussion, but the matter was returned to on December 16 when Representative Garrett of Tennessee declared that the only reason for the more rigorous discharge provision was the fear of the Republican majority that before the end of the session they would have

[27] *Congressional Record,* 69th Congress, 1st Session, Dec. 7, 1925, pp. 9-10.

to face a vote upon the revision of certain schedules
in the Fordney-McCumber Tariff bill. If discharge
of the Ways and Means Committee was impossible,
this subject could be kept off the floor of the House.
Representative Tilson, the Republican floor leader,
justified the new provision because the old arrangement placed in the hands of a majority of five more
than one-third of the membership of the House
(that is, 150) the power "to take control from the
responsible party and force action on any bill." [28]
This, however, is an extreme statement of the situation. All that the 150 signers could do was to force
the House to go on record as to whether a majority
desired to discharge a committee. Now, as an inspection of the provisions of the new rule will disclose, *a majority of the membership of the House*
must act three times: (1) by signing the motion;
(2) by voting to submit the motion to the House,
and (3) by voting to adopt the motion. To anyone familiar with procedure in the House and the
customary percentages of absent members, the subterfuge is transparent. But even if a majority of
the membership of the House favoring the motion
could be secured and kept in attendance, *it may act
on only one day of the month* (and only then if the
signatures have been secured seven days previously),
and if the motion prevails the committee is instructed to report the bill or resolution "within 15
days thereafter and such bill or resolution shall be
referred to its appropriate Calendar." Indeed, it
would have been more generous to say that dis-

[28] *Congressional Record*, December 16, p. 538.

charge motions could be made on February 29 or at the Greek Calends.

This action, however, was consistent with the theories of control held by the Republican leaders of the House. The Republican Steering Committee is headed by the Floor Leader (now Mr. Tilson). Mr. Mondell, when Floor Leader, was also Chairman of the Committee on Committees, and thus held three positions.[29] His authority approached that of Cannon or Reed. In the Sixty-ninth Congress Mr. Madden, Chairman of the Committee on Appropriations became Chairman of the Committee on Committees. This made the leadership but slightly less concentrated. The sessions of the Steering Committee are usually attended by the Speaker and Chairman of the Rules Committee, and the party programme is determined upon. Mr. Longworth, when the Congress was organized, indicated his hope that the Speakership might be revived and that leadership could be more concentrated. The Sixty-ninth Congress has seemed thoroughly under control—so much so that it has not been necessary to make any spectacular use of the special order.

The increasing activity of the Rules Committee in reporting special orders for the consideration of legislation has not been given the attention it deserves. The practice, as I have said, began with the Speakership of Mr. Crisp in the Fifty-second Congress. It was in part an attempt to prevent filibustering which had been freely resorted to in the previous Congresses. The special orders, which

[29] See Brown, *op. cit.*, p. 212.

could be reported by the Rules Committee at any time, limited both amendments and debate and made it certain that the House would take action at a time and in a way determined upon by the leaders.

Increasing use has been made of special orders. At the first session (special) of the Sixty-third Congress (April 7 to December 1, 1913) only six special orders were reported and four of these applied to appropriation bills. This, it will be recalled, was the session when the new Democratic administration (making full use of the caucus) was passing its currency, trust, and tariff legislation. These six special orders were hardly in excess of the number at the first session of the Sixty-first Congress (March 15 to August 5, 1909). Then the Census Bill, the Tariff Bill, the conference report on the Tariff Bill, and an amendment to the urgent deficiency bill were the only matters on which the Committee on Rules proposed to suspend the general procedure of the House. By the Sixty-seventh Congress, however, important business was largely regulated by special orders imposing a rigorous form of closure. Frequently the special orders were presented without any notice, and there was thus raised in an acute form the difficult question which, as I have said, confronts every legislative assembly: how to square the necessity for certainty and a timetable in legislative business with due notice to members and freedom of discussion. The matter is, of course, more acute in the American Congress because there is no centralized authority over legislative business such as is found in a

Cabinet form of government. When the House of Representatives revised its rules at the beginning of the Sixty-eighth Congress, it was provided that a special order shall lie over one day unless immediate consideration was authorized by a two-thirds vote.

Neither the number of the special orders nor their applicability to important legislation, however, has of itself a decisive influence on the deliberative functions of the House of Representatives. It matters little that at the second (short) session of the Sixty-eighth Congress eight special orders were reported, or that in the first session there were nineteen and at the second session of the Sixty-seventh Congress twenty-nine.[30] Nor is it important of itself that these rules covered the whole ambit of congressional business—appropriations, buildings, interstate commerce, agriculture, taxation, and constitutional amendments. From the standpoint of the House as a deliberative assembly or a rubber stamp, the vital thing is what the orders provided in opportunities for debate and amendment. Their ungenerous character is not difficult of demonstration.

Take for example what were probably the major international questions of the last quarter of a century. The procedure in the House when war was declared against Spain has already been referred to.

[30] For the lists see below, Appendix p. 271.

For methods of filibustering and the early forms of special orders, see Charles R. Atkinson, *The Committee on Rules and the Overthrow of Speaker Cannon*, pp. 35–70.

Of debate there was practically none, and the resolution as reported by the committee had to be accepted or rejected without dotting an "i" or crossing a "t." Or take the McLemore Resolution of 1916. This proposed that the House request the President to warn all citizens of the United States against travelling on armed merchant vessels. A special rule was brought in for its consideration.[81] The previous question was first adopted on the rule so that it could not be amended, and then, after the four hours of general debate, the resolution itself was laid on the table. Opponents had no opportunity to offer a substitute in the nature of a resolution declaring that, in the opinion of the House, American citizens should refrain from travelling upon ships carrying belligerent flags. The House could simply vote for or against, and the resolution was tabled.[82]

One of the most extreme cases of this sort occurred in May, 1920, when the House acted on the first bonus bill. This provided for insurance, edu-

[81] On March 7, 1916, Mr. Pou reported from the Committee on Rules the following resolution:

"That immediately upon the adoption of this resolution, the House shall proceed to the consideration of H. Res. 147; that there shall be four hours of general debate, one-half to be controlled by the gentleman from Virginia, Mr. Flood, and one-half by the gentleman from Wisconsin, Mr. Cooper; that at the conclusion of the said general debate the said resolution shall be considered under the general rules of the House." *Congressional Record*, p. 3720.

[82] Debate on the Joint Resolution declaring a state of war between Germany and the United States was freely permitted (*Congressional Record*, 65th Congress, 1st Session, p. 306 ff.) and on the final passage two amendments were proposed and defeated. (*Ibid.*, p. 412).

cation, land settlement, and "adjusted compensation," and levied taxes to raise the billion dollars that would be required. It was an extremely complicated measure, approved as a whole by probably only a tiny section of the House, but the leaders had determined that it should be passed as part of the Republican campaign strategy. It was certain that it would not be considered in the Senate. The Republican Steering Committee considered various forms of closure, and at first determined upon a rule limiting debate to five hours, preventing any amendment, and allowing a single motion to recommit to the committee that had reported the bill. There was a great deal of opposition to this proposal and it was abandoned, but in the end the measure was forced through with the House even more effectively, although not so openly, gagged.

On May 29, 1920, with Congress slated to adjourn on June 5 to permit the members to attend the presidential nominating conventions, the Rules Committee proposed a rule, "That it shall be in order for six legislative days, beginning May 29, 1920, for the Speaker to entertain motions of members of committees to suspend the rules under the provisions provided by the general rules of the House." [33] This proposal but poorly concealed its real purpose; suspensions for the final six days of a Congress had been resorted to, almost without exception, only during the short sessions, when Congress must adjourn on March 4, and when there is

[33] *Congressional Record,* 66th Congress, 2nd Session, p. 7921.

the greatest congestion of business. There were no special reasons to make such a procedure necessary at this time. Nevertheless, the rule was adopted, and Representative Fordney immediately moved "that the rules be suspended and that the House pass H. R. 14157, known as the soldiers' bonus bill." Twenty minutes a side were allowed for debate, the rules were suspended, and the bill was passed. As Representative Mann, one of the ablest parliamentarians in the House, said, no bill as important and complicated had ever been forced through with no opportunity for amendment:

"Here is the situation: Congress has been in almost continuous session for more than a year. The Republican side of the House has had a reasonably large majority. If we say to the country, as we will if this resolution be passed, that the Republican majority in this House, with a year's time, has been unable to bring in legislation and perfect it where it is subject to amendment, it acknowledges its impotency and its incapacity. It will be called to your attention and to your constituents on every stump that the Republican majority of the House has not enacted much reconstructive legislation, and then it will be told in addition that the Republican majority of the House was afraid to enact legislation under ordinary rules and was incapacitated from following the ordinary practice. What will you answer when men say to you that a Republican majority in the House passes a revenue bill raising a billion and a quarter of dollars without a chance to amend it? No party in the history of the country has ever passed a revenue bill under the suspension of the rules.

"No party in the history of the country has ever proposed

to pass a revenue bill without the right to amend it—a bill
that takes a billion and a quarter dollars out of the pockets
of the people." [34]

Two years later a substantially similar procedure
was followed, although by this time the bill had been
somewhat changed.   Again a special rule was reported authorizing the suspension of the rules, and
four hours instead of the usual forty minutes of debate.[35]   The only decision of the House was approval or disapproval of the measure reported by
the committee.   Its members were much more effectively shackled than they ever were by a President forcing obedience to his orders.   Opinions may
differ as to the merits of taxes on sales and excess
profits in order to raise the money, but the advocates of these expedients ought at least to have had
an opportunity of voting for their beliefs.   Members may well have objected to particular sections
of the bill, but they were not allowed to put themselves on record as opposing certain details before
they accepted the whole measure.

Again, the House of Representatives twice voted
to terminate the state of war, but in neither case was
it allowed to express an opinion on how the resolution should be worded.   The Committee on Rules

[34] *Congressional Record,* 66th Congress, 2nd Session, p. 7929.

[35] "That it shall be in order on Thursday, March 23, 1922,
after the adoption of this resolution, to move to suspend the rules
under the provision of Rule XXVII of the House of Representatives:
providing, however, instead of twenty minutes debate being allowed to each side for and against the motion, there shall be two
hours of such debate to each side." *Congressional Record,* 67th
Congress, 2d Session, p. 4350.

reported (April 8, 1920) a special rule for the consideration of the peace resolution. Debate was to last from 11 o'clock to 5 o'clock the next day, and at 5 P.M. the previous question was to be considered as ordered without any intervening motion except one to recommit the resolution to the Foreign Affairs Committee. No amendments were possible; the House had to accept or reject the resolution as the Committee reported it. President Wilson's veto forced the House to act again at the next session of Congress, and then exactly the same procedure was followed,[36] except that this time the approval of the House was asked for a different resolution. The formal approval was given, just as it had been given at the previous session for the other resolution.

Even on money bills—the special concern of lower chambers everywhere—the House of Repre-

---

[36] *"Resolved,* That immediately upon the adoption of this resolution the House shall proceed to consider in the House S. J. Res. 16, as amended by the House Committee on Foreign Affairs terminating the state of war between the Imperial German Government and the United States of America and between the Imperial and Royal Austro-Hungarian Government and the United States of America. The amendment reported by the House Committee on Foreign Affairs as a substitute for S. J. Res. 16 shall be read in extenso. General debate shall continue on the said resolution as amended until 5 o'clock p. m. on Saturday, June 11, 1921, the time to be controlled, one-half by the gentleman from Pennsylvania, Mr. Porter, and one-half by the gentleman from Virginia, Mr. Flood. At the conclusion of the general debate the previous question shall be considered as ordered on S. J. Res. 16 and on the amendment as reported by the House Committee on Foreign Affairs to final passage without intervening motion except one motion to recommit." *Congressional Record,* June 11, 1921, p. 2437 (67th Congress, 1st Session).

sentatives abdicates all deliberative functions: it allows discussion and amendments to be guillotined, whereas the Senate permits a full debate and opportunities for change. Hence the primacy of the Senate in respect of finance—a primacy which is especially remarkable since bills for raising revenue are, under the Constitution, the special concern of the House. The Emergency Tariff Act has been mentioned.[37] The House was forced to pass this in the form in which it was vetoed by President Wilson. Such, Representative Fordney said, was the "instruction" of the Senate Finance Committee. "If we send the bill back just as it was vetoed by President Wilson, they will pass it, but we must make no change in it. If we add anything or take anything out, they will not give it consideration." The House (according to the *Congressional Record*) showed a curious sense of humor and greeted this statement with "laughter." Further reflection, however, changed the senatorial mind. The House passed the bill the day after it was reported, but the measure did not go through the Senate until a month later, and then was considerably a-mended.

While the Senate was not so openly exacting on the Tax Revision Law of 1921 the result was substantially the same so far as the influence of the House was concerned. The Senate added 833 amendments and yielded to the House on only 7 of them. The procedure in the House was just as effective a gag as the Senate's mandate that the

[37] Above, p. 111.

Emergency Tariff Bill must be passed unchanged. On its face, the special rule for the consideration of the tax bill was a liberal one.[38] Two days of general debate were allowed, and then the bill was to be considered for amendment under the five-minute rule; but "committee amendments to any part of the bill shall be in order at any time and shall take precedence of other amendments." When the two days allowed for amendment elapsed, there was no time left for the individual member to propose changes. The hour fixed for a vote arrived, and the House had but a single opportunity to express

[38] *"Resolved,* That immediately upon the adoption of this resolution the House shall resolve itself into the Committee of the Whole House on the state of the Union for the consideration of the bill H. R. 8245.

"That general debate shall be confined to the bill, and be equally divided between and controlled by the chairman and ranking minority member of the Committee on Ways and Means and shall terminate when the Committee of the Whole arises on August 18, 1921.

"Thereafter the bill shall be considered for amendment under the five-minute rule, but committee amendments to any part of the bill shall be in order any time and shall take precedence of other amendments.

"That clause 3 of Rule XXI shall not apply to committee amendments.

"That consideration of the bill for amendment shall continue until Saturday, August 20, 1921, at 3 o'clock in the afternoon, at which time the bill with all amendments that shall have been adopted by the Committee of the Whole shall be reported to the House, whereupon the previous question shall be considered as ordered on the bill and all amendments to final passage without intervening motion except one motion to recommit: That the vote on all amendments shall be taken in gross.

"That all Members shall have leave to extend their own remarks in the *Record* on the bill until August 31, 1921." *Congressional Record,* August 17, 1921, p. 5123.

an opinion on a schedule.[39]   This was afforded by
the Democratic leader's motion to recommit to the
Ways and Means Committee.   In the Senate, the
bill was pending for six weeks and there were one
hundred rollcalls; in the House, which under the
Constitution has the greater responsibility, there
was a single rollcall on what should go into the
bill.   Similarly the House voted on but five amendments [40] to the Fordney-McCumber Tariff Bill of
1922, which emerged from the Senate Committee
with 2428 changes.[41]

Procedure on more recent Mellon revisions has
given the House greater opportunities for deliberation.   The bill brought before the House of Representatives on February 14, 1924 was not guillotined,
and a unanimous consent agreement was entered
into that general debate (to be limited to the bill)

[39] *Ibid.,* p. 5358.

[40] *Congressional Record,* July 21, 1921, p. 4194.

[41] The Fordney Bill the holds record for time consumed in the
consideration of tariff measures. Hearings were begun on the
measure January 6, 1921; it was introduced in the House June
29; reported by the committee on ways and means July 6, and
passed the House on July 21. It was referred to the Senate finance committee July 22, 1921, but was not reported until April 2,
1922. It passed the Senate on, August 18, but the conference committee could not agree until September and then the House ordered the bill back to conference with instructions to strike out
the dye embargo provision and to place potash on the free list.
Fourteen months thus elapsed between introduction and passage.

The McKinley bill was introduced in April and became law in
October; the Wilson bill was introduced in December and became law (without the President's approval) the following August; the Dingley bill was introduced in March and was agreed
to in July; the Payne bill was introduced in March and was concluded in August; and the Underwood bill was introduced in
April and became law in October.

should be in order for four days. A special order was adopted by the House determining a procedure which would permit it to vote on the alternative Garner and Frear schedules for the income tax. On February 29, the House had seven record votes on amendments and on the passage of the bill.[42] One of these votes was on a motion by Representative Mills to recommit the bill to the Ways and Means Committee, since it had been somewhat mutilated by the combination of Democrats and Progressive Republicans. This procedure was unusually deliberative, and it may or may not be connected wth the fact that the draft was not greatly changed in the Senate. Certainly, however, the ideas of the House as a whole were farther from those of their leaders than they were from those of the Senate; yet this may account for the willingness of the House leaders to permit record votes. Deliberation may have been forced on them. In the Sixty-ninth Congress, however, the "Insurgents" had been so completely routed and the leadership was so securely in control that the extraordinary plan was adopted of having the Mellon bill considered under the ordinary rules of the House. Five days of general debate were allowed and then consideration began in the Committee of the Whole for amendment and debate under the five-minute rule. The measure passed on December 18.[43]

But if more deliberation has recently been permitted in respect of tax measures, an absolutely

[42] *Congressional Record,* p. 3345.
[43] *Congressional Record,* p. 732.

summary procedure is too frequently resorted to on important legislation, without a guillotine by the Rules Committee, with no opportunity whatever for amendment, and with privileges of debate so meagre as to be worthless. The procedure used is suspension of the rules. A two-thirds vote is necessary to do this—a requirement designed to prevent such action by the vote of a single party—and it is interesting to note that this safeguard breaks down when, as in the Sixty-seventh Congress, the Republicans have more than two-thirds of the total membership. Motions to suspend are in order on the first and third Mondays of each month and during the last six days of a session; their justification is that they enable the House to act expeditiously on non-controversial matters, or, during the last days of a session, to break up the inevitable legislative jam. Recently, however, the House leaders have been suspending the rules in order to pass legislation that would normally come up according to ordinary procedure and be open to amendment. The case of the bonus bill has already been referred to, but there are numerous other no less significant illustrations. Several of these merit enumeration.

On Monday, February 7, 1921—a "suspension day"—the House Steering Committee proposed to suspend the rules and pass a joint resolution permitting payments (involving about $400,000,000) to the railroads under the Transportation Act of 1920. This procedure would have allowed twenty minutes of debate a side, and no amendments. In this case, however, the House revolted—a very rare occurrence—members objecting not so much to the bill as to the method. The Rules Committee had pending a special rule under which the bill could be amended, but the Steering Committee had apparently vetoed this procedure and had determined to take no chances. The revolt against the House leadership was far more voluble than is usually the case, many criticisms coming from members of the majority party and when the proposal to suspend the rules was defeated,[44] the leaders had to bring in the bill the next day, under the Rules Committee's original proposal, and allow amendments. Only one change was made, but it was an important one. Much as the House seemed to dislike this summary method of procedure, it passed, nevertheless, under suspension of the rules, a measure providing five hospital plants for the treatment of neuropsychiatric and tuberculous ex-soldiers. The bill required the location of these hospitals in specified sections of the country—three of them being of doubtful suitability for tuberculous cases—and was denounced as a pork-barrel allotment; but it went through with no amendments possible.[45]

In the first session of the Sixty-seventh Congress, when the House was far ahead of the Senate in its consideration of legislation and had ample time on its hands, it used the same procedure for two fairly important measures. The Rural Post Roads Bill, providing for grants-in-aid by the Federal Govern-

[44] *Congressional Record,* p. 2740.
[45] *Ibid.,* p. 2736.

ment to the states for road construction was passed under suspension of the rules with the House not allowed to propose amendments, and the same day (June 27) the leaders put through the anti-beer bill.[46]   This was intended to overturn a ruling by the Attorney General on medicinal use and was an emergency measure, introduced by the Chairman of the Rules Committee himself because he thought that the pending Volstead Supplemental Act had too many details, and covered too many subjects to throw it open at that time for debate, amendment, and vote in the House.   On this occasion, however, by unanimous consent, debate continued for four hours instead of the customary forty minutes. It was said in defense of such a procedure that, thus limited as to its action, the House would deliberate "in a much more dignified manner."

In the Sixty-eighth Congress suspension was used for a number of important matters.   A $150,000,-000 public buildings bill was passed on February 2, 1925 [47] and on February 10, the Committee on Rules reported a resolution (H. Res. 433) making it in order to suspend the rules under the provisions

[46] *Congressional Record*, p. 3135.

[47] Representative Kvale said:

"I am opposed to it, were there no other reason, because of the steam-roller methods employed to pass the bill. You gentlemen can spend hours and sometimes days in discussing matters that are relatively of minor importance, and you have only 40 minutes to discuss a bill that embodies $150,000,000.

"I would vote for a reasonable public building bill, but I can not vote for anything as unreasonable as this, nor will I subscribe to the indefensible steam-roller methods employed by this body in order to put this bill through with only 40 minutes of discussion." *Congressional Record*, p. 2885.

of Rule XXVII. Mr. Snell, Chairman of the
Rules Committee, said that there was nothing un-
usual about the proposition. In the Sixty-sixth
Congress, the soldiers' bonus and the good roads
bill had been passed under the suspension of rules;
in the Sixty-seventh Congress the bonus was again
passed under suspension; in the Sixty-eighth Congress the public buildings bill and the veterans' reorganization and hospitalization measures had been
so enacted. In respect of postal employees, on
September 19, 1919, their pay had been increased
under suspension; on June 3, 1922, another increase
in pay and a general reclassification of the service
had been agreed to under a suspension of rules;
the bill then pending (it had been vetoed by President Coolidge) had been passed with the rules suspended at the first session of the Sixty-eighth Congress. Of course the point was that if the rules
were suspended the House was forced to vote for
the increase of postal rates at the same time that it
was voting for an increase in salaries. The bill
could not be amended and members who opposed
an increase of rates had to accept it in order to approve of larger salaries. The House passed the
resolution by a vote of 245–97. Not a sufficient
number of members demanded a record vote. The
postal bill was also passed without a record vote
and then the House, suspending the rules, proceeded
to pass the agricultural credits bill (H. R. 12000)
and the deportation of aliens bill (H. R. 11796);
and a measure (H. R. 151) providing for increased
appropriations for federal experiment stations in

each state of the Union. This had been recommended by the President's Agricultural Commission. In no case was there a record vote.[48]

Little can be said for such procedure except that it is expeditious. Of course there are dangers when the House is turned loose on a bill. Amendments are offered with slight attention to grammar, consistency, or intelligibility. A crowded assembly which acts in a rapid-fire manner, with its members anxious to gratify their vanity or ambition and have a finger in the legislative pie, and with other members willing to take advantage of the confusion to secure the adoption of an amendment with a sinister purpose, is no proper body to perfect statutory projects.[49] The House may be stampeded into endorsing some "radical" proposal that the "conservative" leaders object to. The bonus bill, for example, might have revived the excess profits tax. Such dangers, however, should be guarded against by responsible party leadership rather than by limiting the House to a vote of "yes" or "no." The procedure is old, but this makes it no more justifiable except in rare cases. When

[48] *Ibid.*, p. 2885.

[49] One may with truth use for American legislative procedure Sir Courtenay Ilbert's figure with regard to the passage of a law through its stages in the Commons: "the much buffeted craft, with tattered sails, the deck encumbered with wreckage, and with several ugly leaks in her hold, labours heavily into a temporary harbour of refuge. There is a short interval for the necessary repairs, and then the struggle begins again at the report stage. There may or may not be a sufficient opportunity for making such formal amendments as are necessary to make the measure decently consistent and intelligible. If not, they must be left for the House of Lords." Ilbert, *Parliament*, p. 82 (New York, 1911).

it is used, the assertion of its power by the Senate is directly invited, and the upper chamber has lost no time in accepting the numerous invitations extended to it; gagging is inevitably synonymous with weakness. This was pointed out by Representative Cockran in discussing the procedure on the Revenue Bill of 1921:

"The decline in consequence of this body has been so rapid of late that we are now reduced to about the same level as the Electoral College. And how could it be otherwise? What possible weight or value could be attached to any discussion or action of ours concerning this measure when not one of us is allowed to propose an amendment or even to understand the grounds on which the reductions it proposes are based? Discussion of a revenue bill under these conditions is about as intelligible, about as comprehensible, about as defensible, as if some enterprising gentleman should undertake to discuss after a general election the merits of presidential candidates with a view to affecting the vote of the Electoral College.

"Action by the electors is now a mere formality required by the Constitution to make legally effective the vote of the people which in choosing them has already decided the election and the choice of a President. Yet the Electoral College, as the framers of the Constitution planned it, was to be the most independent body in our whole political system. . . . In spite of every precaution the functions of the college have shrunk to a mere formality, because its members were incapable of defending its independence. And the same fate seems to be impending over this body, if it has not already overtaken us. There is now but one real legislative chamber in this country. A mere formality remains to be observed by us. Before the real legislative body can take jurisdiction of a revenue measure this House must adopt the clause 'Be it enacted.' " [50]

The analogy of the Electoral College should not be pushed too far; there is ample justification for the shrinkage of its functions. In one respect, however, Mr. Cockran exaggerated. The Electoral College must vote in silence; some members of the House may speak and all of them may publish their views in the *Congressional Record* at a cost to the Treasury of $48 per page. Some aspirant for the Ph.D. degree in Statistics should calculate the relative expense of different members of the House (and the Senate) to the country over a period of years.

Of course, the danger that leadership will be flouted is greater in the House of Representatives than it is, say, in the House of Commons, but dominated as the British chamber is by its executive committee—the Cabinet—it would never submit to the ignominy that is the lot of the lower branch of the American legislature. Perhaps the only solution in the congressional system is for the President to take advantage of all the possibilities of his office and lead, even dictate to his party in Congress. There are worse things than the executive lash on the legislative back; that at least is in the open and must work by argument and mobilizing public opinion. Now, if members revolt and defeat their leaders, they defeat completely irresponsible persons, and there are few penalties in the withdrawal of party favors. There is no possibility of punishment in respect of a change of government or a dissolution. Yet complete absence of party control would hardly be more objectionable than the existing abdication by the House of any functions except those of a rubber stamp. It is the willingness of the House of Representatives to be a rubber stamp that contributes so largely to the greater power of the Senate. The second chamber is really the first chamber.

2. *The Senate*

Procedure in the Senate presents quite a different picture. The upper house of the American Congress enjoys freedom of debate, or, as the critics would say, unrestrained garrulity. Almost alone among legislative assemblies of the world it refuses to limit discussion and apply closure; its rules safeguard a free and equal right of amendment. Excessive loquacity as the weapon of a minority can, on occasion, be more lethal in the Senate than elsewhere, for it is a gun that cannot always be spiked by the endurance of the majority. It is the more effective if used during the closing days of the short session of Congress, which comes to an end on March 4 of the odd years. In these sessions a filibuster cannot be overcome if it is begun near the time for adjournment. The minority cannot be exhausted. There is not sufficient time, and even in the long sessions, the chances of victory are not always with those that desire action.

This *lacuna* in the Senate rules has been frequently

pointed out and objected to.   The attitude of particular Senators toward unrestricted debate has been conditioned in large measure by their interest in particular controversies.   Thirty years ago, when his Force Bill was being successfully filibustered against in the Senate, Senator Lodge was of the opinion that parliamentary obstruction was "a travesty of representative government.   Where it exists the majority cannot rule, while the minority in the nature of things is unable to govern.   It is, in fact, the absolute overthrow of majority rule on which popular government rests.   Worst of all, it destroys responsibility, for by it the majority is enabled to go to the country, and to declare that it has done nothing because the minority would not permit it to act."   A legislative assembly "ought to have always both debate and action, but if we must choose between them, action must have the preference, for endless debate without action would soon bring any government into contempt.   Moreover, the surest way today to get intelligent debate is to make it impossible for the minority to stop legislation by obstruction." [1]   The same arguments, as we shall see, have been frequently voiced, and since his election in 1924 Vice-President Dawes [2] has been leading a

[1] These opinions were expressed in an article on "Parliamentary Obstruction in the United States," *Nineteenth Century,* March, 1891, reprinted in Senator Lodge's *Historical and Political Essays,* p. 169 ff. (Boston, 1892).

[2] In his inaugural address as Vice-President, Mr. Dawes said that the Senate rule "which at times enables Senators to consume in oratory those last precious minutes of a session needed for momentous decisions, places in the hands of one or of a minority of Senators a greater power than the veto power exercised under the

movement to force the Senate to revise its rules. That success does not seem exactly imminent makes his proposal none the less worthy of examination.

Various considerations are put forth favoring such action by the Senate, but most of the arguments take little account of the fact that the Senate is a unique legislative body on the basis of its representation, and they pay no attention whatever to the peculiar position of the upper house in the congressional system. It is easy to say, as does Senator Pepper, that "the Senate, by sanctioning unlimited debate and by requiring a two-thirds vote to limit it, has, in effect, so amended the Constitution as to make it possible for a 33 per cent minority to block legislation." Incidentally, of course, this 33 per cent minority may nearly or even actually represent a majority of the population of the coun-

Constitution by the President of the United States, which is limited in its effectiveness by the necessity of an affirmative two-thirds vote. Who would dare to contend that under the spirit of democratic government the power to kill legislation providing the revenues to pay the expenses of government should, during the last few days of a session, ever be in the hands of a minority or perhaps one Senator? Why should they ever be able to compel the President of the United States to call an extra session of Congress to keep in functioning activity the machinery of the government itself? Who would dare oppose any changes in the rules necessary to insure that the business of the United States should always be conducted in the interests of the Nation and never be in danger of encountering a situation where one man or a minority of men might demand unreasonable concessions under threat of blocking the business of the Government? Who would dare maintain that in the last analysis the right of the Senate itself to act should never be subordinate to the right of one Senator to make a speech?" *Congressional Record,* 69th Congress, special session of the Senate, Vol. 67, pp. 1–2.

try; but to state the argument as does Senator Pepper, or to say that *every* legislative assembly should be able to reach a decision when its majority desires it to act is to ignore certain important questions: What kind of a Senate majority has a "right" to act? If it has such a "right" quickly enforceable, do the checks and balances of the American Constitution remain unaffected? For the fact of the matter is, as I hope to show, that, as the much vaunted separation of powers now exists, unrestricted debate in the Senate is the only check upon presidential and party autocracy. The devices that the framers of the Constitution so meticulously set up would be ineffective without the safeguard of senatorial minority action. It is perfectly correct to say that in all foreign legislative systems debate can be restricted, but it is not proper to argue, by analogy, that there should therefore be restrictions in the Senate, for that body is *sui generis*. Foreign practice reads no lesson to the United States, for ours is practically the only system which separates the powers of government, divides and confuses responsibility, and makes things move by the calendar rather than by popular will. Had we executive leadership of, or control by, the legislature, the problem would be quite different. As things are, the justification of unrestricted debate in the Senate is the nature of our governmental system, and to this, in the discussion of closure, practically no attention has been paid.

John Adams who, as Vice-President, presided over the Senate, described it as "A select council of statesmen, true to their duties, not ambitious of logomachy, and not making their honorable station subsidiary to other objects." Procedure in the Senate, as now conducted, has gotten far away from that ideal, and the phrase from Jefferson's *Manual* which still appears in the Senate rules has much humor: "No one is to speak impertinently, or beside the question, superfluously or tediously." [3] This, indeed, could once be prevented, for closure in the Senate has not always been impossible. The rules adopted on April 16, 1789, provided for the previous question. This was invoked four times in the succeeding seventeen years, but was ruled out of order on one of these occasions. During the first session of the Sixth Congress, Jefferson (as Vice-President) ruled that the previous question was not in order on an amendment, but when a new code of rules was agreed to on March 26, 1806, the previous question was not mentioned. It was not expressly barred, but the rule was simply dropped, and from that time to this the Senate has had freedom of debate.

There were few abuses until 1841, when Clay endeavored to get his fiscal bills through the Senate

[3] Sec. XVII, *Rules and Manual of the United States Senate.* Senators follow the advice which has been given to professors: "Talk slowly and indistinctly, at a little distance from the point. No academic person is ever voted into the chair until he has reached an age at which he has forgotten the meaning of the word 'irrelevant'; and you will be allowed to go on until everyone in the room will vote with you sooner than hear your voice another minute." F. M. Cornford, *Microcosmographia Academica, Being a Guide for the Young Academic Politician,* p. 41 (Boston, 1923).

against the opposition of the Democrats. Four days after the hour rule had been introduced in the House of Representatives (July 12), Clay proposed its introduction in the Senate. "Let our contests be contests of intellectuality, and not of physical force in seeing who could sit out the other or consume the most time in useless debate" was Clay's appeal to the Senate. But it met with little response. The debate is summarized by Benton:

"Mr. King said the Senator from Kentucky complained of three weeks and a half having been lost in amendments to his bill. Was not the Senator aware that it was himself and his friends who had consumed most of that time? But now that the minority had to take it up, the Senate is told there must be a gag law. Did he understand that it was the intention of the Senator to introduce that measure?

"Mr. Clay. I will, sir; I will!

"Mr. King. I tell the Senator, then, that he may make his arrangements at his boarding-house for the winter.

"Mr. Clay. Very well, sir.

"Mr. King was truly sorry to see the honorable Senator so far forgetting what is due to the Senate, as to talk of coercing it by any possible abridgment of its free action. The freedom of debate has never yet been abridged in that body since the foundation of this government. Was it fit· or becoming, after fifty years of unrestrained liberty, to threaten it with a gag law? He could tell the Senator that, peaceable a man as he (Mr. King) was, whenever it was attempted to violate that sanctuary, he, for one, could resist that attempt even unto death." [4]

[4] *Thirty Years' View*, Vol. II, p. 253.

The attempt was successfully resisted, and this
manœuvre, as Benton says, was the last that was
heard of the hour rule and the previous question in
the Senate.[5]

Numerous proposals have been made by various
Senators—among them Douglas, Wade and Ham-
lin—for reintroducing the previous question, but
there was little interest in the matter because, until the Force Bill of the winter of 1890–91, there
was no spectacular and successful filibuster. These
obstructionist tactics lasted for two months. Meanwhile, however, a Senate Committee had actually
reported a closure rule. On December 10, 1883,
Senator Frye of Maine, Chairman of the Committee on Rules, reported a general revision of the
rules. This revision included a provision (Rule
XXII) for the previous question, but amendments
adopted in the Senate struck this out and there is
no record of the debate on the subject. "Moreover,
except for the speech by Senator Cockrell of Missouri opposing the closure proposals in connection

[5] "The secret history of their silent abandonment was afterwards
fully learnt. Several whig senators had yielded assent to Mr.
Clay's desire for the hour rule under the belief that it would only
be resisted parliamentarily by the minority; but when they saw
its introduction was to produce ill blood, and disagreeable scenes
in the chamber, they withdrew their assent; and left him without
the votes to carry it: and that put an end to the project of the
hour rule. The previous question was then agreed to in its
place, supposing the minority would take it as a "compromise";
but when they found this measure was to be resisted like the
former, and was deemed still more odious, hurtful and degrading,
they withdrew their assent again: and then Mr. Clay, brought to
a stand again for want of voters, was compelled to forego his
design; and to retreat from it." *Ibid.*, p. 257.

with the Force Bill, there would be no record of the rule, since all copies of the Report apparently were collected and destroyed." [6]   The nearest the Senate ever came to shackling itself was in considering Senator Aldrich's resolution in September, 1890. On five test votes this proposal commanded narrow majorities, but in the end it could not be carried in the Senate because of a filibuster against it which merged into the filibuster on the Force Bill.   The Senate battle over that bill and the Aldrich closure resolution ran for thirty-five days—six of them devoted to the rule.

For the next quarter of a century the Senate was the scene of filibusters but gave no serious consideration to devices for making them impossible.   The details or the justification of particular "tieups" are not pertinent here, but it is worthwhile to list a few of the more important obstructionist manœuvres.   What there was of drama can now only be faintly sensed from the dry and cluttered pages of the *Congressional Record,* but it is a remarkable fact that practically every proposal defeated by a filibuster has been unregretted by the country and rarely readvocated by its supporters.   Such mi-

[6] H. H. Gilfry, *New York Sun,* March 11, 1917.   Mr. Gilfry adds that "Rule XXII as proposed to the Frye report is almost identical in its general provisions with the rule proposed thirty-four years earlier by Stephen A. Douglas, and with the rule proposed by Senator Nelson W. Aldrich as a means of getting the Force Bill through the Senate in 1890.   It provided for closure by a majority and limited amendments to those pending when the previous question was moved."   Mr. Gilfry was the compiler of *Precedents; Decisions on Points of Order with Phraseology in Senate from 1st to 62nd Congress, 1789–1913.*

nority omniscience, of course, must be more accidental than wise, and the danger is always present (it
was barely avoided in 1917) that the interests of the
country will be adversely affected.   Yet although
fortuitous, it is an extremely important argument
that the opponents of closure can make: the absence of closure has been justified by its results;
no really meritorious measure has been defeated
and some vicious proposals have been killed.

The principal items on the list are the bill to re-
charter the Bank of the United States, the Blair
Education Bill, the Force Bill, two ship subsidy
proposals, two River and Harbor Bills, the Ship
Purchase Bill of 1915, the Armed Ship Resolution
of 1917 and the Dyer Anti-Lynching Bill of 1922.
Of course numerous appropriation bills have failed.
Sometimes they have been deliberately held up in
order to shut off supplies and force the President to
call a special session of Congress.[7]   This was the
case, for example, in March, 1919.   More frequently they have been lost in the jam that resulted
from a filibuster against a piece of proposed legislation, and there have been cases of supply measures being talked to death because they failed to
include items that particular Senators desired for
the benefit of their states, or because grants that
they made were considered too profligate.   Obstructionist tactics may be used positively as well as
negatively.   They are effective not only in defeat-

[7] A long list of bills that failed (from 1876 to 1916) and made
it necessary to bring in a special bill containing the appropriations
of the previous year is to be found in the *Congressional Record,*
June 28, 1916, p. 11.

ing measures that minorities object to, but in forcing the Senate to favor a particular section of the
country, or to sanction a special improvement.
Thus in 1903, Senator Tillman of North Carolina
was aggrieved because a deficiency appropriation
bill failed to include an item paying his state a war
claim.   The Senate conferees agreed that it should
stay out.   Tillman thereupon took the floor with
a copy of *Childe Harold* and assured his fellow
Senators that unless they would put back the item
he would read this and other poems until the session ended.   The item was replaced.   Laws were
made to prevent ballads being read.   Similarly
Senator Stone of Missouri forced the inclusion of
an appropriation for a public building in St. Louis
in February, 1913.[8]

[8] "The first instance of this sort after I took my seat here occurred in February, 1913. The occasion was the consideration
of the omnibus public buildings bill. About 9 o'clock one evening
the then senior Senator from Missouri, Mr. Stone, entered the
Chamber and took his seat at his desk, being next to the one I
now occupy. He brought with him a package of papers about
half a foot in thickness, and consisting principally of typewritten
matter. He then offered an amendment to the bill providing for
the appropriation of forty-five or fifty thousand dollars for im-
provements needed in the public building at St. Louis. It went
out promptly on a point of order, and then the Senator, who was
nothing if not deliberate, announced to the Senate that he felt it
his duty to put in the *Congressional Record* the very important
reasons underlying his amendment. He then began to read, in a
slow monotonous voice, and consumed about an hour of the
valuable time of the Senate, when the Chairman of the committee
having charge of the bill, in order to secure its passage, was
forced to accept the amendment and allow the appropriation.

"That is one instance of scores of others which have disfigured
our consideration of appropriation bills ever since I have been
here. But I do not recall a single instance in which a Senator

To accomplish single-handed the defeat or modification of a measure is an endurance test of no mean severity, and the Senate has been the arena in which the records for long speeches have been made.[9]   In the debate on the Force Bill of 1890, Senator Faulkner of West Virginia spoke for thirteen hours.   Senator Allen of Nebraska held the floor for fourteen hours in the controversy over the repeal of the Silver Purchase Act in 1893, but this filibuster failed.   On March 3, 1901, Senator Carter of Montana talked a River and Harbor Bill to death with an oration of fourteen hours, and in September, 1914, Senator Burton held the fort for a twelve hour stretch against a similar dip into the "pork barrel."   A filibuster that failed was that conducted in 1908 against the Vreeland-Aldrich

exercising that authority was rebuked or even censured for his efforts to thus secure money from the Treasury." Senator Thomas of Colorado, February 14, *Congressional Record*, p. 3113.

[9] These are possible, of course, because the Senators care nothing about an audience but only desire to consume time. Indeed, ordinary speeches are made to seats that are usually more empty than filled. In June, 1918, Senator Sherman said that it was impossible for two persons to occupy the floor at the same time, "But in the Senate it is a rule more honored in the breach than in the observance, because here it is generally understood that a dozen conferences may take place on the floor of this chamber; that frivolous gossip to relieve mental tension, neighborly visits and general office affairs are transacted; that every Senator may dive through the door to the cloakroom, and return with perfect impunity after refreshing himself with newspapers and mineral waters; and that such action is not a breach of courtesy, and that it is not a reflection upon the Senator who occupies the floor if every Senator withdraws and goes about his ordinary business in his office. Will that condition be changed by the proposed new rule if it be adopted? I apprehend not." *Congressional Record,* June 8, p. 7531.

Emergency Currency Law. Senator La Follette held the floor continuously for more than eighteen hours, and sustained himself by drinking a mixture of egg and milk. During occasioinal rollcalls, to secure a quorum, he ate sandwiches, and for part of the time he sat on the arm of his chair. The arrangement was that Senator Gore of Oklahoma, a member of the filibustering group, would speak until relieved by Senator Stone of Missouri, who in turn was to be succeeded by Senator La Follette. Mr. Gore, however, who was blind, suddenly stopped talking in the belief that Senator Stone was in the chamber, and ready to procure the floor. Stone was not there, and Senator Aldrich who had obtained an agreement that, when the vote finally came upon the adoption of the Conference Report, the roll would be called without further action, promptly put his motion. Aldrich's name was the first on the roll, and when the Clerk began to call, Aldrich responded, and there was no possibility of resuming the debate.

Such performances of strength are of doubtful success unless they are participated in by several Senators. One man, that is to say, can never filibuster successfully unless he takes the floor in the final hours of a congressional session, when important business remains to be put through before the moment fixed for adjournment. A group of obstructionists is necessary if there is to be effective delay during the session. Indeed, when one comes to investigate the dates of the most important filibusters it is found that practically all the successful ones have come in the short sessions of Congress, which must end on March 4 of the odd years. Abolish the short session, then, it is argued, and the obstructionists will be greatly handicapped. This would indubitably be the case. A resolution proposing such an amendment to the Constitution has passed the Senate three times. The last occasion was on February 15, 1926, when the vote was 78 to 3.[10] If ratified it would have a Congress begin its session two instead of thirteen months after its election; it would abolish the "lame-duck" session—that is the one in which Congressmen and Senators defeated in November continue nevertheless to legislate from December to March, and it would also have the President, in the event that the Electoral College cannot decide, chosen by a House elected at the same time instead of two years previously. Incidentally the leaders of the House have prevented the resolution proposing this amendment from coming to a vote—an index of their control over procedure. The importance of this change in connection with closure in the Senate is two-fold.

In the first place, as Senator Norris has pointed out, "a filibuster cannot be successfully waged, and is never even attempted unless, within a comparatively short time ahead, the date for final adjournment is definitely and irrevocably fixed." The

---

[10] *Congressional Record,* p. 3668. For a discussion of the refusal of the leaders of the House to permit action see *ibid.,* March 25, 1926, p. 6062.

remedy, therefore is not arbitrarily to "close discussion and deny to Members the right to offer
amendments and fully analyze proposed legislation,
but rather to do away with the short session of Congress. If this were done, filibusters would be a
thing of the past and much bad legislation would be
prevented." [11] Of more importance, however, is
the fact that the short, lame-duck session of Congress, by bringing forth doubtful legislative proposals, invites filibustering. One of the best
illustrations of this was President Harding's Ship
Subsidy scheme in 1922. In the long session of the
Congress no attempt was made to put it through;
with reëlection staring them in the face, Representatives and one-third of the Senators would have
been unwilling to vote for the measure, and indeed,
the party machine was anxious to delay it until after
the polling. When the election was over, however,
the bill was strongly urged. President Harding got
it through the House, but in the Senate it was fili-

[11] "The filibuster is in fact a legislative revolution. It defies
the apparent legally constituted majority; it stands, for the time
being, in the way of their progress, and through main strength
prevents the constituted majority from having its will. If this
majority were uncoerced, if its entire membership were unselfish
and standing for the highest type of legislation, unmoved by the
selfish desire to trade votes for office—in short, if the entire membership were absolutely free to follow the dictates of their several consciences, then I concede there would be no excuse for a
filibuster. But on examination of the history of every filibuster
that has ever come to my notice—and I have participated in quite
a number—I find none that would have been even attempted if
one or more of these elements above described had not existed
and stood out in bold relief." George W. Norris, "The Reform
of the Senate Rules," *Saturday Evening Post,* February 13, 1926.

bustered against. The Executive's influence was probably great enough to command a majority of Senators in its favor, for patronage could be used effectively—particularly patronage to take care of the Senators who had been defeated and permit them to continue to live off the Government; [12] but the filibustering Senators were sufficiently numerous and persistent to cause the Republican leaders to lose heart. In order to save the appropriation bills and other legislation, the measure was abandoned and has not been heard of since. The election had shown that the country did not desire a subsidy, and the new Congress would have defeated the bill. This particular filibuster therefore, probably voiced the sentiments of a majority of the people.[13]

[12] Incidentally executive influence through patronage could be enormously increased but for the possibility of obstructionist tactics in the Senate which is the most effective answer to it that the workings of the congressional machine have yet disclosed.

[13] In a lengthy speech which Senator Sherman made in the Senate on June 7 and 8, 1918, on the pending proposal to amend the rules so as to provide for limitation of debate, he included an analysis of the senatorial sentiment in favor of and opposed to the Ship Purchase Bill of 1915 which was successfully filibustered against. The states represented by the thirty Senators who opposed the measure had 41,000,000 inhabitants, while the states represented by the thirty-six Senators who solidly voted for the bill had 37,000,000 inhabitants. The delegations of the other states were divided or the Senators did not vote so consistently on the various proposals that they could be counted in favor or against. Since much of the support of the measure came from the South, it was easy for Senator Sherman to show that the total vote represented by this group was considerably less than that represented by those against—4,314,000 to 7,987,000.

"If, to follow the argument of the Senator from Oklahoma, a majority means voters, then the majority by senatorial votes in this body, applying a limitation upon a right of debate, does not pro-

There was, during the fight over the subsidy bill, ample time to invoke the closure rule which the Senate adopted in 1917. Perhaps two-thirds of the senators could not have been secured to make up the necessary majority, but there was time. These two factors make that closure provision unenforceable except in emergencies when the bill filibustered against is *prima facie* meritorious and when there have already been ample opportunities for debate. The rule was adopted on March 8, 1917, after two days' discussion by a vote of 76 to 3.[14] It resulted from public resentment at the filibuster against the Armed Ship Bill. The Senate was promptly summoned in special session and public opinion was successfully mobilized in support of the President's assertion that,

"In the immediate presence of a crisis fraught with more subtle and far-reaching possibilities of national danger than any the Government has known within the whole history of its international relations, the Congress has been unable to act either to safeguard the country or to vindicate the elementary rights of its citizens. More than 500 of the 531 members of the two Houses were ready and anxious to act; the House of Representatives had acted, by an overwhelming majority: but the Senate was unable to act because a little group of eleven Senators had determined that it should not." [15]

mote the rule of a majority of votes; it promotes the rule of a minority of votes; it promotes the denial of the right of a majority of votes even to be heard, much less to vote." *Congressional Record,* p. 7539.

[14] *Congressional Record,* 65th Congress, Special Session, p. 45.

[15] *Current History,* April, 1917, p. 51.

There was, Mr. Wilson said, but one remedy—

> "that the rules of the Senate shall be so altered that it
> can act.   The country can be relied on to draw the moral.
> I believe that the Senate can be relied on to supply the
> means of action and save the country from disaster." [16]

Only under great pressure from the President could
the Senate have been persuaded to act even to the
limited extent that it did.   How limited the action
was is indexed by the fact that unrestricted debate
in the Senate is criticized when the rules actually
provide for a form of closure.   The rule, however,
has been put into effect only twice in nine years, and
an inspection of its provisions will disclose that the
procedure is so cumbersome as to be possible only
in emergencies.   The Rule (XXII) is as follows:

> "If at any time a motion, signed by sixteen Senators, to
> bring to a close the debate upon any pending measure is
> presented to the Senate, the presiding officer shall at once
> state the motion to the Senate, and one hour after the
> Senate meets on the following calendar day but one, he
> shall lay the motion before the Senate and direct that the
> Secretary call the roll, and, upon the ascertainment that
> a quorum is present, the presiding officer shall, without
> debate, submit to the Senate by an aye-and-nay vote the
> question:
> " 'Is it the sense of the Senate that the debate shall be
> brought to a close?'
> "And if that question shall be decided in the affirmative
> by a two-thirds vote of those voting, then said measure shall
> be the unfinished business to the exclusion of all other
> business until disposed of.

[16] *Ibid.*, p. 52.

"Thereafter no Senator shall be entitled to speak in all more than one hour on the pending measure, the amendments thereto, and motions affecting the same, and it shall be the duty of the presiding officer to keep the time of each Senator who speaks. Except by unanimous consent, no amendment shall be in order after the vote to bring the debate to a close, unless the same has been presented and read prior to that time. No dilatory motion, or dilatory amendment, or amendment not germane, shall be in order. Points of order, including questions of relevancy, and appeals from the decision of the presiding officer, shall be decided without debate."

As is not unnatural, the Senate has been extremely reluctant to take action under this rule. Senator Chamberlain attempted to invoke it two months after it had been accepted by the Senate and to apply it to the national defense legislation then under consideration, but the motion was withdrawn and a unanimous consent agreement was entered into setting a day for a vote.[17] Closure was actually applied for the first time in the debate on the Treaty of Versailles, when, after a discussion which had run for several months, Senator Hitchcock on November 13, 1919, presented the petition required by the Senate rule with twenty-three signatures—seven more than the necessary number. Two days later the motion was voted on by the Senate and closure was adopted by 78–16.[18] The vote on adherence to the League Covenant came on November 19.

In January, 1921, when the Emergency Tariff

[17] *Congressional Record,* 65th Congress, 1st Session, pp. 4838, 4899–4902.
[18] *Ibid.,* 66th Congress, 1st Session, pp. 8413, 8555.

Bill was pending in the Senate and was being filibustered against, Senator Penrose presented the required petition. It came before the Senate on
February 2, but secured a bare majority of one instead of the necessary two-thirds.[19]   The Senate
finally voted on the tariff bill (which was vetoed by
President Wilson), but its long continued debate
on the measure threatened a legislative jam which,
it was feared, would prevent the passage of several
appropriation bills.   The result was, however, that
Congress finished everything except the Naval Appropriation Bill, which was withdrawn in the Senate
because of disputes with the House—not because of
lack of time.   The second successful appeal to the
rule was in the debate on the World Court.[20]   The

[19] *Ibid.*, 66th Congress, 3d Session, pp. 3311, 3432. On June 1,
1926, the Senate refused (46 to 33), to adopt closure for a migratory bird bill (S. 2607), *Congressional Record*, p. 10357.

[20] That the Senate was not forced to be unduly precipitate may
be seen from the timetable of America's relation to the World
Court. It was in February, 1920, that Mr. Elihu Root was named
a member of the Committee of Jurists which met to draft the
statute of the Court. This was completed in December, 1920, and
in September, 1921, Professor John Bassett Moore of Columbia
University, the most distinguished American authority on international law, was elected a judge of the Court. For the first
two years of Mr. Harding's administration, which began in
March, 1921, there was extreme reluctance—indeed, almost complete refusal—to admit the existence of the League of Nations or
any of its works. In February, 1923, however, Mr. Hughes and
President Harding—who were much less irreconcilable than certain senators—decided that adherence to the protocol of signature
of the World Court with certain reservations would be a forward
step that the United States could take with safety, and which might
be possible without a too violent party fight. The Senate, however, took no action, and in his first message to Congress on December 6, 1923, Mr. Coolidge (who had become President) com-

measure had been discussed off and on for at least three years, but formal debate did not begin until December 17. Closure was applied on January 25, and the final vote came on January 27 when the Senate decided by 76 to 16 that the United States should adhere.

Two applications in nine years are assuredly not excessive, and those who now argue in favor of a more stringent closure maintain that the rule is unworkable. That is an extreme statement of the situation. A delay of several days is necessary before a final vote can be taken, and the rule, therefore, cannot be invoked towards the end of the short session. It would not have sufficed to get through the Armed Ship Bill in 1917 except perhaps at the price of suspending action on the reports of Conference Committees. Curiously enough, the two resorts to the rule have been not on bitterly controverted domestic legislation, but on foreign relations. This has served to emphasize the extraordinary nature of the remedy at the same time that it has indicated a paucity of issues that now divide

mended President Harding's proposal of the previous February and requested its favorable consideration. Between June, 1923, and June, 1924, arbitration treaties between the United States and Great Britain, France, Japan, Portugal, Norway, the Netherlands and Sweden were renewed, with the proviso that certain disputes might be referred to the Court after the United States adhered to the protocol. The Senate still refused to act, and in his next annual message (December 3, 1924) Mr. Coolidge repeated his recommendation, but proposed an additional reservation relating to advisory opinions. In March, 1925, as Congress adjourned, the Senate agreed that consideration of the Court proposal should begin on the December 17 following. The Senate finally acted on January 27, 1926.

the Senate on party or sectional lines.[21]   Yet the advocates of closure wish to go much further. Senator Underwood, for example, proposes the following addition to the rules of the Senate:

"Resolved, That the rules of the Senate be amended by adding thereto, in lieu of the rule adopted by the Senate for the limitation of debate on March 8, 1917, the following:

"1. There shall be a motion for the previous question which, being ordered by a majority of Senators voting, if a quorum be present, shall have the effect to cut off all debate and bring the Senate to a direct vote upon the immediate question or questions on which it has been asked and ordered.   The previous question may be asked and ordered

---

[21] The most spectacular filibuster for a number of years, and one which used new methods occurred in the Senate during the third session of the Sixty-seventh Congress. The measure objected to was the Dyer Anti-Lynching Bill (H. R. 13; House Report, No. 453). The Senate was tied up completely through the use of a new expedient: refusal of unanimous consent to dispense with the reading of the journal, the reading of the journal, and then amendments and corrections proposed and speeches on them. Such items as the exact hour that the Vice-President entered the chamber, and the important question of whether the prayer should be included in the journal, were the pegs on which the Senators opposed to the Dyer bill hung their speeches designed to consume time. The filibuster was so successful and showed such promise of continued existence after several days, that the leaders admitted defeat and withdrew the measure. This system of filibustering, it should be remarked, would hardly be possible towards the end of a session. Then the Senate recesses and operates for a number of calendar days with a single legislative day. This does away with the necessity for the approval of a daily journal and saves the time usually spent in "morning business." During the consideration of some important bills, the legislative day may be a calendar day weeks before. *Congressional Record.* November 28, 1922, p. 325 ff.

upon a single motion, a series of motions allowable under the rules, or an amendment or amendments, or may be made to embrace all authorized motions or amendments and include the bill to its passage or rejection. It shall be in order, pending the motion for, or after the previous question shall have been ordered on its passage, for the presiding officer to entertain and submit a motion to commit, with or without instructions, to a standing or select committee.

"2. All motions for the previous question shall, before being submitted to the Senate, be seconded by a majority by tellers if demanded.

"3. When a motion for the previous question has been seconded, it shall be in order, before final vote is taken thereon, for each Senator to debate the proposition to be voted for one hour." [22]

This, as an examination of its provisions will show, is an extreme form of closure. To be sure, after the motion for the previous question was carried, each Senator would have the right to speak for one hour, but if the rule were adopted really effective obstructionist tactics would become impossible. This would, of course, profoundly change the character of procedure in the Senate. Considering the federal character of this body, and its vagarious proportions to the population, it would, even if the majority principle were accepted, be a doubtful proposition.

Mr. Dawes's proposal now seems to be that a closure rule should apply only to the appropriation bills. They, the argument is, ought not to be held

[22] *Congressional Record,* March 5, 1925, p. 9.

up by a controversy over some other piece of legislation. Considered by itself this argument is good: the efficiency of the government services may be menaced and the President may be forced to call a special session which, on other grounds, is inadvisable. The fact of the matter is, however, that only by menacing supply can a filibuster be made effective; the obstruction of the Ship Subsidy Bill in 1923, for example, might not have been successful if the leaders of the Senate had not seen that in persisting in its advocacy they were endangering the passage of the appropriation bills. This outcome they did not care to risk, and consequently yielded; the subsidy proposal was so doubtful that its espousal was not sufficient justification for fighting further. The gravamen of the controversy was shifted from the minority to the majority. This could never happen if closure could be applied to the appropriation bills. A majority might steam-roller them through and the power of the obstructionists would weaken. This would not be so important if the filibuster were simply to prevent the passage of a law; but it would be vital, as will appear shortly, if the filibuster were to force the majority of the Senate to consent to some action—for example, an investigation of an executive department. This consideration is not mentioned—and may be purposely ignored—by the advocates of closure. Making little or no headway in respect of their proposals for the previous question on all pending business, they seek a specious plausibility in respect of appropriation bills. These, however, would prove to be the Achilles heel of the filibusterers. So far as the congressional system is concerned, the axiom that a representative body, through its control of the purse can control the executive has little application; shutting off supplies can rarely be used to supervise administration. But this principle, so honored by the theories of constitutional government, is invoked indirectly and quite effectively. It is through their ability to hold up the appropriation bills that a filibustering minority can win a victory.

What has been said in respect of freedom of debate may seem to suggest that the Senate is unable to get through with the proper proportion of business presented to it. That, however, is not the case. Much of what the Senate does is independent of party lines and is of particular concern to individual Senators. There has thus developed a kind of senatorial courtesy to expedite the passage of such bills. On Mondays, under Rule VIII,[23] the Senate proceeds to the call of the calendar. By unanimous consent numerous bills are passed—amendments necessary to correct the defects of existing legislation, private bills, and those relating to

[23] ". . . bills and resolutions that are not objected to shall be taken up in their order, and each Senator shall be entitled to speak once and for five minutes only upon any question; and the objection may be interposed at any stage of the proceedings, but upon motion the Senate may continue such consideration; and this order shall commence immediately after the call for "concurrent and other resolutions," and shall take precedence of the unfinished business and other special orders. But if the Senate shall proceed with the consideration of any matter notwithstanding an objection, the foregoing provisions touching debate shall not apply."

particular sections of the country. It has been suggested occasionally that objections by two or three Senators (instead of one) should be necessary to shut off consideration, but as the rule now stands it permits the Senate to get through with an adequate amount of business.

Unanimous consent agreements are frequent also to fix an hour at which the Senate will vote on a pending proposal of great importance. There must be some definite expectations as to when action will be taken; Senators wish to be present to be recorded on the rollcalls. There must, also, be safeguards against surprise; those having a particular bill in charge must not call for a vote when those who desire to speak are not present. These requirements can sometimes be met by informal announcement of the leaders' intentions and by notices that particular Senators desire to make speeches before a vote is taken. To get some business through, however, more formal action is frequently necessary. As the Senate rules now stand [24]—with a closure provision

[24] Rule XXII provides that:
"When a question is pending, no motion shall be received but—
"To adjourn.
"To adjourn to a day certain, or that when the Senate adjourn it shall be to a day certain.
"To take a recess.
"To proceed to the consideration of executive business.
"To lay on the table.
"To postpone indefinitely.
"To postpone to a day certain.
"To commit.
"To amend.
"Which several motions shall have precedence as they stand arranged; and the motions relating to adjournment, to take a recess,

that is unworkable except in emergencies—there
must be some safeguard against endless delays by
reason of individual idiosyncracies.   Hence it is a
familiar practice for unanimous consent agreements
to be entered into that the Senate will vote on a
certain day, or that after a certain day speeches will
be limited.   These usually suffice to secure action.[25]
This, in reality, is a species of closure.

Mr. Dawes has argued that obstruction keeps
the Senate from acting on important laws which go
over to the next session.   At the same time, however, he thinks that the inability of the Senate to
apply closure by majority vote "contributes to multiplicity of laws." [26]   These laws, however, are

to proceed to the consideration of executive business, to lay on
the table, shall be decided without debate."

There is thus no provision for stopping a single Senator who
desires to talk further and proceeding to a vote.

[25] A typical unanimous consent agreement, entered into February 27, 1922, was as follows: "It is agreed by unanimous consent that at not later than 2 o'clock p. m., on the calendar day of
Thursday, March 2, 1922, the Senate will proceed to vote, without
further debate, upon any amendment or reservation that may be
pending, any amendment of reservation that may be offered, and
upon the resolution of ratification of Executive R. "A Treaty between the United States and Japan with regard to the rights of
the two Governments and their respective nations in the former
German islands in the Pacific Ocean, lying north of the equator,
in particular the island of Yap, signed at Washington on February 11, 1922," and that after the hour of 5 o'clock on the calendar day of Wednesday, March 1, no Senator shall speak more
than once or longer than thirty minutes upon the treaty, or
more than once or longer than 30 minutes upon any reservation
that may be offered thereto."

[26] "In the last five Congresses the Senate bills and resolutions
passed by the Senate, with ninety-six members, exceed by 182 the
House bills and resolutions passed by the House, with 435 mem-

mostly of a private and sectional character.   Closure would not eliminate them, for they are a result of senatorial courtesy and they would not be
possible but for the fact that, in the United States,
there is no executive control over the initiation of

bers. The exact figures are 3113 for the Senate and 2931 for the
House.

"But more significant even than this, as evidence of the inevitable
exactions of selfish human nature when given a chance, and the
effect in forcing favorable reports on bills in committee, referred
to by Senator Thomas, is the fact that the Senate, without majority
cloture, passes these 3113 bills and resolutions out of a total of
29,332 introduced, while the House, with a majority cloture,
passed its smaller number of 2931 out of a total of 82,632 introduced.

"During the last five Congresses, therefore, the Senate passed
10.5 per cent of the bills and resolutions introduced in the Senate, while the House of Representatives passed only 3.5 per cent
of the bills and resolutions introduced in the House. In other
words, of bills and resolutions introduced, the Senate, without
effective cloture, passed in proportion three times as many as
did the House of Representatives, with cloture.

"As further proof, if any is necessary, that filibustering contributes to multiplicity of laws, it may be stated that it has
caused the President to call, during the last eight sessions of
Congress, seven extra sessions. No one can contend that more
laws were not actually passed in the twenty-three sessions actually held than if only the sixteen regular sessions had been held.
As a matter of fact, in these extra sessions, a total of 386 laws
and 98 public resolutions were passed. Again, as a result of
filibustering, not only more laws are passed but the laws which
are passed often do not receive due consideration." "Reform
of the Senate Rules," *Saturday Evening Post*, November 28, 1925.
Cf. G. W. Pepper, "Senate Cloture," *University of Pennsylvania
Law Review*, December, 1925.

These figures, it is hardly necessary to point out, mean nothing
unless there is some analysis of the relative merits of the bills
introduced in the two branches. Many—perhaps most—of the
bills presented are not expected by their authors to be reported
from committee.

legislation.   This absence of any prior veto, as I
have said, is an additional argument in favor of a
minority having opportunities to obstruct in order
to criticize and secure a time for the focussing of
public attention on what is proposed.   Were responsibility for legislation not enshrouded in committee secrecy and vicariously parcelled out, the inability of the majority to act would have less justification.   As it is, therefore, Mr. Dawes's reasoning
can be used against his closure proposal.   On the
other hand, as has been said, the powers of delay
given individual Senators force into pending bills
some amendments that the Senate leaders would not
accept were they free to act as they desired.[27]   By
and large, however, the astonishing thing is that,
in spite of its rules, the Senate gets through a credit-
able amount of business,[28] and that the log-rolling
opportunities are not more abused.

The strength of the case for closure seems the

[27] Senator Underwood complained of this to his constituents
at Birmingham:

"I had served with your permission for twenty years in the
House of Representatives. I had been the leader of that body; I
was responsible for the legislative conduct of a great party; and
I have gone to the conference table with Senate amendments on
my bill, and convinced a conference—the representatives of the
Senate in conference—that their amendments were wrong, and
then they would calmly tell me they would not yield because a
Senator So-and-So would talk the bill to death if I did not
accept his amendment; and with great governmental issues at
stake, I have been compelled to accept minor amendments to great
bills that I will not say were graft, but they were put there for
the purpose of magnifying the importance of one man with his
own constituency, at the point of jeopardizing good legislation in
America."

[28] See Appendix below, p. 274.

more doubtful when one considers the changing positions of its proponents and antagonists. This is not to say that political consistency is always to be desired, but we find the same Senators approving closure at a time when obstructionist tactics are being used against a measure in which they are interested and advocating unrestricted debate at other times when they are to be found in the filibustering minority. The case of Senator Lodge has already been referred to.[29] Senator Owen, who took a leading part in the enactment of the 1917 closure rule (and later desired to make it more severe) filibustered in 1911 against the bill to grant statehood to Arizona and New Mexico. In 1915, when the Ship Purchase Bill was being delayed, Senator Stone denounced obstruction. "Debate is one thing," he said, "a defiant filibuster without pretence of legitimate discussion intended to enlighten the Senate or the country is quite another thing. I believe now as ever in allowing a wide range for legitimate discussion on any question before the Senate; but when Senators band together merely to stop the wheels of legislation by processes only intended to prevent action by the Senate, then those engaged upon that enterprise are grossly abusing the privilege of debate." Yet in 1907 Senator Stone had filibustered against a ship subsidy bill by reading *Pilgrim's Progress*.

Such tergiversations are doubtless inevitable, and opinions favorable or unfavorable to closure will be determined by views on pending legislative business

[29] Above, p. 162.

or on particular senatorial functions. My own rather decided feeling, that it would be clearly inadvisable to change the present rule, results from the importance that I attach to senatorial investigations of the executive. These, to my mind, would become less numerous and less effective if a Senate majority could act whenever it cared to, and this, as I argue, is the most important, but as yet a largely unnoticed, aspect of the controversy over closure.

CHAPTER VI

CONGRESSIONAL INVESTIGATIONS

"It has been said that England invented the phrase 'Her Majesty's Opposition'; that it was the first government which made a criticism of administration as much a part of the polity as administration itself."

—WALTER BAGEHOT

The congressional system is organized on a principle exactly the opposite of that which Bagehot praised. Our plan, as Secretary Seward told a London *Times* correspondent, is to "elect a king for four years and give him absolute power, within certain limits, which after all he can interpret for himself." [1]   The expanding functions of government and the increase of appointed officials have vastly increased that power, which has become even more absolute.   Impeachment and public opinion apart—the one medicine is poison and the other is too weak to matter—only congressional supervision can attempt to cure the ills of executive inefficiency or wrongdoing, and the patient is by the Constitution separated from the doctor.   They never meet and diagnosis has to be made in the face of objections not only as to inexpediency but as to unconstitutionality.

[1] Quoted by Ford, *Rise and Growth of American Politics*, p. 291.

Legislatures in modern constitutional governments, it is hardly necessary to remark, have a three-fold purpose: they legislate, they control expenditure, and they supervise the administration. The educative and informing functions that Bagehot talks about are incidental to the performance of these major tasks. Successes and failures vary in different parliaments. One assembly may make a legislative rain that is much needed and that waters without flooding, but at the same time it may also be profligate. Another assembly may be legislatively inefficient but may keep the executive on starvation rations; and still another may administer better than it legislates. Foreign assemblies, like the House of Commons and the Chamber of Deputies, to judge from their recent debates and procedural reforms, have many qualms as to the adequacy with which they represent their peoples and the efficiency with which they do their work. It is clear also that the framers of the post-war European constitutions who, though more verbose and meticulous than our own Founding Fathers, were at least not politically illiterate, believed that no existing parliamentary system was worth transplanting without experiments with new grafts, which they deemed necessary because of imperfections and not because of the strange soil in which the borrowed institutions were to burgeon. These new constitutions attempt to make legislation less delayed and imperfect; to make executives less profligate and legislatures less complaisant in paying bills; to control executive policy, and to prevent bureaucrats

from becoming autocrats either from devolution of
powers upon them or because they work in unex-
amined security.   These ambitions cause little concern to American legislators, and signs are not in-
frequent that Congress (to paraphrase Gladstone's
remark about the American Constitution) considers
itself the most wonderful work ever achieved by the
brain and purpose of man.

Yet the fact of the matter is that the American
Congress performs its three major functions most
incompetently.   The reason for this is not personal
but structural.   Generally speaking, the ability and
honesty of the House and the Senate are far greater
than the average of the country.   Indeed, considering the conditions of American public life, the influence of time and chance rather than merit or
skill in determining political preferment, the obscurity to which any but Senators and Representatives of long service are doomed, and the duties of
a harassed attorney which the solons must perform, without, in Burke's phrase, the meanness of
the business being raised by the dignity of the object, Congress is a much better body than one has
any reason to hope for.   Nevertheless, as I have
said, it is incompetent.   Failures in respect of control of the purse and of legislation do not greatly
concern us here, but they have one aspect that deserves consideration.

Since the inauguration of a budget system (1921)
and the concentration of the estimates in the hands
of single committees of the House and the Senate,
Congress has been much more efficient in controll-

ing expenditure. It is a fact not well known that each year since 1921 Congress has reduced the total estimates submitted by the Bureau of the Budget. The inefficiency comes in the petty and piggling restrictions which invite waste in expenditures. Knowing that it can secure but slight knowledge of administrative activities, and that the executives are not responsible, except to the President, Congress attempts to retain some control by statutory provisions limiting administrative discretion. These appear in the appropriation acts but also in non-fiscal legislation.

This, as I have already said, is vicariously initiated and is guided by unrelated, irresponsible committee leaders. That of itself would make the statute book more fearful and wonderful than, say, the British one, which has two special advantages: one—that the statute book is blue pencilled by the prior veto of the executive—is not found in the United States, and the other—that it is edited by trained draughtsmen—has only recently been sought after by Congress and even yet meets with criticism, for it seems to deny congressional omniscience. More serious, however, in its drain on the legislature's time and energy and in its deleterious effect on the output of laws is the insistence of Congress that it must be the final authority on many matters of local and non-public concern. An astonishing proportion of the time of Congress is spent in authorizing the construction of bridges, changing the names of steamers, permitting the coinage of silver pieces to commemorate various anniversaries, sanctioning monuments and memorials, regulating minor Indian affairs, paying private claims against the government, authorizing the conveyance, sale, or transfer of public lands, and regulating military and naval property.   It is difficult to believe that these picayune matters—to say nothing of the private legislation which is by all odds the chief interest of many members—merit the collective wisdom of 531 statesmen who draw substantial salaries, enjoy extensive perquisites, meet in a magnificent building for the greater part of the year, and publish their emanations on this petty business to the extent of millions of words.   What Congress gains (in comparison for example with the House of Commons) by being given only limited authority—the residue being reserved to the state legislatures—is completely neutralized by its attention to questions which in other systems are settled under general laws by administrative agents.

Nor is this the most serious aspect of the matter. Congress habitually meddles with administration; it endeavors to be as explicit as possible on questions of administrative detail.   It decides, for example, to promote certain officers and retire others; to regulate promotions to the grade of captain; to classify retired officers who are professors of military science in civilian colleges.   Bills dealing with these matters do not involve any broad legislative policy.   "Each of these questions, from the detail of an officer for specific duty to the question of which officer to promote, and how and when and why to promote him, was a matter of administration; properly the business of administrative officers and not of a legislature. The Army, however—and fifty other executive agencies in Washington as well—can testify that no such considerations keep these questions out of Congress. . . . Congress hurries tirelessly from one administrative problem to another: from technical details of reforestation to causes of the hoof-and-mouth disease; from the right way to protect fish in Alaskan waters to the regulation of left-hand turns in the District of Columbia; from the proper temperature for a botanical garden to the loan of the Marine Corps Band for a centennial in Florida. It is a common practice nowadays for Congress to spend days debating such administrative questions as which gun shoots best, how long paint lasts, how mail tubes are operated, why somebody ought to be made a captain in the Navy." [2] In thus interfering, Congress does not realize that it is really doing harm; that it is meddling with the administration, causing and discovering inefficiency, attempting corrections by further meddling, and so around and around a vicious circle of distrust and irresponsibility.

In spite of its finical legislation, Congress has less power than any foreign parliament in controlling executive activity. This is occasionally realized in specific scandals, but as a general proposition, it commands scant attention. Yet it is indubitably the case, for the devices of legislative control used by European parliaments are unknown in the United

[2] Charles Merz, "Congress Invades the White House," *Harper's Magazine*, May, 1925.

States. The American executive and legislature never meet face to face; they remain at opposite ends of Pennsylvania Avenue. There is no control by reason of the fact that tenure of office depends upon legislative support; there is never any debate upon the policy of the administration. In France, on the other hand, the executive is interpellated; in the House of Commons there is a daily hour for cross-examining the Government by oral questions. To be sure, the answers of Ministers are sometimes adventures in precocity rather than disclosures of the truth, but the interrogations do nevertheless serve a valuable purpose. Furthermore, the adjournment of the House can be moved to call attention to an urgent matter of public importance, and while in practice this motion is hedged about by so many restrictions that it is infrequently used, it is a valuable safety-valve which can be opened in times of emergency. It is safe to say, for example, that the adjournment of the House of Commons could have been moved to call attention to such matters as the oil leases, or the failure of the Department of Justice to proceed against the Aluminium Trust. The leader of the Opposition can put down a motion of censure of the Government for some act of commission or omission; there is unlimited discussion on the motion for adjournment over the holidays, and there are some opportunities for general debate on the adjournment in the evening. The debate on the Address to His Majesty thanking Him for His gracious Speech from the Throne runs over a number of days; amendments are proposed to the

Government's proposals, and the House of Commons has an opportunity to discuss and divide on the issues in dispute between the parties. In these verbal battles executive and legislature meet face to face.

"Grievance before supply" has long been one of the cardinal principles of the British parliamentary system, and the rules of procedure in the House of Commons have so developed as to provide numerous opportunities for criticism of the Government. The Opposition and private members object occasionally to the meagreness of these opportunities, but in comparison with procedure in Congress they seem more than ample, for the debate on supply and appropriations in the House of Commons turns not on the extravagance or economy of particular grants, but on the whole policy of the Government. This is objected to as relaxing the control of the House over expenditures and permitting profligacy, but on the other hand there are elaborate criticisms of administrative activities. From this standpoint it is better that the debate on the War Office appropriation, say, should turn on a motion to reduce the salary of the Secretary of State for War by £100 in order to call attention to inadequate military discipline or to charges of corruption in furnishing supplies. Several weeks of the time of the House of Commons are taken up with such grievances and there are numerous other opportunities as well. Grievances in Congress can never be so expressed; discussion of appropriation bills turns on the amount of a particular item, and there is no method by which supply can be used as a legislative warning to the executive.

There is also, in France, a special effort to supervise the functionaries through parliamentary commissions. These assist the Chamber in administering as well as legislating, and it is hardly an exaggeration to say, as does M. Faguet, that the country "is governed eight months by the Chamber and four months by a Ministry." [3] These commissions have been so successful in holding Ministers to some continuous accountability and in informing Deputies and Senators that their institution has been ordered by the German and Czecho-Slovak constitutions and has been discussed in England,[4] where there are critics who point out the inadequacy of the existing checks. Thus the Webbs say that control by the House of Commons is now largely a sham. "Ministers and officials have the excuse that, as things are at present arranged, the pertinacity of Members of Parliament is almost always badly informed, the criticisms are ill-instructed, the discussion in Parliament usually extraordinarily futile; and Parliamentary control seems to them to mean merely an increase of official work and anxiety without the counterbalancing advantage of useful criticism or constructive suggestions." [5]   The

[3] *Problèmes politiques*, p. 10 (Paris, 1914).

[4] "Parliamentary Commissions in France," *Political Science Quarterly*, September and December, 1923.

[5] S. and B. Webb, *A Constitution for the Socialist Commonwealth of Great Britain*, p. 173 (New York, 1920). "The great mass of government today is the work of an able and honest but secretive bureaucracy, tempered by the ever-present appre-

important fact is, however, that even though the
devices of European parliaments may be considered
inadequate, they do not exist in Congress. Grievances must be aired in occasional speeches, which
cannot be germane to the legislation that is pending, and which are *in vacuo* so far as executive
officials are concerned. They cannot be called upon
to answer and they need pay no attention. As
Woodrow Wilson wrote forty years ago—and in the
interval events have strengthened rather than challenged his opinion:

"Congress stands almost helplessly outside of the departments; even the special, irksome, ungracious investigations
which it from time to time institutes in its spasmodic endeavors to dispel or confirm suspicions of malfeasance or of
wanton corruption do not afford it more than a glimpse of the
inside of a small province of federal administration. Hostile or designing officials can always hold it at arm's length
by dexterous evasions and concealments. It can violently
disturb, but it cannot often fathom, the waters of the sea
in which the bigger fish of the civil service swim and feed.
Its dragnet stirs without cleansing the bottom. Unless
it have at the head of the departments capable, fearless men,
altogether in its confidence and entirely in sympathy with
its designs, it is clearly helpless to do more than affright
those officials whose consciences are their accusers." [6]

hension of the revolt of powerful sectional interests, and mitigated by the spasmodic interventions of imperfectly comprehending Ministers." *Ibid.*, p. 69.

[6] *Congressional Government*, p. 271. "Congress cannot control
the officers of the executive without disgracing them. Its only
whip is investigation, semi-judicial examination into corners sus-
pected to be dirty. It must draw the public eye by openly avow-
ing a suspicion of malfeasance, and must then magnify and in-

Investigations by congressional committees, as Mr. Wilson said, are the only control that the system permits, and they must be entered upon with ofttimes inadequate information as to their necessity or the matters to be scrutinized.[7] Ignorance of what the administration does is forced upon Representatives and Senators; they have few if any normal opportunities for gaining knowledge.[8] The

tensify the scandal by setting its Committees to cross-examining scared subordinates and sulky ministers. And after all is over and the murder out, probably nothing is done. The offenders, if any one has offended, often remain in office, shamed before the world, and ruined in the estimation of all honest people, but still drawing their salaries and comfortably waiting for the short memory of the public mind to forget them. Why unearth the carcass if you cannot remove it?" *Ibid.*, p. 278.

[7] "Public administration is not criticized enough. Good criticism contributes to efficiency. But the first qualification of the critic is that he should understand his subject-matter. Musical criticism, dramatic criticism and literary criticism are often unfair and prejudiced; but it is not usual for men without any knowledge of music, drama, or literature to come forward as critics. In public affairs there is no such disqualification. The standard of criticism is low because administration is not recognized as an art. It is treated as a branch of party politics." E. M. H. Lloyd, *Experiments in State Control*, p. 392 (Oxford, 1924).

[8] I do not overlook hearings before congressional committees, which are an extremely important, but largely unnoticed feature of the American Government. Whether the pending measure is a tax law, whether it relates to ships, to agriculture or to railroads, most if not all of the interests to be affected have an opportunity to state their case. The issues raised by the legislation are fought out in a much more informed and non-political way than they can be on the floor of the House or in the Senate Chamber—even though in the latter body there is complete freedom of debate. Indeed, it would be hardly too extreme to say that the real discussion in Congress takes place in committee hearings. The scrutiny which sub-committees of the House Com-

schemes of foreign governments have no counterparts in the United States, and it has been worth while stressing this point, for the value of senatorial investigations becomes very obvious when it is realized that they stand alone. I say "senatorial" investigations because party control in the House of Representatives is now so strong as to shut that body off from embarrassing inquiries into executive performances. Only when the majority of the House and the President belong to different political parties do the latter's agents suffer any scrutiny. This, for example, was the case during Mr. Wilson's last two years. Then fifty-one congressional investigations were in progress.[9] But when a President has a Congress of his own political faith, inquisitions are not so frequent; their institution by the House of Representatives is extremely rare, and Senate majorities are not anxious to act. The House, as I have pointed out, is almost completely in bondage to a few leaders. A resolution authorizing an investigation, in order to escape death, must pass several lines of defense

mittee on Appropriations gives to the budget estimates are the American counterpart of the questions and interpellations of a parliamentary system. Cabinet members and Bureau Chiefs appear before the Committees with their requests for money. It is in this device of hearings that we have the most adequate articulation of American Executive and Legislature, but it is most inadequate in comparison with the opportunities under other constitutions, and since it is focused on embryonic legislation, it is of little utility as a check on the executive.

[9] See the speech of Senator Carter Glass, *Congressional Record*, April 15, 1924 p. 6358 ff., and the list of investigations asked for and agreed to during the Sixty-fifth Congress, p. 6363 ff.

which the masters of the House have made impregnable.[10] Committees cannot be discharged; even though they may make favorable reports, special facilities must be given to bring the matter before the House. This body, in short, by reason of its rules of procedure, must fail completely as a critic or watcher of the executive. Of course, it may be said that the House could revolt, but this possibility is extremely remote. It may, obviously, defeat something that the leaders propose, but the present discharge rule is so unworkable that holding up the entire legislative programme is the only weapon that the House could use to compel particular business to be submitted. Naturally, many factors are at work to prevent such a repudiation of the controlling group. When the Speaker, through his power of recognition and committee appointments, could raise a new member of the House to early prominence or keep him permanently in impotent obscurity, few members dared to question Mr. Cannon's right to rule as he saw fit. Now

[10] "It is the hardest thing in the world to undertake to get a resolution through this House to find out what we do with the people's money. First, you have to run the gauntlet of the Committee on Rules, the Steering Committee, and the other powers that be, and then of the House itself. Then you have to go to the Committee on Accounts to get the means to employ clerical and expert help, for members of the committee have not the time, and it takes all of a man's time to do these things. To get a resolution through the Committee on Accounts is not an easy matter, because the committee is busy and it is difficult frequently to get a quorum of its Members to attend. You will have two or three meetings to explain over and over, which makes it such a tremendous job." Mr. Nelson in the House of Representatives, April 22, 1924, *Congressional Record*, p. 6901.

that control has been transferred to a directory and that committee nominations are made by a Committee on Committees, members still hesitate to revolt.   Regularity is the shortest—and perhaps the only road—to greater preferment.   The shadow of the always imminent congressional election makes the majority party of the House reluctant to probe for possibly embarrassing disclosures, and the interests of the popular chamber are not in administrative efficiency but in sops for parochial interests. Even though, in the United States, therefore, a branch of Congress may run wild with no definite effects on *party*,[11] there are a number of important factors that strengthen the oligarchical control of the House of Representatives.   The result is that so far as the majority of the House is concerned, an executive of the same party is an unsupervised king.

That this is the case clearly appears from a list

[11] Of course I recognize the fact that the House of Commons is rarely permitted free decisions, and that a Government (as Lord Palmerston once put it) insists on support not only when it is right but when it is wrong. If members vote against the Government they risk its resignation and a dissolution with the expensive uncertainty of standing for reelection. Consequently there is much blind party support, but this situation is the exact opposite of that in the House of Representatives. The House of Commons may by a majority vote have its own way, and the result is that the Cabinet, realizing this latent power of the House, watches its step; it changes administrative policies that are complained of, or even sacrifices an inefficient member of the Government. The House of Representatives, on the other hand, in adopting its rule of procedure, put on a straitjacket. It deliberately consented to enslavement and it has no latent power that is a continuous threat.

of the investigations asked for in the House and
the Senate, and refused by the former but allowed
by the latter. With the exception of the Graham
committee that scrutinized military expenditures during the war [12] (the inquiry cost half a million dollars) practically every important investigation of
the last three Congresses has been conducted by a
Senate Committee. House Committees have, of
course, held hearings and have conducted some inquiries; but the inquisitorial power of Congress has
been the inquisitorial power of the Senate. The
House has inquired into relatively harmless matters; the Senate investigated the charges of corruption in the Veterans' Bureau, the oil land leases,
the Bureau of Internal Revenue and its tax refunds,
Mr. Daugherty's conduct of the Department of
Justice, the failure to prosecute the Aluminium
Trust, and the internal workings of the Tariff Commission. Most of these inquiries had been proposed
in the House; the Department of Justice resolution,
indeed, had been favorably considered by the Rules
Committee, but was nevertheless not presented to
the House,[13] which, while the Senate searched for
possible corruption, was content to investigate the
administration of the Stockyards Control Act, the
operations of the Army Air Service, the Shipping
Board, charges of duplication of securities in the
Bureau of Printing and Engraving, and charges that
two members of Congress had accepted bribes.
That the Senate, and not the more popular branch

[12] See *Congressional Record,* March 5 and 6, 1920.
[13] See above, p. 134.

of Congress, was the grand inquisitor resulted, as I have said, from the differences in procedure. The leaders of the House refused to permit it to act; the leaders of the Senate hardly tried to keep it from acting. The Senate is such a forum that the need for investigations could be clearly set forth; closure could not be applied, and were the party steamroller to be brought out, the minority could have an effective answer in the form of a filibuster that would endanger the majority's timetable.

To be sure, much has been said against the methods—and even against the theory of senatorial investigations. Much time is wasted. A dragnet is thrown out blindly and brings in irrelevant and innocent matters. Investigations are sometimes little more than fishing expeditions and are pursued not because of situations that need scrutiny but because of the idiosyncracies of individual Senators. Partisan advantages are rarely overlooked. All these evils were abundantly manifested in the investigations of 1923–24. Rumor and innuendo were poured into the record along with competent testimony, but whatever the abuses, the investigations were, I think, valuable, and, indeed, indispensable. As Professor Frankfurter has said, "The safeguards against abuse and folly are to be looked for in the forces of responsibility which are operating from within Congress and are generated from without." [14]   If the alternatives are no inquiry at

[14] "Hands Off the Investigations," *The New Republic*, May 21, 1924.

all, or an inquiry that is abused, then the choice must
be for the latter.   If it is not, then there is no
method by which Congress may perform its duty of
seeing to it that the administration of the law which
Lord Morley called "the keystone of all civilized
government" is neither corrupt nor incompetent.
What the 1924 investigations disclosed is not pertinent here; nor is it necessary to discuss the attitude
that the press and the country took toward them.[15]
It is sufficient to remark that three out of ten
Cabinet members were permitted or pressed to resign; that there were several indictments and two
suicides.

The importance of the Senate *vis-à-vis* the executive is increased by reason of the fact that the
Cabinet is simply a body of chief clerks.   The
President's "official family" is not provided for by
the Constitution; its existence depends solely on
custom.   Congress creates executive departments
whose heads make up an informal body known as
the Cabinet.   This may not be consulted for weeks
on end; it is scattered all over the country during
the summer months but then again it may be frequently summoned to the White House.   The
legend may even spread, as it did during Mr. Harding's administration, that the secretaries are the
President's executive associates; that the Cabinet is an institution.   A German professor of
physiology is reported to have begun a lecture as

[15] William E. Dodd, "Political Corruption and the Public: Fifty
Years Ago and Today," *The New Republic*, June 11, 1924.

follows: "We come now to the spleen. Nothing is known about the functions of the spleen. So much, gentlemen, for the spleen." A professor of politics could say the same of the American Cabinet, for it keeps no records, and apparently reaches no collective decisions.[16]

The Harding Cabinet, for example, incredible though it may appear, seems not to have considered the question of the oil leases. This is the view of Secretaries Hughes and Weeks who said that they did not recall that the matter was ever brought before the Cabinet. Thus Mr. Hughes declared: "I had no occasion to consider the questions of law and fact involved, and I have not been called upon to take any responsibility in the matter." The question may be raised as to whether all Cabinet officers should not be expected to take some responsibility for such decisions of the Government. This might improve the quality of Cabinets individually and collectively, and it might also improve administration. If the "best minds" in a President's Cabinet had to feel some interest in the decisions of inferior minds, the "best minds" would be reluctant to sanction what they did not understand and approve. The possessors of the "best minds," moreover, would not be anxious to serve in a body in which their reputations might be affected by the tergiversations of inferior minds. Of course, in view of the presidential system, such a result

[16] The memoirs of various Cabinet members throw little light on the workings of the body on a whole.

could only be realized in part. It has long been axiomatic that the English Cabinet contains, generally speaking, the ablest men in the party. Collective responsibility seems to eliminate most of the unfit. Without some direct responsibility of the Cabinet to Congress, a similar elimination of mediocrity or venality could not be achieved, but it is a grave defect of the governmental machine that the Cabinet as a whole attempts no supervision over administration.

Nor, as I have said, is there any scrutiny of the individual departments, for they have no regular and frequent contacts with Congress. It is probable, that had Cabinet members been in the habit of making appearances on the floor of Congress, some of the 1924 scandals would have been avoided. It is certainly true that in England such a plethora of wrongdoing and inefficiency never appears. This articulation has long been urged by writers on the American Government and by bills introduced in Congress,[17] but the possibility of its institution is exceedingly remote. Meanwhile there would be nothing to prevent some development of the functions of the Cabinet by custom; it could be institutionalized by having a secretariat and minutes. This at least would be an immense gain. As it is, administration must be viséd by a President who may be too busy with political preoccupations to care much about administrative problems, and

[17] A Senate Committee recommended it in 1881; Senate Report No. 837, 46th Congress, 3d Session (February, 1881).

whose attention can rarely be secured until abuses have actually developed and have caused congressional or public clamor. Even then the tendency is to stand by the criticized official and to argue that all is well.

The fact of the matter is, therefore, that Senate inquiries are indispensable. They have been, however, under considerable fire since the excesses of 1924. As part of the Republican programme of economy, party leaders in Washington have proposed to call a halt on investigations because of the matter of expense. Senator Warren, Chairman of the Senate Appropriations Committee, compiled figures showing that in the last sixteen years the Senate had spent $1,383,500 on various inquiries, and that the cost of those in progress in February, 1926, would reach $275,000. These, of course, seem large amounts, but the price is a small one for some legislative scrutiny of administration. The 20,000 questions which are annually asked in the House of Commons cost a guinea apiece, so that in sixteen years the cost of the daily question hour in Great Britain has been considerably in excess of the cost of senatorial investigations, and this in spite of the fact that Great Britain has many other opportunities for criticism.

Again, as I have suggested, senatorial investigations have to run the gauntlet of presidential antagonism. There have been frequent cases in the past in which Presidents have protested against what they considered unwarranted intrusions by the Senate on executive functions. President Jackson's

attitude was conspicuous.[18]   President Coolidge, of
course, has been bitterly resentful of the attitude of
the Senate.   In a special message to the Senate on
April 11, 1924, he protested vigorously against
certain phases of the Couzens investigation of the
Bureau of Internal Revenue.   He said:

"There exists and always should exist every possible
comity between the executive departments and the Senate.
Whatever may be necessary for the information of the
Senate or any of its Committees in order better to enable
them to perform their legislative or other constitutional
functions ought always to be furnished willingly and expeditiously by any department. . . .

"The constitutional and legal rights of the Senate ought
to be maintained at all times.   Also the same must be said
of the executive departments.   But these rights ought not
to be used as a subterfuge to cover unwarranted intrusion.
It is the duty of the executive to resist such intrusion and
to bring to the attention of the Senate its serious consequences." [19]

The "constitutional and legal rights of the
Senate" are not definitely known, and it is argued
that certain congressional investigations are *ultra
vires*.[20]   It is not necessary to discuss the legal
questions here.   The constitutional law on the
subject is both complicated and incomplete.
There seem to be differences of opinion as to

[18] See Bassett, *Life of Andrew Jackson*, Vol. II, p. 649 (New
York, 1911), and the speech of Senator Goff on the Aluminium
Report, *Congressional Record*, February 25, 1926, p. 4262 ff.

[19] *Congressional Record*, p. 6087.

[20] See the speech of Senator Cummins, *Congressional Record*,
February 23, 1926, p. 4134 ff.

the extent of committee authority (backed by the respective chambers) in punishing contumacious witnesses when the inquiry is for legislative purposes, and the committee power to investigate the conduct of an administrative officer—entirely apart from the question of legislative action. It is argued that, under the separation of powers theory, neither house has explicit warrant to investigate executive derelictions. No permissive clauses of the Constitution can be pointed to, but there have, of course, been many congressional investigations of administrative conduct when no legislation was contemplated.[21] Nor would it seem to be proper or necessary to restrict senatorial authority in this respect by reason of the fact that the House of Representatives has the sole power to impeach. "To restrict congressional investigation to cases where there is avowed legislative purpose would force Congress to pass upon the desirability of legislation in certain cases before the facts of the situation were known. The congressional power to acquire information necessarily preliminary to an actual legislative intent should not be confined by too great adherence to the niceties of constitutional construction." [22]

[21] Some instances are given in Hinds' *Precedents of the House of Representatives,* Vol. III, sec. 1725 ff. *Cf.* H. Berthélemy, "Les limites du pouvoir legislatif," *Revue politique et parlementaire,* December 10, 1925.

[22] "The Power of Congress to Subpoena Witnesses for Non-judicial Investigations," *Harvard Law Review,* Vol. 38, p. 234 (1924). *Ex parte Daughterty,* 299 Fed. 620 (D. C. 1924), and C. S. Potts, "Power of Legislative Bodies to Punish for Contempt," *University of Pennsylvania Law Review,* May, 1926. Professor J. H. Wigmore has argued (*Illinois Law Review,* May, 1924)

On grounds of policy, of course, the obligation on Congress is clear:

"It is the proper duty of a representative body to look diligently into every affair of government and to talk much about what it sees. It is meant to be the eyes and the voice, and to embody the wisdom and will of its constituents. Unless Congress have and use every means of acquainting itself with the acts and the disposition of the administrative agents of the government, the country must be helpless to learn how it is being served; and unless Congress both scrutinize these things and sift them by every form of discussion, the country must remain in embarrassing, crippling ignorance of the very affairs which it is most important that it should understand and direct." [23]

In short, as Mr. Wilson argued, "The informing function of Congress should be preferred to the legislative function." Otherwise the "informing" is left to the President and this, as we shall see, is open to grave objections.

that senatorial investigations repudiate the constitutional mode of impeaching executive officials, but he overlooks the point that the Senate is performing political functions and that, therefore, "all the guarantees of a fair trial" are not to be expected. The rôle of the Senate is somewhat analagous to that of the legislature in a parliamentary system.

[23] Wilson, *Congressional Government*, p. 303.

Admiring as he was of the House of Commons and sceptical of the Lords, Bagehot nevertheless thought that the Peers were extremely useful critics: "An assembly in which the mass of members have nothing to lose, where most have nothing to gain, where everyone has a social position firmly fixed, where no one has a constituency, where hardly anyone cares for the minister of the day, is the very assembly in which to look for, and from which to expect, independent criticism." *op. cit.* p. 194.

CHAPTER VII

PRESIDENTIAL PROPAGANDA AND THE SENATE

"Where through the long-drawn aisle and fretted vault,
"The pealing anthem swells the note of praise."
—THOMAS GRAY

The success of American political institutions has been in the main the success of a written constitution, setting up republican government over a huge territory for peoples in different stages of economic and political development. This was a tremendous experiment, and gloomy forebodings of disaster were well-nigh universal. The experiment was assisted by several important inventions. In respect of the separation of powers, bicameralism, astronomical elections, constitutional protection of the individual, and judicial supremacy, the Constitution placed in the governmental machine wheels and valves which, though adapted in part from England or the Colonies, were put to novel uses, and in this sense were original creations.

Nor did the inventions end with the drafting of the Constitution. That instrument of government but inadequately explains our political processes, for we have developed conventions and customs in such number as to defy complete enumeration, and of such importance as to challenge the primacy of the written word. Direct election of the President, political party machinery, nominating conventions, the importance of congressional committees, the universal connection of Congressmen by residence with the districts they represent, senatorial prerogatives —dictation in foreign policy, "courtesy" in appointments, investigations of administration—all these matters are outside the Constitution. They profoundly influence, if indeed they do not determine, the character of our political life. Their importance is only equalled by their novelty, for these conventions are distinctly our own; they have few counterparts in other popular governments, and it is a striking fact that with all our wealth of experiment, the American Constitution has had slight influence on foreign systems. Our political institutions function without imitation; our proprietary right is protected, not by patent but by foreign distrust. This, I fancy, will be the fate of our most recent, but not the least important invention—the White House "Spokesman." This newly appointed, anonymous, extra-legal official is undergoing no evolution; he has sprung forth full panoplied from the forehead of the God of Publicity. He is important enough to warrant consideration, and, as I hope to demonstrate, dangerous enough to deserve reprehension. His existence is an additional, and a well-nigh irrefutable, argument against closure in the Senate.

It is now trite to say that the American President is the most powerful elected ruler in the world.

The Constitution grants him enormous authority, and he is almost completely free from the checks which many governmental systems place upon the chief of the executive. He is, that is to say, not dependent upon a majority in the legislature; he holds office by the calendar, and not by parliamentary or public approval; and he can be removed only by the cumbersome and almost impossible process of impeachment. He governs in his own name, and by his own authority; no ministerial counter-signature is necessary to validate his acts. The party machine is for the time being the machine of the President. His tremendous appointing power can be and is used to give him a national body of supporters who constitute a personal caucus to rally to support his side, and, if he desires, to work for his renomination and election. His powers of appointment and veto, and his position as the only elected representative of the nation permit him on occasion to make Congress do his bidding; and apart from legislation, in the field of administration there are ample areas in which the President has from the Constitution and statute, full and irresponsible authority. Indeed, impeachment aside, the principal check upon the executive power of a President is the vague and frequently impotent restraint of public opinion. Hence the importance of the methods by which the President creates or encourages a favorable public sentiment. The principal method is newspaper publicity: the exploitation of a willing President by a complacent press. If such a circle of partiality were only personal, it would do no more than turn up a few political noses; but unfortunately the relationship is institutional as well, and it has consequences which are possible only under a system of government such as that set up by the Constitution of the United States.

The President gives audiences to all the Washington newspaper correspondents on Tuesdays at noon and on Fridays at four o'clock. From fifty to one hundred correspondents troop into the executive offices and listen to the President answer or refuse to answer written questions which have been given to him in advance, and supplementary oral questions which arise out of the written interrogations. The correspondents' primary concern is not with the President's point of view, so that they may write more intelligent critiques or analyses of the course of politics. Above everything else they are anxious for news, and consequently all kinds of questions are asked. If the President can be persuaded to express an opinion that the wide-bottomed trousers so popular among college boys are too extreme a style (an actual presidential emanation from one White House conference), a dispatch results; news has been created. The papers, therefore, rarely appear on Wednesdays and Saturdays without devoting considerable space to the opinions of the President on various subjects, both connected and unconnected with politics. The only limitation on this process of getting the views of the President before the country is that there must be no direct quotations. This means no more than that the President's opinions must not be put in quotation marks or too directly attributed to him. Consequently the dispatches read somewhat as follows: "It was stated by a high authority at the White House today"; or "callers at the White House were today informed that President Coolidge is of the opinion"; or "a high official of the government is authority for the statement"; or "a White House Spokesman said"; or "a spokesman for the President let it be known." This anonymity is thinly veiled. Everyone knows that the opinions attributed to these mythical personages are the opinions of the President given by himself to the listening correspondents. The views expressed, as has been said, do not relate exclusively to public affairs. "A White House spokesman" has delivered a long dissertation on angling which, in his opinion, was a sport suitable for children but not for adults. Again, "callers at the White House" have learned that the President believed the Easter season not to require any large expenditures for clothes, and that he himself was to wear an old suit to church. The government's economy should set an example for personal economy. But this advice from the President gave rise to a chorus of protest from haberdashers who saw their sales diminished by persons anxious to emulate the President's boasted sartorial restraint. In order to encourage business, therefore, a "White House spokesman" announced that the President would have a new suit, and that too stringent economy was not a good thing for the prosperity of the country, a *volte face* which embarrassed neither the mythical spokesman nor the newspapers. Perhaps because they had only a traditional and not an economic interest, college sophomores did not challenge the President's opinion that hazing was not a proper form of discipline for freshmen.

Such injunctions to an expectant, and for the most part docile people might seem to indicate Mr. Coolidge's belief that his election as President gave him a mandate to offer advice on matters of ettiquette and personal habits. This, however, is not the case. The President's semi-weekly emanations —though in some cases presumptuous and cheap— have a political significance. He uses the press to keep himself in the public eye. A few years ago only opera stars, actors, and circuses had press agents. Now partly as a result of the war which showed the tremendous power of propaganda, organized publicity is a great American industry. Getting into print is the ambition of banking houses, hotels, business men, charitable enterprises, universities, bearded ladies, and statesmen. The most eminent statesman—the President—has a secretary who is little more than a glorified press agent, and who devotes continuous thought to keeping the White House on the front pages. The publicity organization of the party uses every avenue of information—newspapers, magazines, the cinema, the radio, the stage, the pulpit, the school; and the President in his conferences with the Washington correspondents makes successful semi-weekly plunges into print. An opera star, a business man, or an ordinary politician is not so fortunate unless he has something to say, or unless marriage, divorce, or landing from Europe makes him at the moment of particular interest. The President's eminence, however, is such that the newspapers will publish whatever he says, whether it be trivial, important, dull, acute, exact, or incorrect. Hence there is no difficulty whatever in having the papers devote space to the occupant of the White House and his thoughts on political and non-political subjects. It is the amount and regularity of the space that count, not the pertinence or the sense of the thoughts. This would not be of political importance if the President were only a titular, a ceremonial executive; but he, unlike European Kings or Presidents, combines the theatrical and the efficient functions of government, and in the White House conferences with the correspondents these functions are inextricably mixed.

Conferences at the White House are not an old institution, and ex-cathedra utterances from that edifice on sport and manners are even more recent. In President Cleveland's time the Washington correspondents rarely saw the President. They got information about public affairs as best they could, and then wrote their own analyses of the political situation in Washington. They were political journalists rather than news gatherers. Mr. Roosevelt, however, was accustomed to see correspondents whom he especially liked, and to get them to put his views on certain questions before the public as their own guesses. These *ballons d'essai* enabled him to estimate the country's reaction and shape his course accordingly. Mr. Roosevelt, and his successor, Mr. Taft, limited their contacts with the press to particular journalists in whom they had confidence; and they were only interested in support for their policies. They did not scheme to advertise themselves; they cared nothing about figuring in the papers simply to keep their names before the public.

The new regime, strangely enough, was inaugurated by Mr. Wilson. When the Democratic administration began in 1913 one of the slogans was "pitiless publicity." Mr. Wilson had said that the executive business should be conducted "behind glass doors." It was this theory which led to the holding of semi-weekly conferences between the President and all the pressmen in Washington, but it was not long before the plan was abandoned. The reasons were our acute relations with Mexico and the problems of neutrality which arose after the outbreak of the war. It was not thought desirable that these delicate questions should be discussed by the President (even with direct quotation barred) in the presence of several score newspaper men. After Mr. Wilson was reëlected in 1916 there was just one such conference and then the institution lapsed completely, to be revived and profoundly modified by Mr. Harding. The change was in the greater range of subjects considered at the conferences, and in the deliberateness of the attempt to "get publicity" for the President and his doings. No detail of the personal life of the occupants of the White House seemed too trivial to be told of. An American humorist once said that a person on a surgeon's operating table had no more privacy than a goldfish. The White House submitted to a continuous operation by publicity specialists. Clothes, tastes, pets, amusements, and habits were on public parade. An ex-newspaper man was at-tached to the White House staff to think up ways of "selling" the President to the public.

In his semi-weekly conferences, Mr. Harding at first made it a rule that the correspondents could ask any questions without previous notice to him. He was willing to appear in mental *déshabillé*.   Mr. Harding, however, was not a man of particularly acute perceptions, and his conferences soon dis-closed that many of the journalists were keener and better informed than he was on the public busi-ness about which they inquired.   The President's extemporaneous answers, therefore, were occasion-ally imprudent and inaccurate.   When the Washing-ton conference on the limitation of armament was in session, for example, someone asked the Presi-dent whether the four-power treaty included a guarantee of the home islands of Japan.   Hard-ing replied that it did not, but Secretary Hughes and all the delegates to the Conference were of the opinion that the treaty did cover the islands.   It was necessary, therefore, for Mr. Harding to give out a corrected statement and the ensuing public dis-cussion was such that the treaty was modified and the mooted territory was excluded.   This incident resulted in a rule that the questions must be in writing; that the President must have notice. Mr. Coolidge continued the institution with no change except that the range of subjects discussed has been greatly extended, and on two or three occasions the remarks of "the White House Spokesman" have excited the umbrage of European governments.

In the spring of 1925, M. Jusserand, then French Ambassador to the United States, made a public speech in which he mentioned his government's attitude toward the payment of the French debt to the United States.   A day or two later "the White House" was quoted to the effect that Ambassador Jusserand should not have made his statement to a public audience but to the officials of the American Government.   The newspapers plainly intimated that the President's views (which they were reporting) constituted a rebuke of the Ambassador for his indiscretion.   Such an anonymous rebuke of an Ambassador, however, was rather unprecedented and outrageous.   M. Jusserand promptly protested to the State Department.   The State Department told Mr. Coolidge that he had been indiscreet, and consequently the correspondents were authorized to say that no criticism had been intended or expressed, and the incident was closed.   The anonymity which cloaks the presidential utterances had put the responsibility on the newspapers and it was sought to convey the impression that the indiscretion was theirs.   Something similar happened when the Herriot Government fell.   Mr. Coolidge had a conference with the correspondents on Friday, April 10, 1925.   The next day the papers reported the President's views on the French Cabinet crisis.   According to the New York *Herald-Tribune:* "The President judges that the French Premier has gone out of power on account of great difficulties attending French financing, difficulties which existed before he took office, and for which he was not to blame." The dispatch in the New York *Times* was substantially the same: "The President has read with sympathy the views expressed that M. Herriot's financial difficulties were not of his own making, but were inherited." These remarks were cabled to Paris and there was a chorus of excited protest. It was, as the *Liberté* declared, a "shocking intervention" in French politics; but at the next conference the explanation was made that the President's comments on French politics had been general; he had not meant to interfere, and he had not intended any criticism of the pre-Herriot, Poincaré regime.

Now it may be said, of course, that these incidents simply show the failure of the President to realize the nature of the statements he authorized to be made in his name anonymously (which is what happens at the White House Conferences); but the problem goes much deeper than this. The President of the United States has at his disposal the most powerful publicity agency that any man has ever had. He can get tremendous benefits from it, and, except on rare occasions, when he is particularly indiscreet, he can suffer little or no harm. Responsibility can be dodged, and the indiscretion is promptly forgotten. Yet so far as information to the public is concerned, the White House conference has no value. It is not necessary to enlighten the pressmen or the public on pending legislation or the Administration's programme and policies. The conferences are simply a means of creating news, and it is as *news* that the President's views are reported. Mr. Coolidge on the marriage customs of primitive peoples would receive more space than Mr. Coolidge on the surtaxes, and when public affairs are discussed, the correspondents simply report; they venture no independent criticism or analysis.

Tabulation of the utterances of the White House Spokesman for any fortnight, selected at random, will make it plain that I am not exaggerating. During the two weeks before the close of the Sixty-eighth Congress, on March 4, 1925, for example, the Washington correspondents reported the President's views on the following political matters: farm legislation; the disposition of Muscle Shoals; the flexible provisions of the Tariff Act authorizing the executive to change the rates; the return of German property to its owners; the creation of an independent air service; the fitness of Mr. Warren to be Attorney General; the objections to an increase of the pay of postal employees unless coupled with an increase of revenues; the American attitude toward the French debt; willingness to hold an arms conference as shown by European nations in response to the Administration's "feeler", and, only two days later, willingness to hold an arms conference as shown by European nations in response to their own noble instincts, for there had been no

Administration "feeler". The President in respect of these matters authorized the Washington correspondents to report his position to the country; on the arms conference indeed, he took two conflicting positions. The conferences did not clarify any of these issues. They gave no additional information, but simply kept the President before the public eye. In every case the executive was speaking in an irresponsible manner; he could, that is to say, disavow his statement. In no case could Mr. Coolidge be asked for the basis of his opinions; no congressional critic could ask questions or suggest considerations to show that the President's position was untenable, and no critical correspondent would venture to suggest incorrectness or inadequacy. On the contrary, what happened during the closing weeks of the last Congress—and what happens all the time—is that the President speaks to the country without the danger of being held responsible, and with no fear of embarrassing contradiction or reply. If unhappily the statements made are inaccurate, it is the newspapers that have to appear to take the blame.

If unhappily, there should be unfair criticisms, responsibility can be dodged. Thus at a conference in February, 1926, the White House "Spokesman" declared that some speeches in Congress were being made for political effect and that the country should pay scant heed. The country was "watching with a critical eye the activities of Congress"; it was "quick" to side with the President and to "criticize the Senate for its dilatory methods" in debating the tax bill. "White House officials" had been surprised by "the great number of letters from Democratic states dealing with the tax bill." How many letters was not stated. This vague innuendo, of course, brought forth a couple of frank speeches in the Senate, and so from the the next newspaper conference there emanated the news that the President was pleased with congressional coöperation in respect of the World Court and tax reduction. This retraction shut off criticism of the White House, but the country had been given the impression that its interests were being protected by the executive against the legislature and even the later condescension of a good word for Congress swelled the note of praise for the President. Such a system of recriminating and retracting is, of course, neither straightforward nor sincere. It enables the President to talk all that he cares to, and yet to say nothing that he cannot instantly withdraw. It permits public issues to be confused. Thus Senator Norris' speech in the Senate anent the Lewis appointment,[1] posed the question of whether it was proper for the President to lay down secret conditions before nominating persons to the Shipping Board or the Tariff Commission. The President's "Spokesman" took notice of this question, and the newspapers reported the result: "It was learned at the White House that President Coolidge feels that neither the Executive nor Congress can control a commission, that nearly all commissions are authorized to do certain work by the law creating them, and that they

[1] See above, p. 48.

are not responsible to any particular body." This was all the President vouchsafed on an incident which constituted a serious challenge to his good faith. So far as it went, the reply was impeccable, but its inadequacy and irrelevancy could not be pointed out, for the statement was anonymous and irresponsible.

Perhaps, however, the most audacious exploitation of the President was in connection with the coal strike. This has been largely unnoticed, and it is worthwhile to recall the facts. The miners and the operators were in conference at Atlantic City in July, 1925, and the date of the stoppage was known. The country showed some signs of nervousness, and reassuring statements began to come from the summer White House in Swampscott. On July 18, after a conference between the President and Secretary of Labor Davis, it was announced that "The Government has decided upon positive steps to be taken in case of a coal strike." President Coolidge believed that his undisclosed plan which "had been carefully worked out under his direction" would "be effective in the event the miners and operators failed to reach a settlement by the end of August." The next day an anonymous spokesman for the President declared him to be "determined to prevent the coal strike." The President had "let the operators know that he will exert all the pressure possible to keep the hard coal mines operating and to prevent the condition of three years ago when the public suffered greatly." On July 21, President Coolidge's opinion was that there was "no danger of a hard coal strike," but even then doubts began to appear, and the President assured the country that "the strike cannot be of long duration." On July 25, "Mr. Coolidge indicated" that he was giving the coal situation "earnest thought" and that he "was prepared to exert the pressure of the Federal Government, representing public opinion." By July 27, the President's position was "that it would be premature to assume that this dispute is not going to be settled within the industry," and there were intimations that the President, extremely anxious to act, was handicapped by lack of constitutional powers. The tune changed again. If a strike occurred it could not be of long duration, for there were ample supplies of anthracite in the country, and when these were exhausted substitutes could be used. Such matters were discussed exuberantly, but never quantitatively; the country was not told just how much anthracite was available.

For weeks Mr. Coolidge's thoughts, plans, and hopes were the daily pabulum of the American people, but the hundreds of dispatches which were published had one serious effect; they lulled the country into a false security. Almost without exception, the newspapers aided what was an advertisement for the President at the same time that it was a sedative for the public. It is possible, of course, that real leadership would have failed to arouse the country and to enable the President to force operators and miners to accept a fair agreement, but the point is that if an agreement had been reached and the strike averted, the Swampscott emanations would have made the country think that the President had some share in averting the calamity. Even though the strike occurred, the exploitation of the President made the country believe that he was watching over their interests, and in any event political memories are proverbially short. There were few days during the summer when the President was not on the front pages. After the return to Washington coal was rarely mentioned; other subjects served for advertising purposes. Users of coal learned the reason.

Somewhat the same relationship exists between the executive departments and the press. Members of the Cabinet or their deputies have regular conferences with the Washington news gatherers. Most departments, moreover, have employees whose principal duties are to see that the department gets a large amount of publicity; that the Cabinet member is photographed frequently, and that the public is led to think that affairs are being efficiently and successfully conducted. The attitude of the United States toward Russia is indicated by an "unofficial spokesman" of the State Department. A "high authority of the State Department" announces that American troops have landed in Honduras to protect American lives and property, and the dispatches give the most plausible statements of the reason for and the extent of the intervention. In other words, the newspapers are used as irresponsible agents of the irresponsible departments and of the White House to get certain news before the country. Sometimes this results in a first class *contretemps*. Such, for example, was the Houghton statement which was made without responsibility and caused an even more irresponsible discussion in the Senate.[2]

At best this system is not government by discussion. It is government by favorable publicity. Statements of the government's intentions and activities are *ex parte*. The "spokesman" or the "high authorities" can refuse to answer questions which seek to probe for possible defects or objections. There is no openness of discussion as in a parliamentary system where the executive answers questions publicly, and a failure to answer can be put down as an attempt to conceal, or as ignorance greater than should be found in high places. The Secretary of State in person would never dream of giving to Congress the brief, ofttimes misleading statements with which the press must necessarily be content; and if he did give such statements, a critic of the administration could by questions show their inadequacy and the newspapers would publish an antidote along with the official explanation of the Administration's position.

While he was in office, Secretary Hughes seemed to attach considerable importance to his meetings with the correspondents, and to think that they were an admirable institution. He never seemed to recognize the fact that the State Department was using the press for its own purposes, and that public discussion was being prejudiced, if not prevented. He did realize, however, that more intimate con-

[2] See above, p. 86.

tacts between executive and Congress might be beneficial. In a speech delivered in 1922 he said:

'Whatever the advantages of our governmental arrangements—and I should be the last to underestimate them—I think it should be candidly admitted that they have the effect of limiting the opportunities for the responsible discussion which aids in the understanding of foreign policy. . . . The separateness of the executive power under our system, whilst it has advantages which have been deemed to be of controlling importance, deprives the executive of the opportunities open to parliamentary leaders, of participation in parliamentary debates . . . There is lacking the personal relation to the discussions of the Senate when foreign affairs are under consideration. The advantage of oral explication and of meeting each exigency as it arises in the course of discussion and thus of aiding in the information of public opinion in the manner best adapted to that purpose is not to the Secretary of State. There are numerous situations in which an opportunity for the executive through his department chiefs to explain matters of policy would be of the greatest aid in securing an intelligent judgment." [3]

There is no disposition, however, on the part either of Congress or of the executive to increase the *discussion* of current political problems. The Representatives and Senators can never question the President or Cabinet members except as the latter make rare appearances before congressional committees, and these bodies deal with past events rather than current business. The White House, in other words, is at one end of Pennsylvania Avenue, and the Capitol is at the other, and there are

[3] "Some Observations on the Conduct of Our Foreign Relations," *American Journal of International Law,* July, 1922.

no interchanges in the nature of discussion. There are simply *ex parte* announcements in the press and the President may show a continuous disdain of Congress except as that body's approval is necessary for the Administration's legislative programme. Mr. Coolidge's conferences with the Washington correspondents are simply an index of this separateness and of the fact that the executive seeks for public rather than congressional support and approval.

There are, of course, speeches on the floor of Congress when it is in session, but they are also *in vacuo* so far as controversies between the legislative and executive departments are concerned. Only rarely is criticism of the executive in Congress answered by a legislative spokesman for the Administration, and then he is frequently an unofficial friend of the President. He speaks on personal or party grounds and not because of any relationship between executive and legislature. The American Congress, in other words, is not a successful critic of the executive, and the executive, speaking anonymously at the press conferences, or in vague generalities on the platform, is able to avoid criticism in the press. Indeed, when the Sixty-eighth Congress came to an end, the White House "Spokesman" put forward the suggestion that during the summer the newspapers should devote but little space to the discussion of public affairs. Silence, in the President's opinion, "would be good for business." It would be time enough in December when the new Congress met to begin to talk about legislative measures that might make the business interests feel uneasy. But this suggestion shows something more than solicitude for the financial interests; it shows that government by discussion is held in low esteem.

Nevertheless, few objections have been raised. To be sure, Mr. Coolidge's indiscretions in respect of M. Jusserand and M. Herriot temporarily killed off the White House "Spokesman," but only the opprobrious name was dropped; during the following summer the correspondents quoted "callers" or "those in a position to know the mind of the President." When Mr. Coolidge returned to Washington, the "Spokesman" was resurrected completely and impudently. On September 18, 1925, he called upon the newspapers of the country to support the Administration's attitude in respect of funding the debt. He declared, according to the New York *World,* that "the American press should look after the interests of the United States rather than other nations," and said that "one would be unlikely to find the United States imposing unbearable hardships on other countries." "If newspapers were doubtful, they generally would do right by resolving in favor of the American attitude." At this conference also, the President, through his spokesman, became a book reviewer. He passed critical judgment on the volume entitled "The French Debt Problem" published by the Institute of Economics. This study is a painstaking coöperative effort by American economists to estimate France's capacity to meet her foreign obligations, and may be properly criticized only by a detailed analysis of its statistical material or the conclusions drawn therefrom. Yet the spokesman advised the country to pay no attention to the argument of the book because its estimates were not altogether consistent with the demands of the Debt Funding Commission. This, I imagine, represents the high water mark of presidential omniscience and the irresponsible presumption of his "spokesman."

To him and the exploitation that he makes possible is due, I think, an amazing uncertainty as to the quality of American executives. Mr. Coolidge, for example, enjoys a greater popular support than has been given any previous President. The mass of the people have a quiet confidence in him, which is not justified by his record of achievement in dealing with Congress. Until the session of December, 1925, Congress, indeed, had an almost perfect record of achievement in disregarding the President's recommendations. The Senate repeatedly refused to consider American entrance into the World Court, and when the debate finally began, paid no attention to the executive's wishes. Mr. Coolidge's agricultural recommendations were almost completely ignored; the bonus for ex-soldiers was passed over his veto, when it seemed almost incredible that a President could not have changed the few votes necessary to have the measure fail; the Japanese exclusion clause was put in the Immigration Act over his vigorous protest; his appointments have been rejected, and for the first time in sixty years the President has had to submit to a senatorial veto on the choice of his Cabinet. Against the wishes of the President, Congress raised the salary of its own members. The record really is almost unparalleled, and yet as I say, it seems to have affected slightly if at all the hold that Mr. Coolidge has on the country. Indeed, he seems to have gained strength from his congressional defeats, for the newspapers have published millions of words picturing him as a strong silent man about to veto the Immigration Bill, or about to show firmness in exerting pressure to have the World Court proposal considered. To be sure, this firmness was always pictured in advance of the event, but the country has apparently been unable to contrast lack of performance with the glorious promises. It may be that Mr. Coolidge is one of the strongest Presidents the country has ever had. If so, the idea of him in this rôle is based not upon any specific achievements, but upon a roseate picture that newspaper correspondents have drawn of their interviews with the White House "Spokesman."

Such a newspaper conception of the chief executive is possible because in the United States the President is an important person apart from Congress. The British Prime Minister, on the other hand, is interesting only insofar as he retains office, or as he increases or decreases his chance of doing this, and here the House of Commons is a deciding factor. The outcome is determined in day by day contacts between Cabinet and Commons, and myths about English Ministers cannot long perdure. They vanish before the reality of the Minister's demeanor and skill in dealing with Parliament. He must be his own spokesman. A House of Commons, for example, would have a pretty accurate estimate of the ability of its Attorney General within the first fortnight of a session, and there could be no sudden disclosure after some months in a hearing before a legislative committee that economy of words and a magnificent physique did not mean legal ability—as the country had been led to believe—but only concealed complete ignorance of what the Department of Justice had done. Such a partial picture may frequently be seen in the United States, for the President is never viewed in mental undress and he and his advisers never come to grips with their opponents. The country may know that certain presidential recommendations have been disregarded, but these defects can be easily counteracted by favorable reports putting the President before the country as an exponent of private economy or conservatism in dress.

The matter is important, of course, entirely apart from the fact that Mr. Coolidge happens to be President, and that he has deified his "Spokesman." The semi-weekly emanations from the White House are practically the only utterances that the executive makes on current public questions, and they are indirect and irresponsible. In his responsible statements when he appears in public, the President sticks to platitudes and rarely comments, except in most general terms, upon any matter of legislation or policy. Mr. Coolidge's favorite, if not his only, platform subjects are the need for governmental economy, the excellence of American institutions, the price of freedom, the value of liberty, the equality of opportunity, and "less government in business and more business in government." His remarks upon these topics can mean all things to all men. They are so general, that is to say, that there can be little quarrel with them, and like many generalizations, they glitter and do not illumine. They are more frequently puerile than profound, but their utterance usually demonstrates the truth of the French proverb—that applause is often the echo of a platitude.

There is a vast difference, however, between an occasional resort to such tactics and an exclusive reliance on phrases that sound well and mean nothing. When labored aphorisms and a "Spokesman's" pæans of praise are the only indices of presidential opinions and ability, there must be some branch of the government which can criticize and attempt to call him to account. Hence the importance of unlimited debate in the Senate and the opportunity for senatorial investigations. Were the rules to permit closure, and were germaneness to be insisted upon, legislative criticisms of or questions to the executive would be impossible. There would be no counter-irritant to the favorable publicity that the newspaper correspondents so generously accord the President.

This is not to say that speeches, even by the most eloquent Senators, can make the country realize that the President is speaking vaguely, irresponsibly, and ofttimes inaccurately; but it is to say that only in the Senate can there be any criticisms likely to embarrass the White House "Spokesman" and make him explain as well as exploit. Senator Norris, for example, made it necessary for the White House to take cognizance of his charges in respect of the Tariff Commission and even though the reply was disingenuous, the fact that it was made showed the fear of possible embarrassment. It is true also, I venture to suggest, that the "Spokesman" is the more exuberant when Congress—really the Senate —is not in session. Had the coal emergency been hatching during the winter instead of during the summer the exploitation of the President as a strike preventer could hardly have occurred. It was noticeable that coal was rarely mentioned by the "Spokesman" in Washington. By the time the strike had ended, senatorial criticism had almost forced the President to act, and it had effectively prevented any irresponsible statements of what the President proposed to do. This, I think, is an excellent illustration of the importance that the Senate has *vis-à-vis* the "Spokesman," the rôle being the more obvious because of the simplicity and the acuteness of the coal crisis. Yet it is a rôle that cannot be dispensed with even though it is offstage, and that it may become prominent is the chief danger feared by the extra-constitutional person who increases both presidential influence and irresponsibility. From the standpoint of the executive, he is a desirable fiction; he will be retained until he loses popularity through a realization of his achievements in making popular government unpopular. Meanwhile his existence and his utterances impose important duties on the Senate.

CHAPTER VIII

FORUM OF THE NATION AND CRITIC OF THE EXECUTIVE

"It has not only been demonstrated that the Senate, in its actual organization, is well adapted to the exigencies of the nation, but that it is a most important and valuable part of the system, and the real balance-wheel which adjusts and regulates its movements."

——JOSEPH STORY

My argument, then, briefly put, is that only the Senate can counteract the effects of presidential publicity which lures the country into accepting certain fixed ideas of the executive, and which vouchsafes only favorable information concerning administrative activities. Washington correspondents are no longer interpreters or even news gatherers; were they to use all the "handouts" given them, their papers would have space for nothing else. Everyone in Washington—extra-governmental party politicians, congressmen, and departmental heads— seeks favorable publicity and furnishes the newspapers with ample material. The idea is to be interesting and favorable, not complete or frank, and the separation of executive and legislature makes the situation dangerous. Checks and balances are difficult to apply to such propaganda.

This of course is quite different from the presidential usurpation complained of during the Roosevelt and Wilson administrations. These Presidents attempted to lead Congress. Mr. Wilson in particular, looked upon himself as a Prime Minister. The President, he wrote in February, 1913, just before his inauguration, "is expected by the nation to be the leader of his party as well as the chief executive officer of the Government, and the country will take no excuses from him. He must play the part and play it successfully or lose the country's confidence. He must be Prime Minister, as much concerned with the guidance of legislation as with the just and orderly execution of law; and he is the spokesman of the nation in everything, even the most momentous and delicate dealings of the Government with foreign nations." This frankly expressed intention was acted upon, and it is now trite to say that Mr. Wilson, more than any of his predecessors, exerted an almost absolute authority over Congress. The passage, during the first months of his administration, of the Tariff, Currency and Trust Bills was due to his power of conciliatory but effective leadership. His addresses to Congress were brief and dealt in the main with single subjects. The attempt was consciously made to focus the attention of the country upon a single proposal at a time and to arouse public opinion sufficiently to compel legislative action. When Congress delayed, the President threatened appeals to the country, and actually made them. A closer cooperation between members of the Cabinet and legislative committees of Congress; conferences at the White House between members of the legislature and the President; the drafting of administration measures; the smoother working and more binding decisions of the party caucus; the use of the immense prestige of the presidential office, and frequent public expressions of the desires of the executive—these expedients were used in an attempt to introduce an extra-constitutional but nevertheless, in the absence of great emergencies, a tolerably effective responsible government. The entrance of the United States into the war naturally gave the presidential office a prestige and a chance of leadership far greater than when only domestic issues were to the fore. Until his defeat in the congressional elections of 1918, Mr. Wilson's leadership and commands were rarely challenged with success.

Such a frank acceptance of responsibility and dominance of Congress were of course bitterly criticized, yet the fact of the matter was, I venture to suggest, that during the Wilson administration the legislature was really more important than it has been since. The separation of powers theory gives the country a choice between presidential leadership and congressional inefficiency, and inefficiency is synonymous with impotence. In other words, I think that Congress had a more important function in amending laws initiated by the Cabinet and in refusing to go the whole distance demanded by the President—the Espionage Act is an illustration—than if its score or two of unrelated committees had been the only parents for the legislative progeny, and the executive's wishes had been vaguely expressed through an irresponsible "Spokesman." To be sure, the Presidents who followed Mr. Wilson, while they condemned his dictatorship and did lip service to the idea of Congress playing its "rightful rôle" under the Constitution, have occasionally attempted to exert influence. Little success attended their efforts, for the reason that, to be effective, presidential leadership must be open and continuous, not hidden and spasmodic. This change of emphasis has been partly responsible, I think, for the frequent (and unfair) criticisms of Congress. Left largely to its own devices, Congress, as I have suggested, becomes less efficient; yet unquestionably it more accurately interpreted the temper of the country on the first Mellon tax bill and the ship subsidy proposal than did the executive.

The important point, however, is that a continuous duel between President and Congress cannot be dispensed with except at the price of hodgepodge legislation and bureaucratic security; and without the Senate the executive would have no antagonist. He needs that antagonist whether, like Mr. Wilson, he attempts to be a responsible leader, or like Mr. Harding, he leaves Congress to its own devices; and particularly does he need an antagonist when he refuses to commit himself openly and clearly on public questions and pours out a steady stream of self-advertisement. Hence the importance of the Senate—an importance which closure would greatly lessen and perhaps completely extinguish. For, as I have argued, in respect of legislation the Senate matters little so far as its original purpose is concerned; it matters a great deal considering the way in which the House of Representatives is dominated by a few leaders. The upper chamber is not necessary, in other words, to protect the small states against the large states; it is rarely required to act as a *brake* on the House of Representatives. It is true, as I have said, that the legislative grist of the House is of a low grade and needs considerable purification before it reaches the statute book. Were it not possible, however, for the Senate to be relied upon for this improvement, the House would feel a greater sense of responsibility and would not venture to pass its measures without being certain that they contained no imperfections. There would probably be more deliberation and delay and a better collective judgment on what bills should provide. The appeal is not from Philip Drunk to Philip Sober, but from Philip Shackled to Philip Free. The Wilson Tariff Bill, for example, framed in the House, was discarded by the Senate and a new measure was substituted. Perhaps this was usurpation, but there was hardly a whisper of objection in the House; the judgment of the Senate was admittedly superior. It was the Senate moreover that determined congressional policy in respect of Cuba and the Philippines. The House resolutions declaring that Spanish rule in Cuba was intolerable were abandoned and instead the Senate's views were accepted. The Senate by amendments to the Army Appropriation Bill gave the President authority to govern the Philippines and outlined the conditions for the withdrawal of American troops from Cuba.[1] Many other illustrations could be given of important policies originated by the Senate. This is the case because the House permits its deliberations to be guillotined; it accepts the proposal of a few leaders. The result is that when the Senate comes to discuss the matter it is not difficult to discover a policy superior to that favored by the House. This is not because the collective judgment of the House is less wise than the collective judgment of the Senate, but because the House proceeds on the theory that the opinions of its shifting leaders are so final that they need not be discussed and cannot be improved upon. In view, therefore, of the House rules, the Senate with its complete freedom of debate can play a rôle of the greatest importance.

In another respect also, the Senate has performed great services. The Force Bill was passed by a partisan majority in the House of Representatives. It was defeated by a Senate filibuster. That it was the better course for the measure to fail, will not now, I think, be questioned; the will of a majority of the Senate may have been thwarted, but the minority was right. In other cases the prolonged debates in the Senate on pending legislation or treaties have been extremely useful in giving the country opportunities to form and express opinions.

[1] See H. L. West, "The Place of the Senate in our Government", *The Forum*, June, 1901.

The struggle over the repeal of the Sherman Silver Purchase Law lasted for three months, and this discussion of the country's financial policy was not wasted. It is worthwhile emphasizing the fact that, had the Senate voted quickly, the measure would have been lost; the majority for passage was secured after the debate had explored the whole problem. The Ship Subsidy Bill in the fourth session of the Sixty-seventh Congress is another illustration of the utility of the Senate—or, more accurately, of Senate minorities which the rules do not make impotent. The measure would doubtless have passed if a minority had not obstructed and forced the Republican leaders (who were never much interested in the issue) to withdraw the bill. Similarly a Senate minority, by delaying action until the project could be thoroughly examined defeated a proposed loan to Liberia—a financial transaction that was favored more for the jobs that it would provide for deserving Republicans than for the assistance that it would render a needy republic. The necessity of some agency in the congressional system which will keep legislation of vicarious parentage from being rushed to the statute books is the more immediate because of the separation of powers, and because no definite groups of individuals stand sponsors for a particular proposal. In England, as I have suggested, something is to be said for a majority of the House of Commons being able to act when it desires to act; but in England that majority, headed by a Cabinet, is responsible for what it does and it can be punished at the next general election. This is not to argue that a system of responsible government would be more suitable for the United States with its federalism, extreme bicameralism, and judicial supremacy, to say nothing of the size of the country. The point is that with responsibility divided and confused, the check which is on occasion exerted by senatorial obstructionists is of great value and ought not to be given up. If filibustering Senators have no justification for their course, they will speedily be hoist with their own petard.

The Senate, moreover, is the only available forum, the only assembly that can draw any interest to its proceedings. A nation under presidential government, as Bagehot pointed out,

"is not incited to form an opinion like a nation under a cabinet government; nor is it instructed like such a nation. There are doubtless debates in the legislature, but they are prologues without a play. There is nothing of a catastrophe about them; you cannot turn out the government. The prize of power is not the gift of the legislature, and no one cares for the legislature. The executive, the great centre of power and place, sticks irremovable; you cannot change it in any event. The teaching apparatus which has educated our public mind, which prepares our resolutions, which shapes our opinions, does not exist. No presidential country needs to form daily, delicate opinions, or is helped in forming them.

"It might be thought that the discussions in the press would supply the deficiences in the constitution; that by a reading people especially, the conduct of their government would be as carefully watched, that their opinions about it would be as consistent, as accurate, as well considered, under a presidential as under a cabinet polity. But the same difficulty oppresses the press which oppresses the legislature. It can *do nothing*. It cannot change the administration; the executive was elected for such and such years, and for such and such years it must last. People wonder that so literary a people as the Americans—a people who read more than any people that ever lived, who read so many newspapers—should have such bad newspapers. The papers are not so good as the English, because they have not the same motive to be good as the English papers. At a political 'crisis,' as we say—that is, when the fate of an administration is unfixed, when it depends on a few votes, yet unsettled, upon a wavering and veering opinion— effective articles in great journals become of essential moment. The *Times* has made many ministries. When, as of late, there has been a long continuance of divided parliaments, of governments which were without 'brute voting power,' and which depended on intellectual strength, the support of the most influential organ of English opinion has been of critical moment. If a Washington newspaper could have turned out Mr. Lincoln, there would have been good writing and fine argument in the Washington newspapers. But the Washington newspapers can no more remove a president during his term of place than the *Times* can remove a lord mayor during his year of office. Nobody cares for a debate in Congress which 'comes to nothing' and no one reads long articles which have no influence on events. The Americans glance at the heads of news, and through the paper. They do not enter upon a discussion. They do not *think* of entering upon a discussion which would be useless." [2]

This is somewhat exaggerated, but its main argument cannot be denied. Only the American Senate

[2] *The English Constitution*, pp. 89–91.

can act as a "teaching apparatus" or bring about "a catastrophe" of obstruction that will make politics interesting. The Senate can help the country to form opinions and by its eternal vigilance—sometimes extreme and pettifogging—act as the "real balance-wheel" of the Constitution.

Hence the more obvious, and at the same time the more subtle importance of the Senate in respect of its executive functions. Here, as I have said, the upper chamber is by no means an unmixed blessing. Two of the Senate's powers matter little. There would be, I think, some slight advantages is retaining one and eliminating the other. With American parties organized outside the structure of the Government, and the President separated from the legislature, senatorial confirmation of appointments, though it divides responsibility, is probably a valuable check. Senatorial control over removals, on the other hand, is not desirable except in a rare case as, say, where the officer (for example the Comptroller General) should act as the agent of Congress rather than the subordinate of the executive. The Senate's power over treaties has not been harmless, and contains possibilities of great damage in the future. At first the Senate's power to amend and reserve was conservatively exercised; [3] it was asserted by the two-thirds majority rather than the one-third minority. Now, however, in Cleveland's phrase, almost every treaty may expect the "customary disfigurement at the hands of the

[3] A. Maurice Low, "The Oligarchy of the Senate", *North American Review*, February, 1902.

Senate." The situation would not be so extreme were this power to be exercised to some extent on presidential negotiations and decisions in foreign questions which do not require treaties. On such matters the President has entirely too free a hand; there is less control of such diplomacy in the United States than in any other country save perhaps Japan or Russia, and this failure of supervision is improperly compensated for by a vast excess of supervision over treaties. The international engagements of the United States should, of course, be subject to ratification by a legislative body, but this does not mean that the judgment of one-third of the Senate should be substituted for the judgment of the executive. Such usurpation was not contemplated by the Constitution; it creates an intolerable situation which can only be endured because of the immunity which the United States enjoys from foreign complications requiring expeditious and definite decisions. Were the United States a European country, the Senate would either have learned to be tolerant, or its power would have been taken from it. Much the more sensible procedure, it seems to me, would be to have treaties ratified as ordinary laws—by a majority vote of the Senate and the House of Representatives; but since the consent of the Senate is necessary to submit a constitutional amendment to the state legislatures, this change will not be made unless some extreme minority attitude on a treaty brings down on the Senate a powerful and unanimous denunciation.[4] Mean-

4 Mr. George Stewart Brown has argued ("The Perpetual Cov-

while, as I say, this "irreparable mistake" of the framers of the Constitution does not cost the country a great deal, although the price may increase as contacts with Europe become more numerous and important.

From this angle, as I argue, the Senate is a grave liability. It is, however, a tremendous asset in respect of its general scrutiny of executive activities. This check is indispensable. No inquiry into administration can be secured by a party minority as a minority. The control of the House of Representatives is such that its leaders could prevent an investigation demanded by a sufficient number of the majority party to make the minority a majority, for the Committee on Rules could not be forced to report the resolution. The same thing would be true in the Senate if the previous question were possible, or if germaneness were insisted upon. What happens in the Senate now is that investigations are assented to when urged by the minority or by dissentient members of the majority party and when they are of some *prima facie* justification. The

enant," *North American Review,* January, 1924) that the constitutional prohibition against any state being deprived of equal representation in the Senate without its consent makes any change in the Senate's powers impossible; these must remain as they were when the perpetual covenant was entered into. He argues that it would be "unconstitutional" for the Constitution to be amended so as to abolish the Senate, reduce its legislative authority (as was done for the House of Lords by the Parliament Act), share its treaty authority with the House, permit a national referendum on treaties or statutes, or limit the judicial veto of the Supreme Court. This, it is hardly necessary to say, is an extreme position.

reason is not the generosity of the Senate leaders; it is not their conviction of complete administrative rectitude and consequent willingness for alleged scandals to be investigated. Senatorial inquiries are sometimes permitted because a form of "courtesy" applies to them, but the vital reason is the possibility that an inquisitive minority will obstruct if its request for an investigation is refused. This is a consideration that is almost always hidden, but which is no less important, and its corollary is that, should the investigation be delayed or denied, freedom of debate would permit such exaggerated criticisms and charges that the majority party would suffer almost as much harm as if it allowed the facts to be ascertained.

The Senate, in short, plays a high and unanticipated rôle in the political drama. It is, however, a role that is better described than seen, and one who watches the Senate at work is disillusioned. Bagehot quoted "a severe though not unfriendly critic" of English political institutions who "said that 'the *cure* for admiring the House of Lords' was 'to go and look at it'; to look at it not on a great party field-day or at a time of parade, but in the ordinary transaction of business. There are perhaps ten peers in the House, possibly only six—three is the quorum for transacting business; a few more may dawdle in or not dawdle in." [5] The description could well be that of the Senate. With a dozen members on the floor millions of dollars are appropriated and when there is a fair attendance little

[5] *Op. cit.* p. 181.

attention is apparently paid to the pending business.
The bells ring and the roll is called to secure the
presence of a quorum; a Senator begins a formal
speech and soon he addresses empty desks. He
concludes, another quorum call, another speech—the
facts seem to belie the characterization of the Senate as a deliberative assembly. The absence of
representatives of the executive is largely responsible
for the absence of debate; the principal work is
done in committee; votes are rarely changed by
what is said on the floor; Senators address not the
Senate, but their constituents and perhaps the country. Yet the Senate, to repeat, is the only possible
forum that the Constitution and practice under it
permit. It is the only chamber where minority aspirations can find free expression and where there
can be any criticism of the executive. A member
of the House of Representatives is a private in the
ranks; he must always do the goosestep; he must
almost immediately stand for reëlection. Each Senator, on the other hand, is a staff officer—even a
prima donna. He looks upon himself not as *primus
inter pares* but as *inter stellas luna minores*. Reed
did not exaggerate when, in an unpublished manu-
script purporting to be a "History of the United
States published in 1940" he imagined that, in the
eighties (when there were thirty-eight states) the
people had grown weary of the caliber of their Presidents and had adopted a constitutional amendment
providing that they should be chosen by the Senate
out of the Senate itself. He thus described the
first election:

"So intense was the public excitement that the whole nation left its vocations, flung business to the winds, and assembled in front of the Capitol where, in the open day, the tremendous scene of the choice of the wisest man should be made by and out of the wisest body of men. It was by secret ballot, so that no possibility of influence by public clamor could disturb the serene judgment of the Immortals. When the ballots had been collected and spread out, the Chief Justice, who presided, was observed to hesitate and those nearest could see by his pallor that something unexpected had happened. But with a strong effort he rose to his feet and through a megaphone, then recently invented by Edison, shouted to the vast multitude the astounding result: seventy-six Senators had each received one vote. For a moment a stillness as of death settled upon the multitude. Never until that moment had the people realized that, like the Deacon's One Hoss Shay the Senate of the United States was one level mass of wisdom and virtue, perfect in all its parts, and radiant from North to South with that light of intelligence which never shone on sea or shore." [6]

Senators, perhaps, should not be taken too seriously, but the importance of the Senate must not be underestimated. It is well that, in the United States, there is never a time when

> ". . . the House of Peers withholds
> Its legislative hand
> And noble statesmen do not itch
> To interfere with matters which
> They cannot understand."

[6] McCall, *Life of Thomas B. Reed,* p. 252 (Boston, 1914).
[7] *Iolanthe,* Act II.

The Senate, as I have argued, quite properly acts on a contrary principle. Its collective judgment on legislation cannot fail to be superior to the judgment of the House which too frequently represents no more than the hasty opinion of a few leaders. There is on legislation no prior veto such as exists in a parliamentary system of government and such as there is, in the United States, in respect of treaties. The rigid two-party system of the United States is not hospitable to minority groups, which, reversing the experience of other governments, have secured their most adequate representation in the upper chamber of the American Congress.

But it is as a critic of the executive that the Senate does its most notable work. Here complete freedom of debate and the absence of closure except as a real emergency measure are more indispensable than in respect of legislation. Criticisms of the Senate because time is wasted, irrelevant and extreme talk is indulged in, and logrolling is prevalent, overlook the fact that scrutiny of administration—a normal function of legislative assemblies—can only in the United States be scrutiny by the Senate. Fixed terms and executive irresponsibility make the need for this scrutiny more urgent. The rôle of the American Senate, in short, is a paradoxical but convincing justification of the bicameral theory.

APPENDIX A

SUPPLEMENT TO THE BRIEF OF GEORGE WHARTON
PEPPER, *AMICUS CURIÆ*, CONTAINING COM-
PILATION OF STATUTES RESTRICTING THE
POWER OF THE PRESIDENT TO APPOINT OR RE-
MOVE OFFICERS OF THE UNITED STATES; FRANK
S. MYERS V. UNITED STATES.[1]

EXPLANATION

The following compilation of statutes includes statutes
that provide for appointments by the President either alone
or by and with the advice and consent of the Senate, but
that restrict the President in his exercise of the power to
appoint or remove the appointee. The compilation includes only statutes now in force and does not attempt an
exhaustive but merely an approximately complete and representative list of such statutes. The inclusion of such
restrictive statutes where the statute itself fails to specify
any appointing authority, is made for the reason that the
power of appointment is then to be exercised by the President by and with the advice and consent of the Senate (see,
30 Op. Atty. Genl. 177, 179; 29 Op. Atty Genl. 116 and
opinions there cited; and Scully v. United States [1910]
193 Fed. 185, 187).

Appointees of the President are included without any
attempt to limit the compilation to those appointees only

[1] Prepared by the Office of the Legislative Counsel, Senate
Branch.

who are officers within the meaning of what term as used in Article II, section 2 of the Constitution, or to distinguish between superior or inferior officers of the United States.

Statutes Imposing Restrictions On Appointments

A. RESIDENCE AND CITIZENSHIP REQUIREMENTS

(a) General Statutes

1. Consular Clerks (s. 1704 R. S.)
2. Federal Board for Vocational Education, Appointed Members (39 Stat. 932, s. 6)
3. Federal Farm Loan Board, Members (42 Stat. 1473, s. 301)
4. Foreign Service Officers (43 Stat. 141, s. 5)
5. Postmasters (33 Stat. 441, s. 8)

(b) Statutes applicable solely to a Territory or Possession or to the District of Columbia

6. Circuit Courts of Hawaii, Judges (31 Stat. 157, s. 80, Am. 42 Stat. 119)
7. District Court for Hawaii, District Attorney (42 Stat. 120, s. 86 [b])
8. District Court for Hawaii, Judge (42 Stat. 120, s. 86 [b])
9. District Court for Hawaii, Marshal (42 Stat. 120, s. 86 [b])
10. District Court of the Virgin Islands, Judges (32 Stat. 1132, Am. 42 Stat. 123)
11. District of Columbia, Civil Commissioners (20 Stat. 103, s. 2)
12. Municipal Court of the District of Columbia, Judges (35 Stat. 623)

13. Police Court of the District of Columbia, Judges (Pub. No. 561 68th Cong., s. 3 [a])
14. Supreme Court of Hawaii, Judges (31 Stat. 157, s. 80, Am. 42 Stat. 119)

   (c) Statutes applicable solely to the Army or Navy

15. Army Reserve Corps, Officers (41 Stat. 775, s. 32)
16. Naval Reserve Force, Officers (39 Stat. 587)

B. POLITICAL AFFILIATIONS

17. Board of General Appraisers, Members (42 Stat. 972, s. 518)
18. Civil Service Commission, Commissioners (22 Stat.. 403)
19. Federal Farm Loan Board, Members (42 Stat. 1473, s. 301)
20. Federal Trade Commission, Commissioners (38 Stat. 718, s. 1)
21. Interstate Commerce Commission, Commissioners (41 Stat. 497, s. 440)
22. U. S. Shipping Board, Commissioners (41 Stat. 989, s. 3 [a])
23. U. S. Tariff Commission, Commissioners (39 Stat. 795, s. 700)

INDUSTRIAL GEOGRAPHICAL OR GOVERNMENTAL REPRESENTATION

(a) General statutes

24. Advisory Committee for Aeronautics, Members (38 Stat. 930)
25. Aircraft Board, Military and Naval Members (40 Stat. 296)
26. Bureau of Fisheries, Commissioner (16 Stat. 594, s. 1)
27. Capital Issues Committee, Members (40 Stat. 512, s. 200)

28. Consular Service, Inspectors of Consulates (34 Stat. 100, s. 4)

29. Federal Board for Vocational Education, Appointed Members, (39 Stat. 932, s. 6)

30. Federal Reserve Board, Appointed Members (42 Stat. 620)

31. Internal Revenue Collectors (s. 3142, R. S.)

32. Mississippi River Commission, Commissioners (21 Stat. 37, s. 2)

33. Railroad Labor Board, Members (41 Stat. 470, s. 304)

34. U. S. Shipping Board, Commissioners (41 Stat. 989, s. 3 [a])

(b) Statutes applicable solely to a Territory or Possession or to the District of Columbia

35. Rent Commission of the District of Columbia, Commissioners, (42 Stat. 544 s. 4)

36. Isthmian Canal Commission, Members (32 Stat. 483, s. 7)

37. Municipal Court of the District of Columbia, Judges (35 Stat. 623)

38. Police Court of the District of Columbia, Judges (Pub. No. 561, 68th Cong., s. 3 [a])

39. Territorial District Attorneys, (s. 1875, R. S.)

40. U. S. Court for China, District Attorney (34 Stat. 816, s. 6)

41. U. S. Court for China, Judges (34 Stat. 816, s. 6)

D. PROFESSIONAL ABILITY

(a) General Statutes

42. Advisory Committee for Aeronautics, Members (38 Stat. 930)

43. Bureau of Fisheries, Commissioner (16 Stat. 594, s. 1)
44. Bureau of Mines, Director (37 Stat. 681, s. 1)
45. California Debris Commission, Members (27 Stat. 507)
46. Consular Service, Inspectors of Consulates (34 Stat. 100, s. 4)
47 Mississippi River Commission, Commissioners (21 Stat. 37, s. 2)
48. Parent Office, Examiners-in-Chief (s. 482, R. S.)
49. Public Printer (14 Stat. 398, Am. 18 Stat. 88)
50. Rio Grande Commission, Commissioners (43 Stat. 118)
51. Solicitor-General (s. 347, R. S.)
52. Steamboat Inspection Service, Supervising Inspectors (s. 4404, R. S., Am. 40 Stat. 740)
53. Superintendent of Indian Schools (25 Stat. 1003, s. 10)
54. U. S. District Attorneys (s. 767, R. S.)

(b) *Statutes applicable solely to the Army and Navy*

55. Department of the Navy, Chief of the Bureau of Economics (42 Stat. 140, s. 8)
56. Department of the Navy, Chiefs of Bureaus (ss. 421–426, R. S.)
57. Marine Corps, Major General Commandant (39 Stat. 609)
58. National Guard, Officers (on Federal Service) 41 Stat. 784, s. 49
59. Navy, Judge-Advocate-General (21 Stat. 164)
60. Officers' Reserve Corps, Army (41 Stat. 775, s. 32)
61. Regular Army, Officers (41 Stat. 771, s. 24)

E. FITNESS TO PERFORM DUTIES OF OFFICE

62. Board of Tax Appeals, Members (43 Stat. 336, s. 900 [b])

63. Steamboat Inspection Service, Supervising Inspector General (40 Stat. 739)
64. Interstate Commerce Commission, Chief and Assistant Chief Inspectors of Locomotive Boilers (36 Stat. 913, s. 3)
65. U. S. Shipping Board, Commissioners (41 Stat. 989)

F. SUCCESSFUL COMPLETION OF EXAMINATION OR PERIOD OF PROBATION

66. Civil Service Appointees (22 Stat. 403)
67. Consular Clerks (s. 1705, R. S.)
68. Foreign Service Officers (43 Stat. 141, s. 5)

G. SELECTION FROM LIMITED NUMBER OF NOMINEES

69. Civil Service Appointees (22 Stat. 403)
70. Railroad Labor Board (41 Stat. 470, ss. 304, 305).

STATUTES IMPOSING RESTRICTIONS ON REMOVALS

Note: Restrictions as to methods of removal below listed are not intended to exclude or deny the power to remove an incumbent appointed by the President by and with the advice and consent of the Senate through appointment of a successor by the President with like advice and consent (see Wallace v. United States (1922) 257 U. S. 541, 545; Parsons v. United States (1897) 167 U. S. 324). There are not included under this heading judges of constitutional courts who are appointed by the President but whose removal is barred under the "good behavior" clause in Article III, Section 1 of the Constitution. Variations in terms of office of original appointees, for the purpose of providing overlapping terms of office, are not included, but only the permanent terms of office are specified.

A. DENIAL TO THE PRESIDENT OF ALL POWER TO REMOVE

(a) Genera Statutes

71. Comptroller General of the U. S. (42 Stat. 23, 24).
    Appointed by President with consent of Senate.
    Term of Office: 15 years.
    Removal by Joint Resolution of Congress.
    Restriction on removal: "After notice and hearing
    * * * when permanently incapacitated or * * *
    inefficient, or guilty of neglect of duty, or of mal-
    feasance in office, or of any felony or conduct in-
    volving moral turpitude, and for no other cause and
    in no other manner except by impeachment."

72. Court of Claims, Judges (40 Stat. 1157, s. 4).
    Appointment by President with consent of Senate.
    Term of office: None specified.
    Removal: None specified.
    Restriction on removal: "hold their offices during good
    behavior."

(b) Statutes relating exclusively to the District of Columbia

73. Court of Appeals of the District of Columbia, Justices
    (31 Stat. 1224, s. 221).
    Appointed by President with consent of Senate.
    Term of office: None specified.
    Removal: None specified.
    Restriction on removal: "shall hold office during good
    behavior."

74. Municipal Court of the District of Columbia, Judges,
    (35 Stat. 623; 41 Stat. 555, 556, s. 65; Stat. 1312,
    1313, s. 13).
    Appointed by President with consent of Senate.

Term of office: 4 years and until successor is qualified.

Removal by Supreme Court of the District of Columbia.

Restrictions upon removal: "May hear charges * * * and remove * * * from office for cause shown."

75. Supreme Court of the District of Columbia, Judges (31 Stat. 1199, s. 60).

Appointed by President with consent of Senate.

Term of office: None specified.

Removal: None specified.

Restriction on removal: "holding their offices during good behavior.'

2. DENIAL TO THE PRESIDENT OF THE POWER TO REMOVE EXCEPT WITH THE CONSENT OF THE SENATE

NOTE: See also, statutes listed under "E" below.

76. Postmaster-General (s. 388, R. S.).

Appointed by President with consent of Senate.

Term of office: "during term of the President by whom he is appointed, and for one month thereafter."

Removable by President with consent of Senate.

Restriction on removal: None except that consent of Senate must be obtained.

77. First, Second and Third Assistant Postmasters-General (s. 389, R. S.).

Appointed by President with consent of Senate.

Term of office: None specified.

Removal by President with consent of Senate.

Restrictions on removal: None except that consent of Senate must be obtained.

78. Postmasters of the First, Second and Third Classes (s. 3830, R. S.; 19 Stat. 80, 81, s. 6).

Appointed by President with consent of Senate.

Term of office: 4 years.

Removal by President with consent of Senate.

Restriction on removal: None except that consent of
Senate must be obtained.

C. DENIAL TO THE PRESIDENT OF THE POWER TO REMOVE FOR ANY OTHER CAUSE OTHER THAN CERTAIN SPECIFIED CAUSES

(a) *General Statutes*

79. Board of General Appraisers, Members (42 Stat. 972,
    s. 518).

    Appointed by the President with consent of Senate.
    Term of office: None specified.

    Removal by President alone.

    Restriction on removal: "hold office during good be-
        havior, but may, after hearing, be removed * * *
        for the following causes and no other: Neglect
        of duty, malfeasance in office or inefficiency."

NOTE: The statute (26 Stat. 136, s. 12) involved in
Shurtleff v. United States (1903) 189 U. S. 311, merely
provided that the members of the Board "may be removed
from office at any time by the President for inefficiency,
neglect of duty, or malfeasance in office." This statute
was amended by the Act of May 27, 1908 (35 Stat. 406,
s. 3), so as to impose the above restrictions (see also 36
Stat. 98, s. 28).

80. Board of Tax Appeals, Members (43 Stat. 336, 337, s.
    900).

    Appointed by President with consent of Senate.
    Term of office: 10 years and until successor is quali-
        fied.

    Removal by President alone.

    Restriction on removal: "inefficiency, neglect of duty,
        or malfeasance in office, but for no other reason."

81. Railroad Labor Board, Members (41 Stat. 470, ss. 306,
    307).

Appointed by President with consent of Senate.

Term of office: 5 years.

Removal by President alone.

Restriction on removal: "neglect of duty or malfeasance in office, but for no other cause.'

(b) *Statutes relating exclusively to Army or Navy*

82. Army, commissioned officers (s. 1229, R. S.; 36 Stat. 894, ch. 22; 41 Stat. 811, Art. 118).

Appointment: None specified in statutes cited, which relate to removal only. Appointments in Regular Army are made by President with consent of Senate. In Reserve Corps and branches of the service other than the Regular Army, appointments are usually required to be made by the President alone, except that general officers are appointed by the President with the consent of the Senate.

Term of office: None usually specified.

Removal by President or by general court martial.

Restriction on removal: In war time, no restriction on President; in time of peace, President may at any time drop from the rolls any officer absent from duty three months without leave, or absent in confinement in a prison or penitentiary for three months after final conviction.

83. Navy, commissioned officers (ss. 1229 and 1624, Art. 36, R. S.).

Appointment: None specified in statutes cited, which relate to removal only. Appointments in Navy are usually required to be made by President with consent of Senate.

Term of office: None usually specified.

Removal by President or general court martial.

Restriction on removal: In time of peace only by sentence of general court martial.

D. DENIAL TO THE PRESIDENT THE POWER TO REMOVE FOR CERTAIN CAUSES EXCEPT AFTER NOTICE AND OPPORTUNITY TO DEFEND

NOTE: Statutes under this heading are of two classes. First, there are those statutes which provide for removal "for cause." No federal statute with a like provision has been construed by the courts so far as counsel is aware, but the State courts regard statutes providing for removal "for cause" as requiring the removing authority to give notice and opportunity to defend before the removal (see for example, Haight v. Love (1876) 39 N. J. L. 14, affd., 39 N. J. L. 476,; State v. Frazier, [N.D., 1921] 182 N. W. 545; Street Commissioners v. Williams [1903] 96 Md. 232; Andrews v. Police Board [1900], 94 Me. 68; Ham v. Board of Police [1886] 142 Mass. 90; see also, United States v. Shurtleff [1903] 189 U. S. 311, 314). Second, there are those statutes which provide certain specified causes for removal, as for example, "inefficiency, neglect of duty, or malfeasance in office." Such statutes are construed as permitting removal for causes other than those specified unless the statutes provide in term to the contrary. Removal for the specified causes, however, may be had only after notice and opportunity to defend (Reagan v. United States, [1901], 182 U. S. 419; Shurtleff v. United States [1903] 189 U. S. 311). Therefore both classes of the above statutes constitute a limitation upon the President to the extent that he is required to give notice and opportunity to defend before removal and cannot remove at pleasure.

(a) *General statutes*

84. Consular Clerks (ss. 1704, 1705, R. S.).
    Appointment by President.
    Term of office: None specified.
    Removal authority not specified.

Restriction on removal: "for cause * * * submitted to Congress at session first following such removal."

85. Federal Farm Loan Board, Members (39 Stat. 360, s. 3, Am. 42 Stat. 1473, s. 301).

Appointment by President with consent of Senate.

Term of office: 8 years.

Removal by President alone.

Restriction on removal: "for cause"

86. Federal Reserve Board, Members (except *ex officio*) (42 Stat. 620, s. 10).

Appointed by President with consent of Senate.

Term of office: 10 years

Removal by President alone.

Restriction on removal: "for cause."

87. Federal Trade Commission, Commissioners (38 Stat. 717, 718).

Appointment by President with consent of Senate.

Term of office: 7 years.

Removal by President alone.

Restriction upon removal: "inefficiency, neglect of duty, or malfeasance in office."

88. Interstate Commerce Commission, Commissioners (24 Stat. 383, s. 11, Am. 41 Stat. 497, s. 440).

Appointed by President with consent of Senate.

Term of office: 7 years.

Removal by President.

Restriction on removal: "for inefficiency, neglect of duty, or malfeasance in office."

89. U. S. Tariff Commission, Commissioners (39 Stat. 795, s. 700).

Appointed by President with consent of Senate.

Term of office: 12 years.

Removal by President alone.

Restriction upon removal: "inefficiency, neglect of duty, or malfeasance in office."

90. U. S. Shipping Board, Commissioners (41 Stat. 989, s. 3).

Appointment by President with consent of Senate.

Term of office: 6 years.

Removal by President alone.

Restriction upon removal: "inefficiency, neglect of duty, or malfeasance in office."

(b) *Statutes relating exclusively to a Territory or to the District of Columbia*

91. District Court for Alaska, Judges (23 Stat. 24, Am. 31 Stat, 325, s. 10).

Appointed by President with consent of Senate.

Term of office: 4 years and until successor is qualified.

Removal by President alone.

Restriction on removal: "for cause."

92. District Court for Alaska, Marshal (23 Stat. 24, Am. 31 Stat, 325, s. 10).

Appointment by President with consent of Senate.

Term of office: 4 years and until successor is qualified.

Removal by President alone.

Restriction on Removal: "for cause."

93. Juvenile Court of the District of Columbia, Judge (34 Stat. 73, s. 2).

Appointment by President with consent of Senate.

Term of office: 6 years.

Removal by President. Note: Whether the consent of the Senate is required is not clear. The language is as follows: "The judge * * * shall be appointed by the President * * * subject to the removal by the President for cause, and by and with the advice and consent of the Senate * * *, or until his successor is appointed and confirmed."

Restriction on removal: "for cause."

94. Police Court of the District of Columbia, Judges (Pub.
     561, 68th Congress, s 3 [a]).
     Appointed by the President with consent of Senate.
     Term of office: 6 years and until successor takes office.
     Removal by President alone.
     Restriction on removal: "for cause."

95. U. S. Court for China, Judge (34 Stat. 816, ss. 6 and
     7).
     Appointed by President with consent of Senate.
     Term of office: 10 years.
     Removal by President alone.
     Restriction on removal: "for cause."

E. DENIAL TO THE PRESIDENT OF THE POWER TO REMOVE
UNTIL SUCCESSOR IS CHOSEN AND QUALIFIED

96. Governor General of the Philippine Islands (39 Stat
     552).
     Appointed by President with consent of Senate.
     Term of office: None specified.
     Removal by President.
     Restriction on removal: "hold his office at the pleasure
         of the President and until his successor is chosen
         and qualified."

97. Governor of Porto Rico (39 Stat. 955).
     Appointed by President with consent of Senate.
     Term of office: None specified.
     Removal by President.
     Restriction on removal: "hold his office at the pleasure
         of the President and until his successor is chosen
         and qualified."

F. REQUIREMENT OF COMMUNICATION BY PRESIDENT
TO SENATE OF REASONS FOR REMOVAL

98. Comptroller of the Currency (s. 325, R. S.
     Appointed by the President with consent of Senate.

Term of office: 5 years.
Removal by President.
Restrictions on removal: President to communicate reasons for removal to Senate.

99. Director of the Mint (s. 343, R. S.).
Appointed by President with consent of Senate.
Term of office: 5 years.
Removal by President.
Restriction on removal: President to communicate reasons for removal to Senate.

GEORGE WHARTON PEPPER,
Amicus Curiae.

APPENDIX B

At the second session of the 67th Congress (December 5th, 1921 to September 22, 1922) the Committee on Rules of the House of Representatives brought in special orders for the consideration of twenty-nine matters. House Bills included such legislation as the Anti-Lynching Bill, the Amendment of the Interstate Commerce Act, the Amendment of the War Risk Insurance Act, the appointment of additional Circuit Court and District Judges, appropriations for Russian relief, Amendment of the War Housing Act of May 16, 1918, Amendment of the Jones Law for the government of the Philippine Islands, the use of the mails and interstate commerce for the sale of securities contrary to State laws, the Rivers and Harbors Bill, adjusted compensation for war veterans, the pay of the Army and Navy, the retirement of employees in the Civil Service, the scrapping of vessels in accordance with the Washington Treaties, trading in grain futures, citizenship of married women, additional compensation for certain civilian employees, and dealing with the fuel emergency by expanding the powers of the Interstate Commerce Commission and creating the post of Federal Fuel Distributor. The Senate Bills for which the Committee reported special orders related to Amendments of the Interstate Commerce Act, Amendments of the Federal Reserve Act, the extension of the powers of the War Finance Corporation, appropriations for relief in the crop failure areas, the creation of two new positions in the Department of Labor and the continuation of the Land Offices. Two joint resolutions for which there were special orders authorized the purchase of land for cemeteries in Europe, and favored the establishment in Palestine of a national home for Jewish people.

At the fourth (short) session of the 67th Congress, the Committee on Rules reported twelve special orders. These covered certain provisions of the Naval Appropriation Bill relating to the procurement of aircraft, the protection of migratory birds, the appraisal of tribal property of Indians, the Rogers Bill for the reorganization of the Foreign Service, Amendment of the Federal Farm Loan Act, Amendment of the Trading with the Enemy Act. The Committee reported special orders for the following Senate Bills: the erection of buildings for the National Leper Home, the transfer of vessels from the Navy to the Coast Guard, the issuance of exploration permits in Oklahoma, and additional credit facilities for agricultural and livestock industries. There was a special order also on the House resolution proposing an Amendment to the Constitution permitting the taxation of Federal and State securities, and on the Senate resolution authorizing the President to require the Sugar Equalization Board to take over sugar imported from the Argentine Republic.

At the first session of the 68th Congress (December 3, 1923 to June 7, 1925) the Committee on Rules reported nineteen special orders. House Bills: selling Muscle Shoals to Henry Ford, appointing two additional District Judges for the Southern District of New York, for the purchase of the Cape Cod Canal property, for the provision of additional hospital facilities, amending the Vocational Rehabilitation Act, amending the Classification Act of 1923, amending the act providing compensation for injured Federal employees, extending the District of Columbia Rent Law, limiting immigration into the United States, fixing the pay of employees in the Govermental Printing Office, creating an Inland Waterways Corporation, amending the National Banking Act, declaring an emergency in respect of certain agricultural commodities.

There was a special order for the Senate Bill authorizing the deferring of payment of reclamation charges, and on the House Resolution proposing the Tax Exempt Security Amendment (which at this session failed of passage), and on the House Resolution proposing the Child Labor Amendment. There was also a special order for the Senate Resolution for the relief of the drought-stricken farm areas of New Mexico.

At the second session of the Sixty-eighth Congress the Committee on Rules reported eight special orders on the following matters: H. R. 745, a bill to establish migratory bird refuges; H. R. 7190, an amendment of the China Trade Act, 1922 (Public No 484); H. R. 11282, increasing the limits of costs of certain naval vessels (Public No. 399); H. R. 11472, authorizing public works on rivers and harbors (Public No. 585); H. R. 11957, authorizing the modification of visé fees (Public No. 464); H. R. 12348, creating the Federal Coöperative Marketing Board. There were also special orders on S. 2287, permitting the New York Port Authority to acquire the Hoboken Manufacturers' Railway (Public No. 479); and on H. J., Res. 68, amending clause of the federal Constitution (Garrett-Wadsworth Amendment); but the special order was not voted on and the resolution did not go before the House.

APPENDIX C [1]

	64th Cong.	65th Cong.	66th Cong.	67th Cong.	68th Cong.
No. of Senate bills introduced..	8,334	5,680	5,052	4,658	4,410
No. of Senate joint resolutions introduced	221	230	254	290	193
Total bills and joint resolutions	8,555	5,910	5,316	4,948	4,603
No. of Senate bills passed by the Senate	591	464	437	568	713
No. of Senate joint resolutions passed by the Senate........	60	65	56	85	74
Total	651	529	493	753	787
No. Senate bills enacted into law	234	152	181	289	378
No. Senate joint resolutions enacted into law..............	29	33	27	48	53
Total	263	185	208	337	431
No. of House bills introduced..	21,104	16,239	16,170	14,475	12,474
No. House joint resolutions introduced	393	445	481	466	385
Total	21,497	16,684	16,651	14,491	12,589
No. of House bills passed by House	588	310	460	670	689
No. House joint resolutions passed by House..........	39	30	52	69	34
Total	627	340	512	739	723
No. House bills enacted into law	387	244	340	536	540
No. House joint resolutions enacted into law..........	34	23	46	58	25
Total	421	267	386	594	565

[1] Tabulation by Senator McKellar showing that the Senate gets through with a great deal of business. *The Searchlight on Congress*, May 1925, p. 8.

INDEX

INDEX

A

Adams, Henry, 54; quoted, 72.

Adams, John, and removals from office, 32; and Senate, 24; quoted, 164.

Adams, John Quincy, quoted, 62.

Agricultural bloc, in American Congress, 93 ff.

Alexander, De A. S., quoted, 128; cited, 124.

Aldrich, Nelson W., 96, 168, 172.

Alien and Sedition Laws, 99.

Allen, W. V., 171.

Aluminium Trust, proposed investigation of, 197, 205.

Ambassadors, nominations of, and Senate, 28.

Amendments, by Senate to treaties, 250.

Anne, Queen, 65.

Anonymity, of presidential publicity, 218.

Appointments, confirmation of, by Senate, 13, 22 ff., 250; restrictions on, 257 ff.

Appropriations, greater liberality of Senate, 111; congressional procedure on, 143; closure on, in Senate, 184.

Arbitration, U. S. treaties of, 180.

Area, groupings by, in Congress, 104.

Arizona, statehood bill, 189.

B

Armed Ship Resolution, filibuster on, 169; and Senate, 176, 180.

Arms Conference, and Congress, 52.

Asquith, H. H., 105.

Atkinson, C. R., cited, 129, 130, 144.

Austria, second chamber in, 3.

Bagehot, Walter, quoted, 56, 77, 88, 90, 131, 191, 213, 248.

Baker, Ray Stannard, quoted, 54.

Balfour, Lord, quoted, 118.

Bank of U. S., incorporation of, 99, 169.

Bassett, J. S., cited, 211.

Baty, Th., cited, 95.

Baumann, A. A., quoted, 121.

Bayard, James A., 65.

Beard, Charles A., cited, 15 130.

Beck, James M., 32, 43.

Benton, T. H., quoted, 166; cited, 124, 125.

Berthélemy, H., cited, 212.

Bi-cameral theory, and Constitutional Convention, 10; consequences of, 90 ff.; and Senate, 256.

Biggar, Joseph, 122.

Bills, number of, passed by House and Senate, 186, 274.